D1236328

'ace

THE POWER OF CHILDREN

THE POWER OF CHILDREN

The Construction of Christian Families in the Greco-Roman World

MARGARET Y. MACDONALD

BAYLOR UNIVERSITY PRESS

© 2014 Baylor University Press
Waco, Texas 76798-7363

All Rights Reserved. No part of this publication may be reproduced, stored in a retrieval system, or transmitted, in any form or by any means, electronic, mechanical, photocopying, recording, or otherwise, without the prior permission in writing of Baylor University Press.

Scripture quotations, where not an author's own translation, are from the New Revised Standard Version Bible, copyright 1989, Division of Christian Education of the National Council of the Churches of Christ in the United States of America. Used by permission. All rights reserved.

Cover Design: Andrew Brozyna, AJB Design, Inc.
Cover Art: Stone burial monument with relief representing Neumagen school with teacher and pupils, about 180 / De Agostini Picture Library / G. Dagli Orti / The Bridgeman Art Library

Library of Congress Cataloging-in-Publication Data

MacDonald, Margaret Y.
  The power of children : the construction of Christian families in the Greco-Roman world / Margaret Y. MacDonald.
  251 pages cm
  Includes bibliographical references and index.
  ISBN 978-1-4813-0223-4 (hardback : alk. paper)
  1. Children—History. 2. Children—Biblical teaching. 3. Families—History. 4. Christianity and other religions—Greek. 5. Christianity and other religions—Roman. 6. Church history—Primitive and early church, ca. 30-600. I. Title.
  BR195.C46M33 2014
  261.8'358509015--dc23
                                        2014010732

Printed in the United States of America on acid-free paper with a minimum of 30% post-consumer waste recycled content.

JKM Library
1100 East 55th Street
Chicago, IL 60615

CONTENTS

ACKNOWLEDGMENTS

With this book, I bring together two of my main interests in the study of Christian origins: early Christian families and the disputed Pauline literature. Over the past ten years I have been enriched by the work of scholars too numerous to mention. Two groups gathering in conjunction with the meeting of the Society of Biblical Literature, however, have been especially influential: the Disputed Paulines Section and the Early Christian Families Group.

I would like to extend special thanks to the Social Sciences and Humanities Research Council of Canada for supporting my research on children and childhood in early Christian house churches. In particular, funding from this granting agency facilitated fruitful conversations with Carolyn Osiek (Emerita, Brite Divinity School), Adele Reinhartz (University of Ottawa), and Cecilia Wassen (Uppsala University). I have benefited enormously from their collective knowledge of Roman, early Christian, and Jewish sources in interpreting the evidence for the lives of children examined in this book. I would also like to thank my own university, St. Mary's University (Halifax, Nova Scotia), for research support and my former university, St. Francis Xavier University (Nova Scotia), for offering me encouragement in the form of the senior research award in May 2012.

The staff at Baylor University Press has provided excellent guidance and support. I extend special appreciation to Carey Newman for his consistent engagement with the project and many helpful suggestions.

This book is dedicated to my lifelong partner Duncan Macpherson, with whom I have spent many hours discussing children. He is a wonderful husband and father to our children, Delia and Jake. For more than thirty years, his support of my scholarship has been unfaltering.

1

INTRODUCTION
The Codes and Children

In the middle of the first-century CE, in ancient Colossae or Laodicea, a group of believers in Christ is gathered in the house of a woman named Nympha (Col 4:15). Her house is a modest peristyled house or *domus* (a building with a colonnade), but the interior courtyard is large enough for an assembly of about fifty people to gather. It is the same space where earlier in the day children had been practicing their singing of psalms, hymns, and spiritual songs. Newcomers have listened eagerly to the rejoicing and are eager to be taught this spiritual wisdom (Col 3:16). But now people are making an effort to listen quietly, with a slave caregiver doing her best to settle the toddlers in her charge. A letter from the Apostle Paul is being read aloud in the midst of the assembly (Col 4:16). Slave and free children are sitting side by side and are addressed directly, being told that they must obey their parents in everything, for this is their acceptable duty in the Lord (Col 3:20). Older slave children, already aware of the confines of their servitude and constantly reminded of the authority of their masters (Col 3:20-23), are nevertheless surprised to hear a comforting message: like freeborn sons and daughters, they will receive their inheritance from the Lord (Col 3:24).

Not too far away in ancient Ephesus, a father is teaching scriptural traditions (Eph 6:2-3) to his children, along with the stories he knows about Jesus (Eph 6:4). But these children are not only those born to his wife; they also include the slave children who live in the house and children who are playmates from the neighborhood. Some

1

are orphans—street children with very uncertain futures. Not only is he a father and head of the household, he has become a pseudo-father, bringing up all of his children in the discipline and instruction of the Lord (Eph 6:4).

A few decades later, one of these well-raised children is being recognized as an overseer/bishop in the community (1 Tim 3:1-7). His deep roots in the church traditions are celebrated, for he is no recent convert (1 Tim 3:6). An apt teacher (1 Tim 3:2), he is emulating the household leadership he learned from his own father. He too will keep his children respectful and submissive in every way.

At the same time, one of the most prosperous women in the community is hosting a group of girls and young women in another household (1 Tim 5:16). Her teaching and mentoring influence has also been recognized in helping younger women make the transition from childhood to married life, motherhood, and the management of believing households (Titus 2:3-5). The young women are quick learners and are eager to discuss some of the new community teachings that place limits on their activities. A widow herself, the woman has considerable sympathy for the young widows who wish to remain unmarried and devote themselves to ministry (1 Tim 5:11-15). Perhaps, she thinks, community leaders are overreacting to some of the tension with neighbors that has resulted from efforts to win new members.

Today the topic among the gathering of older and younger women is the young male evangelist (1 Tim 4:12) who addressed a group of children, including many adolescent boys awaiting their teacher on the steps of the theater. He claimed to be following the example of Timothy (2 Tim 4:1-5) but may have been imprudent. He encouraged the children to go along with him to the shops adjacent to the house owned by the wealthy widow in the community where they could meet other believing children and learn more about the Lord. Since then, rumors have been flying that the community is overrun with foolish women and slaves who corrupt children and encourage the disobedience of legitimate figures of authority—fathers and school-teachers.[1] The women are worried that this young evangelist is actually making it more difficult to reach out to the children in need.

These early church scenarios are fictional, but they are nevertheless based on the research in this book. New Testament (NT) ethics contained in the rule-like statements about family relations that have come to be known as household codes (e.g., Col 3:18–4:1; Eph 5:21–6:9) reveal that the presence of children was valued in early church communities. Set within the context of family life in the Roman world, brief references to children in Colossians, Ephesians, and the Letters to Timothy and Titus gain new significance. Moreover, the treatment of slaves in early Christianity should not be examined in isolation from the treatment of children. Slave children and slave parents and caregivers were members of the early Christian audience and played a role in the development and growth of early Christianity. Early church literature reveals an interest in the socialization of children as a means of preparing the community for the future and as part of efforts to articulate its identity. More and more, this concern for socialization became an explicit interest in education. Moving children to the center of the interpretation of household ethics in the NT brings one to the heart of church communities; these groups combined elements of household and school existence. Ultimately, a focus on children leads to greater understanding of how early Christians combined their faith commitment with family life; they challenged but also adopted many features of the society in which they lived.

At the outset, however, it will be necessary to discuss the nature of the evidence and how it should be approached. What difference does it make to the interpretation of household code texts when the neglected children are considered? What new questions should be asked?

Historical Questions: The Codes and Children

Probably no passages of the NT elicit such a strong set of emotions as the direct teaching about family life contained in the household codes (Col 3:18–4:1; Eph 5:21–6:9; 1 Pet 2:18–3:7; 1 Tim 2:8-15; 3:4-5; 6:1-2; Titus 2:1-10; 3:1; cf. Ign. *Pol.* 4.1–5.1; Pol. *Phil.* 4.1–6.1). These texts illustrate the importance of family matters in NT times—for some, no doubt a welcome correction to the Paul of 1 Corinthians 7, who seems a little too ambivalent about marriage and the survival of the household. These same texts have seemed to others to be the most obvious sign of an emerging patriarchy that would overshadow the spirit-filled egalitarianism of an earlier time. Perhaps above all, the household codes offer unmistakable evidence of the acceptance of the institution of slavery as a reality of early church communities and, more generally, of the shaping of early Christianity by its Roman context. Such teaching embarrasses and offends contemporary sensibilities no matter what spiritual values can be detected as infusing the rule-like statements. But to understand the meaning and legacy of these ethical codes, it is important to understand as fully as possible how they would have been heard in their own time by a diverse audience that included children. It is not possible to erase the patriarchal and oppressive effect of these codes throughout history. The main goal of this study is to read the codes with an approach that allows for awareness of the interaction of the ethical instructions with the complexities of family life in the Roman world.

The first thing to notice about the household codes is that they contain rules that in their purest form refer reciprocally to three pairs of hierarchical relationships: wives-husbands, slaves-masters, and children-parents. While the Letters to the Colossians and Ephesians offer the earliest and most succinct example of the genre (Col 3:18–4:1 and Eph 5:21–6:9), 1 Peter, the Pastoral Epistles, and the Apostolic Fathers also reflect the same type of household code material, usually displaying a rule-like structure, even if interpreted more freely.[2] The exhortations concerning marriage and slavery have received an enormous amount of attention in the past, probably because at first glance they seem more relevant to contemporary debates.[3] No doubt partially because of the brevity of the exhortations, children and the child-parent relationship have played a very small role in interpretation of the household codes. But the neglect has also been fostered by a very narrow and incomplete understanding both of childhood in the Roman world and of the relevance of familial teaching for the lives of children in church groups. Children play a more important role in these texts than is usually acknowledged. Children were more greatly valued in certain early church groups than is often recognized.

There are no simple explanations for why this type of ethical teaching emerged at a specific period of time: from approximately 60 to 150 CE (from the time of the final stages of Paul's life or shortly after his death to the period of the Apostolic Fathers, the first church authors to write after the NT).[4] This was a key era for transition and construction of identity in the *ekklēsia*, the community of believers in Christ, in the decades immediately following the disappearance of the first apostles and witnesses. At the same time, this was the era when members began to be recognized as a distinct group, apart from Jews and Gentiles. Historians have rightly pointed out, however, that overlapping identity persisted for a long time among Jews and early Christians and manifested itself in a variety of ways in different geographical regions.[5] With emerging visibility and distinctiveness came increasing hostility at the hands of outsiders. And, with increasing hostility came the need for apology: a need to explain and defend the way of life of these first Christians. In particular, these believers wished to illustrate that their familial life matched and even exceeded the best of Greco-Roman ideals. In so doing, they were following the example of their Jewish contemporaries. Little attention has been paid, however, to how children figured in this endeavor.[6] In this book, one new question that will be asked is how a focus on children can influence perception of the household codes as an apologetic response.

To view the household codes as apologetic, however, does not completely explain their origin and function. This ethical teaching also plays a key role in integrating various family members within the community. Household codes created organizational structures that facilitated relations within the community, with an eye to the outside world, to varying degrees.[7] Various factors were at play. For example, against a rising tide of asceticism involving measures to control physical appetites and contain sexuality (which can be detected especially in Colossians and the Pastoral Epistles), the household codes offered community integration to married members within the house church.[8] While some early church teachers called for the rejection of marriage altogether, in contrast, the codes concretized a stable family identity that supported the rearing of children. Admirable family identity—one of the marks of respectable citizenship—was lived out in a group whose societal alienation had been replaced by citizenship with the saints and membership within the household of God (Eph 2:19; 1 Tim 3:15).[9] Thus, a second new question has to do with integration: How does the inclusion of the address to children in the household codes of Colossians and Ephesians, together with various references to the child-parent relationship in the Pastoral Epistles, help to stabilize identity in the family and *ekklēsia*? How is an emerging concern with the socialization and education of children related to integration?

Closely connected to the issue of why NT household codes emerged in the middle to latter decades of the first century CE is the matter of the cultural roots of this teaching. The references to the three pairs of relationships dealing with marriage, parenting, and slavery represent an adoption and adaptation of common advice found in discussions of household management (*oikonomia*) from ancient Greek times to the Roman imperial era.[10] Like other discussions of household management, which envisioned the relationship between household and civic welfare (involving state, economy, and religion), the NT household codes were shaped by a perspective that linked the household to broader social entities, including the welfare of the community. This is especially clear in Ephesians, wherein marriage becomes a metaphor for the community's identity and ultimate commitment to Christ (Eph 5:22-33). The pure bride stands for much more than the inviolability of her own home, embodying the holiness of the whole *ekklēsia*.[11] Beyond recognition of basic thematic similarities, however, it is sometimes difficult to judge whether parallels with Jewish and Greco-Roman sources mean that the household codes merely reproduce conventional ethics or whether the directives are in any way shaped by a distinctive early Christian vision.[12]

In analyzing the household codes, one might distinguish between external influences and early Christian developments. On the one hand, the theme of household management and instructions about superior-subordinate relations appear to reflect wholesale borrowing from the outside. On the other hand, there is an internally developed Christian teaching framework. The specifically Christian framework includes such elements as "justification clauses" referring to "the Lord" or "in the Lord." Thus, both Colossians (3:20) and Ephesians (6:1) call children to obey their parents "in the Lord."[13] Yet, in emphasizing these phrases, it is important not to overplay Christian uniqueness.[14] Jewish Wisdom literature and Hellenistic writings offer striking parallels that can be deeply structural and/or content-specific and not just thematic. In considering the structure of the NT codes, for example, one might consider the fact that Sir 3:1-16 also contains an address, instruction, and motivation in its teaching concerning fathers, mothers, and children (and their bearing on relations with God).[15] In a manner reminiscent of the codes in Colossians and Ephesians, Philo of Alexandria (Hellenistic Jewish philosopher, ca. 20 BCE to ca. 50 CE) attempts to moderate the authority of masters and addresses both masters and, unusually, slaves (albeit indirectly) at one point.[16] There have been a striking range of materials from the Gentile world as well, which have been compared with the household codes in an effort to identify specific parallels in form and content. Examples from Hellenistic street philosophy,[17] inscriptional evidence from family-based religious associations,[18] and the agricultural handbooks (offering advice on farming practice and the management of estates) from the Roman world have all been presented as offering a context for understanding the domestic codes.[19] When children are brought to the center of interpretation, a third question must be asked: While acknowledging the infusion of "Christian" elements, such as references to the authority of the Lord, do any of the household codes reveal evidence of significant change or challenge to the status quo? Do the household codes simply reinforce the traditional role of parents or do they reshape them in certain respects?

Particularly significant is that the direct address to the subordinate groups has been identified as a distinctly Christian innovation to the household codes.[20] Household management discussions from classical Greek times to the NT era certainly refer to relational pairs and often treat each member of the pair reciprocally. But the direct address to subordinate groups as if they are listening members of the audience (especially to slaves) is unusual, if not unique.[21] The much more usual pattern is to address the head of the household directly, the implication being that this household head, as husband, master, and father, would guide and direct the other subordinate members of the household.[22] Thus, despite the fact that a great deal of similarity exists between the household codes and discussions of household management in the ancient world, no precise parallel exists to addressing subordinate members in this direct manner.

In evaluating the significance of the direct address to subordinate groups in the NT household codes, however, two points must constantly be borne in mind. First, the prescriptive tone of the regulations should not be understood as a description of what was actually going on in the communities.[23] Household code texts are idealized family descriptions that do not reveal the tensions, opposing forces, and multifaceted possibilities of lived experience. One must be cautious about drawing broad-reaching conclusions about the historical setting. The call for women to obey their husbands, for example, should not be taken to mean that women stopped exercising leadership roles during this period, as the reference to Nympha as the leader of a house church makes clear (Col 4:15).

Second, the circumstances of various members of subordinate groups should not be considered in isolation from members of other groups. Structures of domination have been shown to be comprehensive and interlocking, extending beyond the patriarchal and gender-based system to include elements of race, class, and colonialism. What this means for an analysis of the place of children in household code teaching is that the circumstances of childhood cannot be separated from the conditions of oppression caused by slavery, hierarchical marriage, or imperial might.[24]

In short, despite the relative brevity and conventionality of the NT household codes, the household codes operate in complex ways. The codes are culture affirming, but also include some countercultural elements.[25] With respect to the latter, perhaps the greatest attention has been given to the promise of inheritance from the Lord to slaves as a reward (Col 3:24), which takes on new poignancy with recognition that under Roman law slaves stood outside the realm of inheritance altogether.[26] It is crucial to investigate what the presence of such a promise could really mean when it is delivered in tandem with a call for slaves to obey "in all things" (Col 3:22) that clearly reinforces structures of domination. If only freeborn children might actually inherit, one must reflect upon what inheritance from the Lord actually implies for the life of the believing slave child.

A focus on children and childhood offers further insight into how the household codes reflect the complex negotiations related to identity formation and preservation that the early Christians shared with

Jews in the Roman imperial world. The recipients of the household codes had identities with multiple dimensions as family members, and these identities needed to be renegotiated in light of a commitment to life in Christ. This leads to a final question that requires detailed investigation: How does one's perspective on the household codes change when one views the instructions concerning children as not highly restricted in scope but instead as overlapping with exhortations directed at other groups?

To address these four questions, the main approach will be to situate the household codes in the context of family life in the Roman world. A natural place to begin, however, is with an examination of some other treatments of children and the child-parent relationship in the ancient discussions of household management.

Children in Household Management Discussions among Gentiles and Jews and in the Ancient World

The child-parent relationship plays a central role in the household management discussions of the Greco-Roman world. Several aspects of this thought are of particular importance for understanding the NT codes. Of fundamental significance, children belong to a somewhat nebulous category. Childhood was a flexible concept rather than one that was rigidly determined by biological age in the Roman world. Sometimes when children are mentioned, adult children are in view or expectations concerning the attitude of children to parents that continue into adulthood are intended.[27] In addition, children are certainly required to obey, but their obedience (and the consequences for disobedience) is viewed as fundamentally different in nature from that required of slaves. The dominion of parents over their children is typically understood as a key indicator of *pietas* (often translated as "piety"), perhaps the most important virtue in the Roman world. This virtue combines emphasis on submissive, obedient behavior, with notions of family loyalty, citizenship, and deference to God or the gods. So important is this virtue that it can override concepts of justice in parent-child relations; for it is sometimes necessary to acquiesce to the unjust will of a parent for the sake of one's *pietas*.[28] Among

Jews and Gentiles, parental authority could be expressed as akin to divine authority, even though there were also clear calls for moderation in the exercise of discipline.

Many of these elements can be detected in the classic discussion of household management in Aristotle's *Politics*.[29] The parallel with the household codes of Colossians and Ephesians can be seen in the treatment of the same pairs of relationships and the focus on the authority of the head of the household. Children, like women and slaves, are "by nature" intended to be ruled. But the child represents a somewhat ambiguous category because of potential to exercise dominion. Clearly shaped with the male child primarily in view, it is acknowledged that the child has the deliberative part of the soul (albeit an undeveloped form) and that "the children grow up to be partners in the government of the state." In contrast, women have the deliberative part of the soul "but without full authority" (slaves lack it altogether); and while the education of both women and children "to be good" is ultimately for the good of the state, the male child is set apart by his latent capacity for dominion.[30] While a child is still a child, however, he or she is subject to the kingly authority of the head of the household who is a ruler by virtue "both of affection and of seniority."[31] Yet in a manner that anticipates the moderation of parental authority in the household codes, *The Nicomachean Ethics* spell out that kingly authority does not mean tyrannical authority following the example of the Persians who use their sons as slaves.[32] The commentary indirectly asserts, of course, that tyrannical rule with respect to slaves is appropriate.[33]

A second example from the classical Greek era (fourth-century BCE Athens) of household management discourse, often compared with the household codes, is Xenophon's *Oeconomicus*, which likewise treats marriage, the management of slaves, and the child-parent relationship. Much of the text is a reported conversation between Socrates and a married householder, Ischomachus, illustrating the relationship between economics, household management, and agriculture especially clearly. Of special significance for this volume is the way it presents the intergenerational bonds between parents and children.[34] While it certainly reflects the indoor (women)/outdoor (men) dichotomy of elite classical Greek society, the manner in which wifely and motherly authority is described is sometimes surprising.

For instance, Ischomachus presents his wife as capable of managing the household affairs independently while he occupies himself with outdoor pursuits. Her skills stem from both the education she received from her parents and from the formation he himself provided upon their marriage. Ischomachus admits that she was young when they married (not quite fifteen) and that she would inevitably have much to learn. But he also states confidently that she had been carefully raised to control appetite and self-indulgence, which is the most important product of education of the young for both men and women. Here we are introduced to concepts that are important for interpretation of household code materials in the Pastoral Epistles: marriage of women when they were (by our standards) still adolescents means that a fluid relationship existed between childhood and adulthood with associated responsibilities. In Xenophon's treatise, the young wife is like a child to be instructed, and ongoing education continues well into the early stages of marriage (cf. Titus 2:3-5). Without denying the existence of patriarchal structures, male and female authority over the household could be presented as taking distinct, but equally important, forms (cf. 1 Tim 3:1-5; 5:14).

In Ischomachus' speech we find several examples of intergenerational influences. The mother is presented as key to promoting sobermindedness or temperance in her daughter (the same quality was instilled in Ischomachus by his father). The couple is to credit their parents for bringing them together in the hope of the best welfare for their household and future children. Likewise, the couple will consult each other as to how best to bring up their children with the promise that they will be looked after in their old age. Procreation is identified as the chief duty of the married couple, but interestingly, the central outcome of this bond is sons and daughters to look after parents as they grow old. The continuum from infancy to old age is even reflected in the manner in which the wife's indoor life is conceived. Women have been created with the capacity to nurture newborn babies and granted a larger share of affection for babies than has been bestowed upon men. The wife's household management is compared with that of a queen bee who sends forth those with outdoor responsibilities, manages the stores of what they bring back, presides over the fabric of carefully constructed cells, and is the guardian of the youth who are nursed and reared under her care, but who are unhesitatingly sent forth when they are ready for work responsibilities. With this analogy, Ischomachus communicates the central role of his wife in "the circle of (household) life." Her role should strengthen with age—as her hair turns gray—for she is to gain even greater honor as mistress, wife, and mother, with increasing skill as guardian of the home and helpmate to husband and children (cf. 1 Tim 5:9-10).

While there is not much detail provided about the family life of slaves in Xenophon's *Oeconomicus*, the presentation of Ischomachus' introduction of the household structure to his wife reminds us of the way children and family relations could be used as a means of controlling slave behavior. We also find such strategies in Roman sources, yet such strict divisions of living spaces largely disappear from sources of the Roman imperial era.[35] In describing the living arrangements of slaves, Ischomachus speaks of the women's apartments being separated from the men's apartments by a bolted door; a measure that prevents household slaves bearing children without the consent of the household head. He goes on to say that while cohabitation can provide opportunities for scheming on the one hand, the rearing of children in slave families can increase loyalty in good servants on the other.[36] Later in the text, on the role of the bailiff (slave estate manager), there are references to motivating slaves with various rewards (or withholding them) such as more praise, more food, better clothing and shoes.[37]

Although there are some subtle differences, most of the same sentiments about parenting and children were articulated in the household management material from the next several centuries. From the Roman era we might consider the *encomium* (a formal expression of praise) of Rome by Dionysius of Halicarnassus, Greek historian and teacher of rhetoric who wrote at the end of the first century BCE. He sought to convince his audience of the merits of Roman rule by telling Rome's history with its mythic past, including the foundation of the Roman state and law under Romulus. Dionysius of Halicarnassus' *Antiquitates romanae* has been viewed as especially important for the thesis that the NT domestic codes have an apologetic function because of its defensive and ideological orientation. The work offers a prime example of the tendency of some authors to discuss the public constitution, with reference to "temperance," which includes a wife's chaste behavior and submission to her husband and the proper training of children.[38] Like the NT household codes, Dionysius praised household relationships involving the three Aristotelian pairs of wives and husbands, children and parents, masters and slaves, in the same order as the pairs in Colossians and Ephesians. Further, as in these NT works, the duties of wives precede those of husbands, and those of children precede those of fathers.[39] The detailed attention he pays to children and parenting among the Romans is particularly interesting for the purposes of this study.[40] In establishing the superiority of the Roman position over the Greek, he notes that the laws concerning women by Romulus were excellent, but "those he established with respect to reverence and dutifulness of children toward their parents, to the end that they should honor and obey them in all things, both in their words and actions, were still more august and of greater dignity and vastly superior to our laws."[41] The same terminology with respect to children occurs in Col 3:20, which instructs children to obey their parents "in all things," and while it is contained within a scriptural reference, honoring parents is encouraged in Eph 6:2.[42] In Colossians, wholehearted obedience ("in all things") is also required of slaves (Col 3:22), and the links between slavery and childhood with respect to authority and obedience call for careful reflection.[43]

It is important to note that comparison between the subordinate states of childhood and enslavement is a key feature of Dionysius' case to establish the superiority of the Romans concerning the value attached to the obedience of children. To build his case, he begins with the time frame of fatherly authority over sons. According to Dionysius, Greeks limit the authority of fathers over their sons to the time frame of early manhood and before marriage. Moreover, punishments for disobedience are not severe, for they extend only to disinheritance and turning sons out. Dionysius defines fatherly authority among the Romans in the strongest possible terms: "But the lawgiver of the Romans gave virtually full power to the father over his son, even during his whole life, whether he thought proper to imprison him, to scourge him, to put him in chains and keep him at work in the fields, or to put him to death, and this even though the son were already engaged in public affairs, though he were numbered among the highest magistrates, and though he were celebrated for his zeal for the commonwealth."[44] Dionysius' point is made sharper and his apologetic rhetoric clearer by the comment that anyone educated in the "lax manners of the Greeks" may view as "harsh and tyrannical" the fact that Roman law gave fathers the right to sell their sons into slavery and that they would remain in the cycle of slavery/fatherly control until they were sold a third time, when they would gain their emancipation. Slaves, on the other hand, remained free after they had been sold once and gained their liberty. With a very frequently cited phrase, Dionysius states that the Roman lawgiver gave "greater power to the father over his son than to the master over his slaves."[45]

Dionysius pays very little direct attention to the slave-master relationship beyond this comparison; his main interest is to stress the value that Romans attach to the obedience of children. His case is overstated for effect, as there is plenty of counterevidence to suggest that slaves were usually treated much more severely than legitimate children in the Roman world.[46] There were several warnings against the use of excessive force in the punishment of children from Roman times; in and of themselves the calls for moderation in Col 3:21 and Eph 6:4 certainly do not point to novel Christian parenting practices.[47] It is the case, however, that the Roman concept of the authority of fathers and heads of households—*patria potestas*—often did increase the emphasis on the obedience of children in comparison with earlier Greek models.[48] In the ancient philosophical circles devoted to neopythagorean traditions (a revival of Pythagorean doctrines combined with elements of Platonism), very difficult to date but which many scholars now locate between the first centuries BCE and CE, we find a strong accent on the obedience of children.[49] Among these fascinating texts are examples of women writers who are purportedly giving advice to other women. In *On the Harmony of a Woman*, Perictyone offers advice on a woman's roles in household management with respect to her husband, children, and slaves, but also provides extensive teaching on a daughter's reverence for her parents, which extends into their old age; the discourse provides further evidence for the intergenerational links we have already observed in household management material. A daughter is told that she is to obey her parents in important and minor matters (recalling the reference to all things in Col 3:20). The one who despises her parents is charged with a sin by the gods—one of the frequent associations of parents with divinity in the ancient world.[50]

Within a century of Dionysius of Halicarnassus and at about the same time as many NT works were composed, the Jewish author Josephus created an apologetic work, *Against Apion*, wherein the obedience of children also figured prominently.[51] Although marriage and the slave-master relationship are certainly discussed, the rearing of children is rarely recognized as a key aspect of Jewish identity in Josephus' apologetic work.[52] This emphasis on proper rearing of children likely played a role in responding to accusations that Jews were disruptive and antisocial; but as comparison with Dionysius of Halicarnassus illustrates, reference to obedient children and reverence for parents was also central to a display of good citizenship and might help one win a hearing. The treatment of children by Jews becomes part of the agenda to convince Josephus' audience that Jewish family values are compatible with Roman imperial values. Josephus' apologetic interests stand out especially sharply, for example, in his first reference to children: "Above all we pride ourselves on the education of our children, and regard as the most essential task in life the observance of our laws and of the pious practices (*eusebeian*), based thereupon, which we have inherited."[53] This is followed by a statement that the law "orders all the offspring to be brought up," with prohibitions of abortion and infanticide—a response to Greco-Roman practices viewed as anathema to the Jews.[54] Josephus wishes to illustrate that the law is more severe than the practices of other nations, so that among Jews "the mere intention of doing wrong to one's parents or of impiety (*asebeias*) against God is followed by instant death."[55] Similar overstatement is found in the following comment, which is also clearly intended to leave no doubt that Jewish law is in keeping with and exceeds the concept of *patria potestas* among the Romans: "Honour to parents the Law ranks second only to honour to God, and if a son does not respond to the benefits received from them—for the slightest failure in his duty towards them—it hands him over to be stoned."[56]

The association of the obedience of children with piety and parental authority with divine authority is completely conventional in the ancient world. Among first-century Jews, an arguably even stronger expression of equivalence between parents and the divine than that of

Josephus was made by Philo of Alexandria: "For parents are midway between the natures of God and man, and partake of both . . . Parents in my opinion, are to their children what God is to the world."[57] Philo's analogy draws upon ancient concepts of the gods as models for fathers/parents. The second-century CE Stoic philosopher Hierocles offers one of the clearest examples of this sentiment in his discussion of family relations and household management:

> After the discourse concerning gods and country, what other person could one mention first if not one's parents? Hence we must speak about these, whom one would not err in calling as it were second and terrestrial gods, and indeed because of their nearness, if it is lawful to say so, even more to be honored than the gods. . . . Thus, to make the choice of our duties towards parents easy, it is best that we propose a summary argument and keep it continually at hand: that our parents are images of gods and, by Zeus, domestic gods, benefactors, relatives, creditors, masters, and most reliable friends.[58]

Whether parental authority receives the same kind of divine sanction in the early church household codes and what this might mean for children in the community is an issue that requires careful consideration. On the surface it may appear that the household codes do not draw a parallel between parents and God/gods in order to encourage appropriate behavior in the manner of many ancient authors.[59] But it is difficult to know how far to push this observation. While it applies to marriage rather than to the parent-child relationship, this kind of analogical principle is certainly at work in Ephesians, in which the authority of Christ as head of the church mirrors the authority of husbands over wives (Eph 6:22-33). Moreover, the parallel call for children and slaves to be obedient in all things to the head of the household, coupled with the play on the use of the term "Lord" (*kyrios*) to mean both divine Lord and earthly master, means that with the household codes we are very close to the worldview of these ancient philosophical texts. Hierocles' use of several analogies to remind readers of the nature of duties to parents—from images of the gods, to benefactors, to masters—also needs to be kept in mind. The analogies point to the flexible boundaries and frequently unspoken assumptions that characterized hierarchical relations in ancient familial contexts. Even the warning to masters that they have a heavenly Lord, which seems to qualify their authority in significant ways, sounds less radical in relation to Hierocles' principle for governing family relations. His principle sounds remarkably like the call to "do onto others": "A person would treat a slave well, if he considered how he would think the other should behave toward himself, if the other were the master and he himself the slave. And the argument is similar for parents in respect to children and children in respect to parents and, in a word, for all in respect to all."[60] At the same time, it is true that human authority is quite clearly presented as secondary to the authority of the Lord in the early church household codes: both parents and children stand side by side under the authority of the Lord.[61] The cultural negotiations required are inevitably complex, for the household codes spoke to audiences that sought divine sanction for rupture within the family. Tension and even breakdown in relations between wives and husbands, slaves (including slave children) and masters, and most probably also children and their parents are all within the realm of possibility.

There are deep similarities between references to children in the NT household codes and material about children in household management discussions among Gentiles and Jews and in the ancient world. These similarities point to the necessity of evaluating evidence on both material and ideological grounds. Discussions of household management were rooted in notions of the household as property and of household headship as control of property. Subordinate family members were subsumed under the category of household holdings, which included not only goods, but slaves and even blood family members.[62] The ancient household was at the heart of the ancient economy, and extended households were defined by an emphasis on production.[63] Both free and slave children were active participants in this multifaceted and bustling family unit; given the domestic context of early church groups, it is crucial to remember that the usually unacknowledged presence of children might have been a far more important factor in the origins of Christianity than has heretofore been recognized.

But the control of children was part of the cultural currency of this society—one of the main means of demonstrating honor and exercising dominion. In fact, the authority of the *pater familias* (the male head of the household) was delineated in terms of persons and things under his legal power (*patria potestas*).[64] References to the rearing and obedience of children were one of the means groups employed to define themselves and to argue for their superiority in relation to others. But as Hierocles' principle for governing family relations makes clear, there is a surprising emphasis on mutuality and even occasional challenges to traditional expectations in some of these texts, leading to questions about the real balance of power. All of this needs to be remembered when evaluating texts concerning children that seem on the surface to be either simplistic or highly ideological (or both) but which may in fact be related to a far more complex social reality.

The Direct Appeal to Children in Context

The direct appeal to subordinate members of the household—especially slaves—has garnered a great deal of attention among commentators on the household codes. Nevertheless, few interpreters have really probed the significance of the direct appeal to children in Colossians and Ephesians. Admittedly, the references dealing with the child-parent relationship are brief, with two reciprocal verses in Col 3:20-21 expanded somewhat in Eph 6:1-4. But these texts leave us with no doubt that children were present in community gatherings where Pauline Letters were read aloud (Col 4:16) and called out for exhortation. The parent-child relationship was valued as something that could be shaped by life in Christ. These verses, therefore, are far more significant than their length would suggest. The presence of children in early church groups was of central importance to the atmosphere and mission of early church groups. We need to consider how early church instruction would have been "heard" by children, and how a recognition of the presence of children might transform our vision of the interactions in church communities.

To some degree one is hampered in understanding by literal translation and narrow and anachronistic interpretation. Debates about whether these texts refer to young children or adult children fail to appreciate the lack of strict demarcation between childhood and adulthood in antiquity and the absence of chronological markers that strictly determine rights, such as our modern age of eligibility to drive or to vote.[65] Especially when we consider the lives of girls who often married when they were only adolescents by our standards, we need to keep in mind a long continuum of ongoing education into adulthood that surpassed marriage and the birth of a first child.[66] In addition, we must move beyond a simplistic analysis of the categories in the houschold codes. Three points need to be made concerning overlapping aspects of familial identity that have not always seemed obvious to interpreters: Slaves must have included child slaves. Not all children were from households headed by Christians. In a house-church context it would be virtually impossible to exclude the presence of children.

It is now generally accepted that the household codes should not be understood as a straightforward description of what was actually occurring. But it is also crucial to come to terms with the fact that the categories themselves fail to reveal overlapping identities. References to slaves would naturally include children, and references to children would also by necessity refer to slaves. Slaves formed varying degrees of stable family alliances. The children of believing slaves would often have shared service to believing masters with their parents. Likewise, the child slaves of nonbelieving masters may well have accompanied their believing parents to church meetings without the permission of their masters, placing the children and the parents in an extremely vulnerable position (1 Tim 6:1-2). The presupposition that slaves must include child slaves is also based upon the shared living spaces of free and slave children. Roman Ephesus and Pompeii offer little solid evidence for separate slave quarters. This means that slaves probably slept wherever they happened to be working or serving their masters; kitchens, storerooms, and the floor of a master's bedroom are all possibilities.[67] Wet nurses and caregivers were usually slaves who reared young free and slave children together; all children, therefore, would share the same spaces during the day, and free children frequently became temporary members of the slave *familia*.[68] Ancient sources speak of both free and slave children being present at celebrations such as banquets and weddings. We must even be prepared to conceive of slave children being assigned ritual roles that grew out of their work as servers, readers, and entertainers.[69]

Not only do the household codes mask the reality of the shared world of free and enslaved children, they offer a form of camouflage to children who were members of households headed by nonbelievers. While they are rarely taken into consideration, it is almost beyond question that early church communities welcomed these children. As early as 1 Cor 7:12-16, the presence of the children of nonbelievers is presupposed. Here Paul encourages believers to remain married to nonbelievers as long as the nonbelieving partner is willing to stay together. There is nothing to indicate whether believing wives, husbands, or both are in view, but later church literature speaks almost exclusively of women being in such circumstances. Nevertheless, the nature of the later evidence is not surprising, given that one might expect married householders (but also widows at the head of households) to enter the church with their whole extended household. There is at least limited evidence in Paul's Letters and in Acts for this pattern of conversion (1 Cor 1:16; Acts 10:1–11:18; 16:11-15, 25-34; 18:1-11). The brief reference to children in 1 Cor 7:14 points to the presence of (or, as a minimum, consideration of) the children of mixed marriage who are now "holy," and we would do well in imagining these children as having believing mothers who brought them to church gatherings.[70]

The use of familial language to refer to slave alliances (despite the fact that slave marriages were not recognized in law) in ancient commemorative inscriptions means that we cannot rule out the possibility that the children of mixed marriage included slaves.[71] First Timothy 6:1-2 refers to the slaves who live under the authority of nonbelievers and children should be considered as part of this group. In addition, 1 Pet 3:1-6 offers indisputable evidence of the presence of women married to unbelievers in the community. These women were also mothers, raising the question of whether their precarious situation was caused by the fact that they not only betrayed their husband's oversight over the religion of the household but encouraged their children to do the same.[72] It is often mistakenly presumed when nonbelief is not explicitly mentioned that the people covered by the named categories in the household codes were all Christian. Yet it is important to note that the codes (most notably Colossians) do not state this. One should assume that the family circumstances of some members of the audience that heard these codes included the tricky complexity of living in the house of a nonbeliever who would not have approved of the new allegiance.[73]

A comprehensive vision of family life in the Roman world, including how families lived in a variety of domestic spaces, allows one to move beyond a literal reading of the household codes.[74] It is vital to give in-depth consideration to various possible identities of the children addressed in the codes: members of believing families, children of mixed marriage with one parent as a believer, neglected children who made their way into church meetings without parents, or slave children, including slave children who may have been biological children of their masters. It is crucial to consider how particular circumstances affected how children heard the household codes. It is also essential to reflect upon the identity of parents who may often have been pseudo-parents in the Lord rather than biological parents. The relationship between childhood and slavery should be of prime interest. Among the many aspects of this relationship, one that needs to be considered in light of inscriptional evidence is the suggestion that some slave children were raised with the expectation that they would one day share in the promise of the free children of the family.[75] In addition to the sharing of domestic spaces by slaves and free children, slaves and free children also shared educational experiences, with slave caregivers often acting as the first educators of children and with much education taking place at home. The emphasis on education/socialization of children in household code traditions (Eph 6:4; *1 Clem.* 21.6, 8; *Did.* 4.9; Pol. *Phil.* 4.2) calls for an examination of the house church as a locus for children's education.[76]

Be they slave or free, the sons and daughters of believers or nonbelievers, one must assume that when early Christians met in houses, children were present. Children seem to have penetrated virtually every social space in the Roman world. The archaeological record does not support notions of separate playrooms or bedrooms for children.[77] Simple two-room dwellings above shops (which might well have served as the meeting places for some church groups) would simply have children, including crying infants and toddlers, as a constant presence. The story in Acts of the youth (*neanias, pais*) Eutychus falling asleep at the window of a dwelling in Troas and then falling to near death is suggestive of such a context (Acts 20:7-12). With respect to lower classes, the neighborhood and street were the playground. Children were also everywhere to be found in more elite spaces, even if one's own inclination might be to think that the bigger the space, the greater the chance that a child could be sequestered. Architectural plans in grander houses were open, and children were mobile within them, ready to witness every activity.

Gospel and Pauline Trajectories

A heightened awareness of the sexual use of children in the Roman world in recent years has led to consideration of whether the association of Jesus with children in the Gospels means that burgeoning church groups should be viewed as offering protection to children. Male and female slaves were sexually available to their masters in the Roman world; this sexual availability extended to include boys and girls.[78] With respect to the Jesus tradition, for example, it has recently been argued that the reference to "cause to stumble" (*skandalizō*) of the little ones in Mark 9:42 followed by mention of body parts in 9:43-48 (which in some contexts carry sexual connotations) actually refers to pederasty. Sexual immorality of various types was typically included in descriptions of the scandals of the Gentile world by Jews.[79] It remains a matter of some conjecture whether such teachings of Jesus were understood as calls for protection of children, including child slaves who were frequently used for the sexual enjoyment of masters, for the NT is not explicit in its prohibitions. But there is significant comparative evidence in Jewish and Christian texts and, therefore, the deep concern for sexual ethics in Colossians and Ephesians should be taken as having a bearing on sexual relations with slaves, including slave children.[80]

That the direct appeal to children in the NT domestic codes might be in some way related to the protection of children is in keeping with other aspects of the Jesus tradition as well. That children offer an example of discipleship (Matt 18:4-5; Mark 9:36-7; Luke 9:47-48) and true greatness is unusual in an ancient context where children could admittedly serve as models of piety (Ps 8.2; Matt 21:16), but where it was also highly unlikely that adults would be viewed as having something substantial to learn from children.[81] Mark 9:33-37 is striking on two counts: Jesus' teaching takes place in a house setting (Mark 9:33), suggesting that the text might have gained significance as it was heard later in a house-church setting where members struggled to work out the meaning of subordination in community life. In addition, this teaching is also set within the framework of an argument among the disciples about who should be greatest. Cultural expectations are reversed, as it is the child who embodies what it means to be a disciple and becomes a representative of Jesus himself. Such reversals are perhaps even more pronounced in Luke's report of the words of Jesus, "Let the greatest among you become as the youngest" (Luke 22:26), and the prayer of Jesus in Matthew, "I thank you, Father, Lord of heaven and earth, because you have hidden these things from the wise and the intelligent and have revealed them to infants (*nēpiois*)" (Matt 11:25).[82] Trajectories from the Jesus traditions to Pauline teachings concerning families might help explain the unusual direct appeal to children and slaves in the household codes as well as the fact that in Colossians and Ephesians the instructions to subordinates typically precede instructions to superiors.[83]

It may also be helpful to reflect upon how Jesus' blessing of children (Matt 19:13-15; Mark 10:13-16; Luke 18:15-17) would have been heard in the household context of early church communities. Here children are presented explicitly as the focus of Jesus' ministry. In Mark's Gospel, the touching of children recalls frequent references to acts of healing (cf. Mark 1:41; 3:10; 5:23, 27-30; 6:56; 8:22); the relevance of healing for the life of children is also reinforced by three accounts that precede the blessing episode (Mark 5:21-24, 35-42; 7:25-30; 9:14-29).[84] Taken together, the blessing and discipleship texts from the Gospels, in which children act as either examples or are the direct recipients of Jesus' ministry, could offer justification for house-church communities to heal, care for, and teach children. This is not to suggest that early church groups revolutionized interaction with children, somehow placing them in positions of authority. Jesus' recognition of parental authority (e.g., Mark 7:9-13; Matt 15:4-6; 19:19) and the household code teaching itself come as reminders that hierarchical concepts of child-parent interaction are preserved in the NT.[85] But Matt 11:25 offers particularly strong warrant from the Jesus tradition that the welcoming of children into the community might sometimes involve the denial of traditions emanating from elders, as in cases in which parents (and more often fathers) were nonbelievers. We do not know that such teachings were familiar in the Pauline and early church communities where household code teaching was proclaimed. But documents containing household code material do point to slaves and wives challenging the authority of nonbelieving heads of households through their allegiance to early church groups. Later evidence confirms the picture. The second-century critic of earliest Christianity, Celsus, presented church groups as specifically targeting children and encouraging them to disobey fathers and teachers.[86] From the same era and in both early Christian texts and pagan reaction to church groups, we find a frequent grouping together of orphans and widows. These texts suggest an atmosphere wherein church groups cared for the abandoned and alone and/or believing widows of some means extended hospitality to destitute women and children.[87]

In some respects it is more difficult to trace a trajectory to the direct appeal to children in the NT household codes from the undisputed Letters of Paul than from the Gospels. The main reason is that Paul is virtually silent about the concrete presence of children despite his frequent description of believers as children (most often *teknon/ tekna* is employed). The only indisputable reference to flesh-and-blood children is 1 Cor 7:14; but to be precise, these are the children of a believing parent rather than a direct reference to believing children themselves.[88] The meaning of the reference to children in 1 Cor 7:14 remains unresolved, and despite the efforts of English translators to infuse the verse with logic, the most straightforward translation renders the verse contradictory and paradoxical: "since therefore they [the children; *tekna*] are unclean, but now are holy."[89] In a manner that draws upon Jewish categories of thought but departs significantly from later rabbinic sources, Paul is speaking about the curious circumstances of children with one parent who is a believer and another who belongs to the nonbelieving (unclean) world. Such children serve as argumentative proof for the necessity of preserving mixed marriage if at all possible. Paul seems to argue from hindsight that such children offer obvious illustration of the transformative power of a believing life (they are holy); yet their concrete circumstances in the community remain far from clear. It is impossible to determine whether these children were attending house-church meetings on a regular basis and whether this was taking place with the nonbelieving parent's knowledge. There is no indication that these children would no longer be holy if, as is made possible by the scenario envisioned in 1 Cor 7:15, the nonbelieving partner separated, taking the children (in case of divorce, husbands typically retained the children).[90] In thinking about the challenges facing these children and their believing parents, we catch a faint glimpse of the ubiquitous presence of children in the Apostle's life despite his clear preference for asceticism expressed elsewhere in the chapter.[91] First Corinthians 7:14 indicates that a preference for celibacy should not be taken to mean that children had no place; sometimes children on the margins of church experience might even have found a temporary haven in the midst of fluctuating circumstances.

First Corinthians 7:14 comes as a reminder that we should not assume that the children addressed directly in the household codes were of uniform identity. We must think in much more diverse terms than that of the free child, with two believing parents. While there is no conclusive evidence, there is much in the metaphorical language and rhetoric used by Paul to describe relationships and convey theological concepts to suggest that even in their earliest stages church groups were nurturing children. In fact, while it has received comparatively little attention, there is a remarkable appeal to concepts of parenting and childhood in the Letters of Paul.[92] Paul's conventional acceptance of the virtue of obedience, including the tendency to view the disobedience of children in relation to parents as a sign of ungodliness (Rom 1:30), is particularly relevant for analyzing the household codes.[93] In keeping with his extensive use of the concept of the child to envision relations, Paul describes Timothy as a faithful and compliant child (1 Cor 4:17), a notion developed further in the Pastoral Epistles.[94] Like the household codes, Paul's metaphors respect the hierarchy inherent in the role of the *pater familias* with respect to slaves, the freeborn, and inheritance (Gal 4:2). The education and discipline of children by their fathers is likewise a central feature of the household code in Ephesians (5:4).[95] The use of metaphorical language in Paul's Letters to refer to the training of believers as they are led to maturity is well known, including the image of the pedagogue (*paedagōgos*), usually a slave, who brought children to school and offered basic instruction (e.g., 1 Cor 4:15; Gal 3:25-26; 4:24-25).[96]

Some aspects of Paul's thought support the role of the house church as nurturing children, even if Paul does not speak of concrete human interactions in this way. The image of adoption is explored, for example, to great theological effect (e.g., Gal 4:1-7; Rom 8:14-17, 18-24; cf. Eph 1:3-14; 3:14-15).[97] In one of the most striking familial images in the NT, Paul describes his interaction with the Thessalonian community (1 Thess 2:7) as being as gentle as a nurse (the slave caregivers who were also wet nurses).[98] In the same text, he appeals to the situation of orphans and appears to describe his situation in relation to the Thessalonians as being that of a helpless orphan, yearning for his parents.[99] Some of the most surprising aspects of the use of childhood images and rhetorical devices involve Paul's reversal of expectations with respect to children or the use of parenting images in unexpected ways. As one might expect, Paul uses the role of the father as an image for relations with communities (e.g., 1 Thess 2:11), including the role of father as a strict disciplinarian (e.g., 1 Cor 4:14-21). But serving as a caution against excluding the role of mother in how the household codes would have been heard in community life, Paul can also conceive of his relationship with believers in terms of motherhood (e.g., Gal 4:19).[100] Perhaps the most daring of Paul's childhood images is the use of the unusual term *ektrōma*, often translated as "untimely born," but perhaps better rendered as "prematurely born, or possibly born with some kind of physical defect" to refer to his own apostolic status based on being the last to receive a resurrection appearance (1 Cor 15:8).[101] Much attention has been paid to Paul's rhetorical tactics and style of argument to gain a following and secure his authority. But in this case his shocking metaphor may be intended to highlight his vulnerability and forge a bond with his addressees whose social positions include vulnerabilities of many forms related to life in an all-powerful, and often brutal, empire.[102] If Paul's paradoxical expressions concerning childhood extend beyond rhetoric to encompass social and ideological meanings, then one might identify a trajectory between the undisputed letters and later Pauline and early church literature containing household codes: unexpected elements and challenges to cultural norms in the codes emerge in relation to imperial ideologies and definitions of family supported by the imperial agenda.

Children, Families, and Empire

The NT household codes are more culturally complex than has previously been recognized. The cultural complexity involves both the multiple identities of the recipients of the codes and the various attitudes toward interaction with the dominant Roman imperial society reflected in the ethical teaching.[103] When the household codes with their hierarchical vision have been compared with the communal arrangements reflected in the undisputed letters of Paul, however, there has been a tendency to characterize the NT household codes as accommodation to the interests of empire in contrast to the anti-imperial Paul.[104] Yet when the disputed Pauline Epistles are examined on their own terms in light of imperial ideologies and iconography, the orientation of the household codes does not appear so straightforward. Anti-imperial notions can be identified and/or multifarious cultural negotiations can be brought to light.[105] The Colossians code, for example, should be interpreted in light of the temple complex at Aphrodisias, located about 100 km from Colossae; this sculptural relief dedicated to the Julio-Claudian emperors celebrates their triumph as they stand together with their families and deities ruling over pacified peoples assimilated in imperial harmony. The iconographic display suggests that the emphasis on harmony in the Colossians code and in Col 3:11 (celebrating new identity in Christ in light of the breaking down of ethnic boundaries and uniting of slave and free) needs to be read in relation to imperial ideology and propaganda.[106] Depictions of both ideal imperial families and conquered families, including women and children, served moral and political purposes in the Empire. This raises many questions about what ideological positions might underlie

the presentation of ideal families in the household codes. An awareness of the presence of slave children among the audience of the NT
household codes, for example, can lead to recognition of the existence
of a countermessage in the codes directed at those who would label
such children as only belonging to the alienated, conquered, and
disenfranchised.[107]

The concept of a "hidden transcript," as typical of oppressed
groups, is illuminating when seeking to situate household code traditions within the context of empire. This line of reasoning suggests that
while oppressed groups appear to be compliant with the dominant
social order, they are in actuality speaking a language that only insiders will understand.[108] It suggests the likely scenario that early Christians may have sometimes used language that made them appear to
be culturally compliant but had a different meaning within their own
groups.[109] In other words, the NT household codes contain language
that had a distinct meaning to insiders, the members of early church
groups. This language may not have been *obviously* countercultural to
neighbors and curious onlookers and operated in conjunction with
conventional values, but nevertheless it challenged the values and
ideologies of the dominant society. The promise of "inheritance" to
slaves in Col 3:24, for example, had a very specific meaning in the
construction of identity of early church groups.[110] At the same time,
however, the complicated historical record revealed by the household
codes must always be kept in mind.[111]

Postcolonial analysis offers insight into the conflicted nature of
the relationship between the early church and the broader society and
a greater appreciation of the complicated interactions required for
church groups to forge their identities in the Roman imperial world.[112]
In brief: postcolonial critics demonstrate a dual interest in the various
strategies by which colonizers (in this case, the Roman authorities)
construct images of the colonized (in this case, the various peoples
conquered and enslaved throughout the regions of the Empire) and
how the colonized themselves make use of and transform many of
those images in order to articulate their identities and empowerment.
The latter is of particular significance for the origins of early Christianity.[113] With respect to the household codes, it is important to investigate how early church authors made use of (and went beyond or

critiqued) conventional appeals to family structures and values found throughout the Empire to exhort community members.

Three concepts from postcolonial theory are especially useful to probe the location of early church groups within the Roman Empire and their apparent willingness to proclaim the very familial ideology that was at the heart of imperial self-conception: ambivalence, mimicry, and hybridity.[114] Only an introduction of these concepts is possible here, but they will lay the groundwork for the analysis in the chapters to come. Briefly put, there is an ambivalent quality to the language and narrative arising from a colonial situation.[115] While a certain amount of assimilation of the colonized to the colonial worldview is inevitable, it is never quite complete. Hence, we may speak of mimicry as being "almost the same, *but not quite.*"[116] With respect to the household codes, early church groups appear to emulate the family structures and values of the dominant society, but certain elements might be transformed, while others are absent or rejected— sometimes in subtle ways that are difficult to detect.[117] The notion of hybridity is especially promising in seeking to understand an ethos that reflects the experience of the colonized and displaced, while at the same time demonstrating points of contact with the strategies of the Roman imperial conquerors.[118] The concept of hybridity can help one to understand the household codes as more culturally diverse, representing a type of intercultural exchange between the emerging early Christian ethos and the values and ethics of the broader society.[119]

This study calls for reflection concerning how the conventionality of the household code teaching on the child-parent relationship should be understood in light of strong indications that house churches were welcoming the children of nonbelieving household heads. It is important to consider the experience of children among subject peoples and how children figured in Roman imperial ideology and propaganda, including iconographic display. By bringing the experience of children to the center of investigation, this enterprise has much in common with studies on women in early Christianity that seek to bring women's lives to the center—to move beyond a simplistic view of the lives of the women based on male attitudes to women in the direction of an effort to hear the women's voices.[120] The lives of children are even more difficult to reconstruct on the basis of evidence than the lives of women, however, for they remain literally silent in our sources. But one may certainly feel their presence and glean something of how it shaped the life of house churches. Perhaps most important is the new perspective one gains in reading the household codes through the lens of children and childhood. The effect is not unlike what has been seen in the study of early Christian women and gender roles: what at first glance may appear to have little to do with children and childhood turns out to be much more about them than was previously thought. Categories that were once thought to exclude children must now be opened up to include them. At the same time, one must pay careful attention to how the representation of children is affected by genre, metaphor, novelistic tendencies, and conventional literary and moral themes such as the household management theme reflected in the household codes. The same caution that applies in the move "from representation to reality" in the case of women should apply in the study of childhood, for like women, children could serve the metaphorical and rhetorical purposes of male authors.[121]

In keeping with the insight that the household codes are prescriptive and not descriptive, it is crucial to reiterate that household codes represent familial idealizations that have a convoluted relationship to real people. Insistence on the obedience of children, for example, should not be taken to mean that parental authority was never contravened in church groups. Moreover, as one explores the child-parent relationship, how gender is constructed becomes central to evaluation of the roles of mothers and fathers. Household codes are prime assertions and defenses of masculinity that involve reinforcement of paternity and male control of household dependents. With a long history of treatment as apologetic discourse, they have often been recognized as focused on church image, but not primarily on parental image. Such a shift in perspective may offer a new way of approaching the long-debated question of how this ethical teaching reflects interaction between church and society, placing new emphasis on children as a point of contact and a point of conflict. Finally, approaching the household codes with a focus on familial ideologies and ideologies of masculinity can be very valuable in illuminating the broader messages conveyed in the exhortations about the honor of the household and house church within the broader imperial society. For example, in analyzing Ephesians, traditional concepts of male dominion and the preservation of honor need to be examined with respect to the role of the house church in the formation of children. An understanding of traditional cultural expectations about family continuity and memory passed from father to son can shed new light upon the role of the father as teacher in Eph 5:4, and the even stronger reinforcement of educational roles along gender lines in the Pastoral Epistles, which become bound up with delineation of church offices (e.g., 1 Tim 3:1-5).[122]

Tracing Developments from Colossians to the Pastoral Epistles

This study of the household codes is ultimately an exploration of the relationship between the ideal relationships described in the ethical exhortations and social reality. It traces an evolution of ideas and strategies as one reads through Colossians, Ephesians, and the Pastoral Epistles, all of which take account of children and child-parent relationships within household code traditions in one way or another. The thematic focus of each chapter is based upon the specific content of the ethical teaching in these NT documents. Colossians sets the stage by singling out children for exhortation, pointing to their value and raising the question of the impact of free and slave children sharing their existence within the church space. In Ephesians, one detects an explicit interest in the socialization of children in a document highly concerned with the boundaries of church identity. In the Pastoral Epistles, this concern for socialization becomes an identifiable emphasis on education, with particular roles assigned to male and female leaders. In fact, in the Pastorals, the community is being depicted as combining elements of household and school.

Tracing this evolutionary development from Colossians to the Pastoral Epistles, however, is only the first step in the investigation conducted here. Informed by research on the life of families in the Roman world, this study will demonstrate that the social environment played a crucial role in the ongoing development. But it is also vital to seek to understand what social realities operate in tandem with or stand outside the ethical prescriptions, or even exist in tension with them. For example, when fathers are mentioned, one must ask about the influence of mothers; when slaves are told to obey their masters, one must question what this might suggest for the sexual treatment of children; when older women are instructed to set an example for younger women, one must probe what this might mean for the education of girls.

2

SMALL, SILENT, BUT EVER PRESENT
Slave Children in Colossians 3:18–4:1

The first direct address to children in the Pauline literature occurs in Col 3:20. Together with the reciprocal address to fathers in Col 3:21, the text has generally been judged to be highly conventional and deserving of only very brief comment. There has been much more interest in the longer treatment of the slave-master relationship in Col 3:22-25. But a wider lens is required. It is a mistake to view the six categories of the Colossian household code as static and clear-cut, without giving careful consideration to the fact that audience members usually belonged to more than one category. Rather, one must consider the overlap in categories between the slave and the child and the slave and the parent. The main question under investigation is how consideration of the perspective and circumstances of slave children might change our understanding of Col 3:18–4:1.

This chapter explores what happens to the portrait of slave-master relations in Colossians when children become the focus of attention. How does such a shift in perspective affect what is being promised to slaves in the community? It is vital to pay close attention to the family life of slaves and the potential threat to family life caused by slave owners' use of slaves as sexual objects. It is also important to consider the various parenting roles that slaves played in ancient families and how this might change the interpretation of exhortations to masters and parents. One needs to keep in mind that slaves were also parents, the child and adult offspring of other slaves, and sometimes the biological offspring of their masters. All of this must be kept at the forefront of the exploration in an attempt to comprehend how children, both slave and free, came to find a place of belonging in house-church communities.

Who Are the Children? Who Are the Parents?

Because one is often dealing with overlapping categories, it is necessary to clarify the difference between "child" and "adult." For the purposes of this book, unless otherwise indicated, "children" refers to all people under the biological age of twenty.[1] Ancient sources usually treat people in this age group as nonadult, but there was great variety and many differences with respect to girls and boys. Here several points need to be borne in mind that set ancient families apart from modern western families.

Childhood in the Roman world is best understood within the broader framework of the life course. Funerary monuments include sarcophagi that present life as journey or even a competitive race with a starting point, turning points, and a final destination. Death in childhood is depicted as the tragic truncation of this journey, depriving the child of expected experiences.[2] In Colossians it is false teaching that veers one off the course culminating in Christ, cheating one of the deserved prize (Col 2:18; cf. Phil 3:12-16).[3] The association of a race with the life course becomes even more explicit in the Pastoral Epistles (e.g., 2 Tim 4:6-8), in which the life-course approach also shapes ethical and pastoral teaching.[4]

Within the broader framework of the life cycle, several ancient authors did have a basic concept of the stages of childhood and adulthood, with seven being a popular number, although there were variations.[5] These stages are often related to stages of education for boys, including knowledge of the Torah for Jewish boys.[6] There were some commonalities. Age seven typically marked the end of infancy and the beginning of childhood. Characterizations of adolescence often exhibit a repetitive and timeless quality, easily paralleled with modern experiences, such as Horace's description of the beardless young man: "As impressionable as wax, he is easily influenced to vice, sharp with any who reprimand him, slow to see what will be beneficial, prodigal with money, high-handed, full of desires, and swift to leave aside the object of his desires."[7] But in ancient society, there was nothing like the connection between rights and biological age or strict definitions of the end of childhood that we find in modern laws such as those pertaining to driving and voting. Instead, the end of childhood occurred in a very flexible manner. Parental discretion was apparently the guide among Romans for determining the age of a boy undergoing the coming-of-age ceremony, the *toga virilis*, in which the boy exchanged his boyhood garb for that of adulthood; ages when boys participated in the ceremony range from thirteen to eighteen.[8] No such coming-of-age ceremony existed for girls; instead, marriage acted as the most visible sign of adulthood.[9]

There remains uncertainty as to when marriages typically took place, ranging from early to late teens for girls, but often to significantly older men. It is probably no accident that Jairus' daughter is presented as a child of twelve (Matt 9:18-26), on the cusp of adulthood and the fulfillment of her potential as a married daughter. While marriage was a marker of adulthood and the taking on of adult responsibilities, young women (adolescents by our standards) often required ongoing education from their mothers in household management and initiation into motherhood.[10] The age discrepancy between women and men in marriage is also a factor in the overlap between parenting and marriage discourse. In an important discussion of household management from the classical Greek era, Xenophon's *Oeconomicus*, the husband is cast almost as the parental instructor of his young bride—taking over the fine work of her parents.[11] When applied to young wives, there is a type of intrinsic continuity between the commands for children to obey parents (Col 3:22) and wives to be subject to their husbands (Col 3:18).

The world of work also blurs the distinction between child and adult, especially for the freeborn poor and slaves. It was expected that a slave child by the age of five could render service to his or her master.[12] The skeletal remains of children recovered at Pompeii and Herculaneum have revealed evidence of sustained physical labor in youth. Adults showed signs of prolonged exertion pointing to labor activity from childhood, and children as young as five, including a number of girls, showed signs of significant injury. The geographical locations of Pompeii and Herculaneum suggest that the labor in question involved farming and activities related to the harbor, such as rowing or unloading cargo. One fourteen-year-old girl was found cradling a baby; while the infant was adorned with bronze jewels indicating upper-class status, the girl (almost certainly a slave) demonstrated signs of severe malnutrition and prolonged exposure to physical exertion involving heavy lifting—she was likely already exhausted from performing hard labor and entrusted to look after her master's baby.[13]

Although the use of slaves for menial tasks and for prostitution is generally well known, slaves were trained from childhood for a variety of occupations, including some requiring significant education to work as copyists or types of accountants; others were trained as actors.[14] There is an allusion to the profit to be made from female slaves in the description of the female slave with the spirit of divination in Philippi; she is left vulnerable by Paul's cure, having lost her ability to make money for her owners (Acts 16:16-19). In Acts, Paul and his entourage are notably unconcerned about her fate. The Apostle, however, would have certainly encountered slaves, including children, in conjunction with his work as an artisan and among fellow craftspeople and traders. One inscription tells of C. Vettius Capitolinus, who at age 13 was very skilled at embroidery or sewing.[15]

Slave Children in the House:
Complicated Family Arrangements

It is not completely certain that slave children were part of the audience listening to the Colossian household code (Col 3:18–4:1), but there is a strong likelihood based on several factors. Most obviously, because the exhortation to slaves is by far the longest section of the Colossian household code, it is reasonable to conclude that slaves formed a significant segment of the house-church community. Moreover, the very nature of ancient domestic arrangements supports the notion that slave children along with adult slaves were part of the audience. It is useful to draw a distinction between a "houseful" as opposed to a "household." Archaeological investigations of Pompeii have been central to this distinction, indicating that several house-holds could function within one domain, especially in large dwellings. "Houseful" refers to the number of people living in a particular house, which could include slaves, freedpersons, clients, and relatives, as well as the head of the household and his wife and children.[16] Within this larger group, there could be several households, such as those made up of freedpersons or slaves with their families. To a certain degree households could operate with some independence within a larger structure, which could also encompass shops with adjacent rented rooms.[17] Such circumstances could offer opportunities for slaves to form a believing community and have access to a significant number of people living within the same structure or in close proximity. Two conclusions can be drawn based on such observations: (1) any kind of meeting of a house-church group would probably have been attended and certainly observed by slaves, including slave children; and (2) even in larger dwellings, it is possible that a community was composed of a large number of slaves (perhaps on occasion, they even represented the majority) who operated as a type of extended family, with slave children having a variety of relationships.[18] The involvement of slave caregivers and attendants (*paedagogi*) with freeborn children meant that in some sense freeborn children were part of the slave commu-nity.[19] Whether attended by slaves in the kitchen, elsewhere in the house, or on the way to school, freeborn children would inevitably be accompanied by slave children who were playmates; these slave chil-dren would also be parented by domestic slaves who sometimes also were their biological parents.

While it is not made explicit, it is nevertheless important to acknowledge that some of the fathers exhorted in Col 3:21 were prob-ably slave parents. Thus, for some members of the audience who were slave children, the command to obey their masters in all things (3:22) was held in inevitable tension with the command to obey their parents in all things (3:20); ownership of and dominion over slave children ultimately belonged to the head of the household. Such tensions would become especially acute in light of the rights of the *pater familias* to make sexual use of slaves: men, women, and children. Slave women could become pregnant because they formed marital partnerships with other household slaves or because they were used sexually by their

masters for enjoyment or for breeding purposes. In fact, it has recently
been argued that the majority of slave children may have been the
biological offspring of their masters, the so-called *fillii naturales*.[20] The
birth of slave children is part of the records of early Christian martyrdom, which include many accounts of the bravery of women. The early
third-century martyrological description of Felicitas of Carthage who
gives birth in prison may be fictional, but it nevertheless captures the
common and potentially fraught experience of the female slave: preg-
nancy, labor, and delivery.[21] Her painful early delivery, which involves
much human suffering, is presented as a counterpoint to her overcom-
ing of the pain of martyrdom because of the strength she receives
from Christ. In the case of Felicitas, no father is mentioned, leaving
many unanswered questions. But whatever the circumstances might
be, it is important to realize that the female slaves who came under
the purview of the household codes could be daughters, wives, and
mothers in addition to being slaves themselves.

Questions remain about the nature of slave family units, but there
is general agreement that the phenomenon was widespread. It is also
generally recognized that to allow families to form family units was a
strategy of slave management and slave control wherein the punishment of relatives along with oneself was a powerful deterrent. The use
of marriage terminology and references to family members in funerary monuments of freedpersons is well documented. Such commemorations make it clear that one must include consideration of slaves and
freedpersons in examinations of early Christian texts dealing with
marriage and family life unless there is good reason to exclude them.[22]
However, it is important to acknowledge that the instability of the
slave family was a key aspect of slave vulnerability; the possibility of
forced family breakup loomed large. Heads of households could break
up slave families on a whim, with spouses separated from each other
and children taken away from their parents. Slaves could be viewed
as merchandise to be sold for profit or sold as form of punishment; or
they could simply be moved from one part of an estate to another or
transported as labor and trade demanded.[23] These hazards suggest that
the preservation of slave families was an aspect of treating slaves justly
and fairly as is commanded of masters in Col 4:1. Certainly the desire
for ongoing family bonds is one of the most clearly visible aspects of

the aspirations of slaves surviving from the Roman world. Funerary window reliefs of the late Republic and early Empire (which belong almost exclusively to freedpersons) clearly mimic Roman norms and ideals, but they also reflect a concern to display newly founded lineage and continuity.[24] They show spouses lined up together with family members of different generations, flexibly incorporating members of both the nuclear and extended families. These visual displays may be more emblematic than literal depictions of particular families with accurate records of membership. They should not be understood as providing straightforward records of the structure of the Roman family, but rather as a statement to the outside world; the family ideals of an emerging social group seeking recognition.[25] If indeed the community to which Colossians was addressed included a majority of slaves and freedpersons, one wonders whether the domestic code—mimicking elite and imperial family ideals—might represent a type of longing for family preservation and continuity within the house church.[26]

The position of slaves as parents (and indeed slaves as children) in church groups could be rendered even more complicated depending on the nature of their relationships. Slaves of nonbelieving masters, partners of nonbelieving slaves, and slave "spouses" separated by circumstance all faced great difficulty in maintaining family ties. The negotiations involved in preserving their family connections, not to mention allegiance to a new religious group, must have been complicated indeed. The slaves of nonbelievers who seem to be of special concern in 1 Tim 6:1 were taking significant risks in their allegiance to early Christian groups. But perhaps these risks were taken, at least in part, for the opportunity to foster family life that the house church provided. There has been a tendency to read the Colossian code as involving regulations directed at believers. This tendency may well have arisen as a result of the influence of the code of Ephesians, in which marriage is used as a metaphor for the relationship between Christ and the church. It is difficult to imagine such a metaphorical application if it were not shaped by a context with marriages between believers in mind. Nevertheless, the concise exhortations of Colossians leave room for the presence of the wives, children, and slaves of nonbelieving heads of households.[27] A believing wife's subjection to a nonbelieving husband can certainly be "fitting in the Lord" (Col 3:18;

cf. 1 Pet 3:1). Obedience of believing children (including slave children) to nonbelieving parents may certainly "please the Lord" (Col 3:22).[28] Slave believers might obey their "masters according to the flesh" in everything (Col 3:22; cf. 1 Tim 6:1). Those deserving obedience must include believers, as they in turn are exhorted as husbands, fathers, and masters. But we cannot even assume that believing pairs were in the majority. For the identity as believers of those deserving obedience is not made explicit as it might have been if, for example, the reason given to obey was that husbands and wives were brothers and sisters in Christ.[29] Thinking especially of the circumstances of slaves as parents, a slave mother whose master was a nonbeliever would be in a particularly fraught position if she attended church meetings with her (and possibly her master's) children. Presumably, the consequences would potentially be brutal; this was a society in which executioners sometimes offered specialized services for the torture of slaves.[30]

The influence of slave wet nurses and caregivers as pseudo-parents has received too little attention as a potential factor in the expansion of early Christianity. The teaching authority and influence of the wet nurse is especially worthy of note. The wet nurse's social function was extensive, and it endured well beyond the weaning period. She could become a lifelong companion. The role of the wet nurse is one of several examples of the importance of non–kin relations and extended family to the experience of childhood in antiquity—connections made of milk and not blood.[31] Ancient authors philosophized about the selection of wet nurses in a manner that makes their educational influence clear.[32] Not only were physical attributes mentioned (e.g., medium size breasts, ideally having given birth a few times), but also virtues (e.g., self-control), nationality (Greek is best so that the infant will be exposed to the best speech), and warnings about excesses in religious matters. Wet nurses and foster parents needed to be carefully selected based on character and the type of lessons they would provide.[33] Christian wet nurses were in a position to teach their young charges. If they were owned or hired by nonbelievers, their teaching would take the form of evangelization.[34] We might even surmise that Christian slave children could share in this task vis-à-vis freeborn children. The Roman rhetorician Quintilian, who commented extensively on educational matters, recognized the influence of playmates on children; he spoke of not only the importance of the nurses' standard of speech but also that of the slaves selected to be brought up with the child.[35]

As childhood progressed, slave attendants (*paedagogi*) were some of the people who coached children in day-to-day behavior; their influence could be compared with that of other family members, such as grandmothers.[36] This coaching might include instructions about polite behavior at dinner parties and social gatherings where children were sometimes present. In addition to being occasions for conviviality, such events could include readings with literary and moral points being brought out by parents or slave attendants.[37] Slave children who were present at dinner parties as servers could experience life in intellectual homes involving elevated dinner conversations or the speeches of learned guests (visiting apostles and prophets come to mind). In such homes, slave children sometimes received literary training and went on to establish their own literary careers as librarians, tutors, and skilled readers.[38] The direct address to children in the household codes needs to be read in relation to such a background. The Pauline Letters were read aloud in the assembly (Col 4:15-16) and most likely were combined with readings, admonition (Col 3:16), and a communal meal (cf. 1 Cor 11:17-34).[39]

While dinner parties and social gatherings were clearly opportunities for public display and family celebrations, literary sources also critique the negative impact of certain rowdy dinner parties on children, who learn bad habits "before they know they are wrong." According to Quintilian the corruption is largely sexual and the scene assumes the presence of slave children; for not only mistresses are in view but also boy lovers—undoubtedly slaves.[40] The propensity for wild and bawdy dining habits is one of the many impressions that outsiders had of early Christians. In his anti-Christian polemic, the Roman orator and grammarian Marcus Cornelius Fronto drew attention to the presence of children at the immoral banquets of Christians.[41] Like all of the earliest pagan comments on the nature of early church groups, there is a strong measure of stereotype and conventional accusation in this account. But at the same time, ancient audiences would not have been surprised by the presence of children at banquets. So too would the scene depicted by the second-century pagan critic Celsus

seem completely believable (at least in the terms of the characters presented), despite its intent to denounce early Christianity in the strongest possible terms.[42] Children accompanied by "stupid" women are
the target of propagation efforts by early church teachers known to
frequent slave spaces and neighborhood workshops (wool workers,
cobblers, laundry workers). The setting is one familiar from antiquity,
with households sharing space in blocks or with adjacent or lower-
level shops; in such a setting one can presume the presence of adult
slaves accompanied by slave and free children alike.[43] Celsus offers an
outsider's perspective on what is also disclosed in some early Christian sources: the possibility of Christian priorities clashing with the
duty to those in positions of authority (including nonbelieving masters who entrust the care of children to believing slaves). We do know
of at least one slave, Onesimus, who is at the heart of a controversy
involving relations to his master, Philemon. In this case, complica-
tions arose from the allegiance of Onesimus to the believing community, suggesting that interbelieving relationships between slaves
and masters were subject to moral dilemmas.[44] The traditional interpretation maintains that Onesimus was a runaway slave who became
a member of the *ekklēsia*. During his flight he finds his way to Paul,
who then advocates on his behalf and seemingly suggests that Onesimus should be granted his freedom. Recent scholarship, however, has
raised many questions about what is being asked of Philemon and the
true nature of the problem. While debate about the issues remains,
there is consensus that Paul issues a much more rhetorically nuanced
plea concerning Onesimus' status as both a slave and a believer than
was recognized by an earlier generation of interpreters.[45]

Some of this new perspective is based on a greater understanding
of slavery in the Roman world. It is especially significant that Onesimus appears again in Colossians with no mention of Philemon.[46] The
reference to Onesimus extends evidence for a slave presence in the
community beyond the household codes. Colossians 4:8-9 makes it
clear that Onesimus is one of the Colossians, evidently traveling with
Tychicus bearing Paul's letter.[47] Together they are to tell the Colossians "about everything here" (Col 4:9). There is an attempt to bolster
the authority of fellow workers in Colossians, and the reference to
Onesimus clearly functions to offer reassurance. Onesimus is a slave

or freed member of the community who is bestowed with some type of leadership role. Given his function in bringing the letter to the Colossian community, it is important to be open to the possibility that he helped interpret or reinforce the instructions in the letter (a phenomenon that—at least from a modern perspective—would be infused with irony, given the call for subordination in the household code). But in a society in which slaves could be slave owners themselves and overseers, it would not be surprising to find a slave or former slave leader, especially if the community were composed of many slaves. Drawing upon skills that he acquired when he was literally a child (cf. Phlm 10) in Philemon's household, Onesimus could be a skilled reader of the type mentioned above and actually deliver the content of the letter to the Colossians in the midst of the assembly.

Vulnerable Children:
The Sexual Use of Slaves and Sexual Ethics in Colossians

The connections between Onesimus, Philemon, and Paul raise many questions about the nature of the transformed relations that occurred when slaves became believers. One issue that must be confronted is the potential impact on sexual relations.[48] Neither the undisputed nor the disputed Letters of Paul address the pervasive sexual use of (freed) slaves; there are no prohibitions, and it is not even clear that sex with one's own slaves constitutes immorality (*porneia*).[49] In this study, the cultural expectation of a master's sexual dominion, which included the sexual of use of slave children, is of prime significance.

The ideology of slaveholding never allowed a slave to reach adulthood. We catch a glimpse of both this phenomenon and the desirability of the slave boy in the condemning remarks of the Stoic philosopher Seneca, who alludes to the presence of slaves at dinner parties:

Another, who serves the wine, must dress like a woman and wrestle with his advancing years; he cannot get away from his boyhood; he is dragged back to it; and though he has already acquired a soldier's figure, he is kept beardless by having his hair smoothed away or plucked out by the roots, and he must remain awake throughout the night, dividing his time between his master's drunkenness and his lust; in the chamber he must be a man, at the feast a boy.[50]

Seneca's main point here is by no means to call for an end to the sexual use of slaves; his comments reflect its inevitability.[51] His main focus is how the sexual use of slaves—probably most especially young people—is a sign of debauchery, an indication of the slippery slope leading to loss of self-control and the need to impose moral limits. Seneca is frequently cited as an ancient author who is concerned for the humane treatment of slaves, and his writing sometimes displays equalizing rhetoric.[52] Elsewhere, however, he emerges as a clear supporter of the dominion of masters over slaves, and his comments reflect the chasm between the two states.[53] Seneca's emphasis is much more clearly on the virtuous behavior of the slaveholder than on the welfare of slaves.

The young person in Seneca's discourse on reprehensible behavior at dinner parties has been interpreted as a type of *delicium* (pet or favorite child).[54] These were slave children, cultivated for their charm and good looks and living in circumstances of pseudo-adoption, known as *delicia*. Quite abhorrent from the modern perspective is the fact that these children (of both sexes) were often used as sexual favorites. The evidence for this practice is iconographic, inscriptional, and textual.[55] The famous Warren Cup (silver drinking cup from the first-century CE decorated with reliefs), for example, reveals sex with a slave boy. Particularly illuminating for understanding the context in which house churches arose is that the cup also depicts a child observing a sexual act as he enters the door of an apparently easily accessible room.[56] As is the case with the Quintilian's description of bawdy dinner partners, sexual acts are depicted by the Warren Cup as easily observable by children. Moreover, house churches developed in such an open atmosphere, in which flexible sleeping arrangements often found children, nurses, slaves, and laborers cheek by jowl. No modern sense of privacy—complete with firm architectural barriers—would separate a master and his wife from the remainder of the household.

It is important to clarify that not all uses of the *delicium* terminology as applied to children carried sexual connotations; such terminology could even be used as a term of endearment for a natural son or daughter.[57] The broad range of applications is related to the diverse notions of parenting in the Roman world. Bonds developed between children and a large group of people beyond the "nuclear" family, in part because of the challenges related to distance separating the houses of children and relatives and to blended families created by divorce, widowhood, and forced breakups of slave families. A divorced woman, for example, might have more "parental" contact with a slave child whom she called *delicium* than with her own son or daughter who remained under the control of and in the house of her ex-husband.[58]

The NT is silent on the sexual use of slaves, including the practice of adopting *delicia* children as favorites. It would be naïve, however, to think that the sexual use of slaves disappeared completely from early Christian communities (the Christian ethos would have no effect, in any case, on the circumstances of slaves with nonbelieving masters). Yet it remains intriguing that epigraphical evidence for Christian *delicia* children is virtually nonexistent.[59]

While the broad cultural expectation of the sexual use of slaves is beyond dispute in the Roman world, rare statements do appear calling for limitations on the practice and carrying implications for the treatment of children. In contrast to a well-attested tendency to advise wives to look the other way when their husbands made use of slaves for sexual enjoyment, the first-century CE Stoic philosopher Musonius Rufus appealed to the issue of the double standard to critique the practice. He asks how a husband would feel if his wife had sex with a male slave. Musonius focuses especially on the condition of the slave girl—the unmarried female slave—pointing to the existence of slave marriages and family units in which the girl presumably could find some family stability.[60] He readily admits that sexual relations between masters and slave girls is not considered adultery and that people will retort that every master has a right to use his slave as he wishes. Recalling some of the language of Colossians (Col 3:5), he describes such actions as "yielding to the temptation of shameful pleasure and like swine rejoicing in its own vileness."[61] In keeping with his usual approach to marriage and issues of gender, Musonius states that one should not expect men to be less moral than women.

Particularly interesting for the points of comparison it offers with the atmosphere of house-church communities is an inscription found on a marble stele from a Philadelphian religious association within a house structure (dated from late second- or the first-century BCE).[62] Like the NT household codes, the inscription is concerned with interaction between various familial groupings. The exhortations are designed to ensure orderly and morally appropriate behavior within the community.[63] In fact, the foundation of the group is presented as rooted in the desire for harmonious familial relations. Most probably the patron of the association, Dionysus, received instructions in his sleep from Zeus to open his house to both men and women, slave and free; the text repeatedly stresses that all of these groups are welcomed (cf. Gal 3:28 and Col 3:11). Offering strong parallels especially to the Ephesian code, the moral exhortations place particular weight on fidelity between husband and wife. As in the case of Musonius Rufus' discourse, men as well as women are held accountable in this regard (the exhortations are cast mainly in the form of an oath), and once again we find an unusual prohibition against sex with slaves: "Apart from his own wife, a man is not to have sexual relations with another married woman, whether slave or free."[64] The text leaves unanswered the question of whether unmarried slave women or prostitutes are off-limits, but with different emphasis, the inscription recognizes the potential inviolability of slave marriages. It is impossible to determine what kind of community produced this monument. But if, as has been suggested, it was erected to serve an elaborate household cult tied to a large extended household, then the relations between master of the house and household slaves would be in view.[65] Relations between household slaves themselves could also, however, come under the purview of the exhortations. The public display nevertheless means that members of other households attending gatherings cannot be ruled out, closely resembling the situation in house churches. In this case, the exhortations would have a bearing on relations between masters and other people's slaves as well between slaves living is separate houses.

In addition to references to relations involving slaves and wives, the Philadelphian inscription refers to children in a way that includes slave children. Once again, there is a focus on sexuality. Men are directed to avoid defiling or corrupting boys or virgins in a manner that seems rooted in a setting wherein slave children were easily accessible for sexual use. There is a further elaboration of the prohibition to warn against commending others to engage in such sexual practices, quite possibly referring to a master's proclivity to offer his slaves to friends for sexual use. The household community reflected in this inscription demonstrates a recognizable interest in the protection of children. That this goal extends to slave children is also revealed by the inclusive prohibition against making use of "a love potion, abortifacient, contraceptive, or any fatal thing to children [a probable reference to abortion and/or infanticide]."[66] Presumably, unwanted slave children should not be put to death.

Careful consideration of the household codes in light of the content of this inscription can alert us to the probability that concern with sexual contact (and its avoidance) runs just under the surface of the household codes, even if such concerns are not made explicit by the codes themselves. The verb used to refer to corruption (*phthreirō*) of boys and virgins is one that occurs frequently in the NT with sexual overtones (e.g., 1 Cor 3:17; 2 Cor 11:3; 2 Pet 2:12; Jude 10; Rev 19:2). Such associations are plain in the use of the verb in Eph 4:22, in the midst of ethical exhortations that are found immediately before the household codes. While it refers to marriage rather than to relations with slaves, sexual purity and control are clear priorities in Eph 5:22–33. Slaves and sexuality, however, are connected in the household code material found in the writings of Ignatius of Antioch at the beginning of the second century. Scholars have puzzled over the precise meaning of Ignatius' exhortation that slaves who desire to become free at the expense of the church are at risk of becoming slaves of lust (*epithumias*; Ign. *Pol.* 4.3). It has been suggested that Ignatius is alluding to the dangers of freedpersons needing to resort to prostitution in order to survive.[67] Turning to prostitution carries implications for the future of children born to these freed slaves who might feel desperate enough to involve their own children in such activities or to seek an opportunity for a child to become the *delicium* of a prosperous patron. But most relevant for the present discussion is the statement found in the *Didache*, a prohibition against the sexual corruption of children (*paidophthoreō*; *Did.* 2.2).[68] Later, the text condemns murderers of children and corrupters (*phthoreis*) of what God has created, which could also be a reference to the sexual abuse of children.[69]

Nowhere does Colossians explicitly condemn the sexual use of slaves (or children), but the broad references to sexual vices and need for restraint frame such expectations.[70] The Colossian household code is preceded immediately by a list of virtues and vices, including four vices (Col 3:5) that probably have sexual connotations: immorality, impurity, passion, and evil desire.[71] The author of Colossians is laying out the vices of the nonbelieving Gentile world while at the same time setting a high moral standard for the community.[72] It is impossible to determine which precise activities are addressed by this list of vices and the virtues inherent in an alternate way of life. But comparison with the Philadelphian inscription (which presumes the same type of familial atmosphere as the house church) points to the adoption of a strong sense of fidelity within marriage (Col 3:18-19), the recognition of slave "marriages," and the relinquishing of sexual relations with slaves for all members. All members of the community would be called to a radically new standard of behavior whether male or female, slave or free. Indeed, the rejection of a past way of life is an ethical priority of the work that flows from baptism (Col 1:21-23; 2:20; 3:5-11). The warning to masters that they also have a master in heaven in Col 4:1 should probably be taken as a corollary of the warning that the wrath of God is coming upon those who continue (or revert to) living in a world of vice (Col 3:5-6). There is at least one early Christian text that views the giving up of sexual escapades with slaves as a sign of conversion. In the middle of the second century, Justin Martyr told the story of Roman matron who became associated with early Christianity but whose husband (whom she eventually divorces) continued to live immorally. Justin contrasts the ongoing debauchery of the husband with the moral rectitude of the wife, who did not consort with household slaves.[73]

Cultural Compliance: Ideologies of Slave-Holding and Pseudo-parenting

The pervasive acceptance of the sexual use of slaves and the NT silence on the matter means that the household code directives concerning slave-master relations must be examined from many angles. Silence might mean acceptance of the practice in early church communities, but one must also consider the following alternative: silence might well mean that the issue was contentious. Moreover, the more general sexual ethics would inevitably have some bearing on relations between masters and slaves and among slaves themselves. When one allows the child-parent relationship to enter the mix, the situation becomes even more complicated.

There are clearly points of contact between the Colossian household code, however, and the ideologies and perspectives of slaveholding. The command that children are to obey their parents "in everything" (Col 3:20) is repeated in the reference that slaves are to obey their masters "in everything" (Col 3:22). Although freeborn children were certainly not equated with the enslaved either in theory or practice (although their daily existences were often shared), one nevertheless senses a parallel between the authority of masters and fathers in the following grammatical construction: there is a shift from obedience to both parents in the instructions to children (Col 3:20) to the emphasis on the authority of fathers *alone* over their children in the instructions concerning parents (Col 3:21). Roman law gave extreme authority over the members of the household to the *pater familias*, even if there is considerable debate over the extent to which it was exercised. In speaking of the authority of fathers over their children, Dionysius of Halicarnassus used the same language of "obedience in all things" as Colossians.[74] To make his point even more forcefully, Dionysius built a case that resulted in the overstatement that the Roman lawgiver gave "greater power to the father over his son than the master over his slaves."[75]

Given the complex range of relationships and scenarios possible within a house-church community, it is difficult to discern how the call to obey in all things would have been heard by audience members. One immediately comes up with contradictory expectations and moral dilemmas. If, for example, both free and slave members were called upon to adhere to the same standards of sexual morality in the community, it is impossible to determine how a slave could avoid participating in immorality when the immorality was the result of obedience to one's master. There are further implications concerning the sexual use of the children of slaves. Obedience to one's master could mean allowing one's child to be adopted as a favorite, a *delicia* child. Even setting aside the issue of sexual use of slave children, a favorite slave child could end up with much less contact with a slave mother or slave parents. There is a notable lack of concern for the natural parents of *delicia* children in the evidence offered by the Roman poet Publius Papanius Statius.[76] For example, in the case of Atedius Melior's favorite boy slave, Glaucias, who died at age twelve, the grief of the boy's quasi-adopted father is presented as surpassing that of his natural parents, who are nevertheless in attendance at the lavish and widely attended funeral; the extent of Atedius' grief astonishes the natural parents, who presumably are less devastated than Atedius. It is Atedius, not the natural parents, who kissed the lips of the deceased.[77] This kind of flexible and inverted relationship between parent and pseudo-parent involving masters and slaves was part of the world of early Christianity. A believing slave child (even a grown child) whose parents were believers could face many challenges, especially if his or her "adopted" parent were a nonbeliever.

There is no reason to doubt the presence of the slaves and slave children of nonbelievers among the audience exhorted by the Colossian household code. For these slaves, it would be impossible to avoid physical contact with immorality, impurity, passion, and evil desire (Col 3:5).[78] Refusal to participate in wrongdoing (from an early Christian perspective) would inevitably lead to accusations of insolence and beatings (cf. 1 Pet 2:18-25). Salvian, the fifth-century early Christian author, in fact stressed the powerlessness of female believing slaves before sexual advances of tyrannical Roman masters: "Women were not permitted by their shameless owners to be chaste, even if they wanted to."[79] It is difficult to avoid the conclusion that the call to obey masters in everything would have been heard by the slaves of nonbelievers as acknowledgment of their situation as owned bodies. Although this is admittedly an argument from silence, it is worth seriously considering that the issue of the sexual use of slaves is not made explicit in the text because the author of Colossians was walking a very fine line. Slaves, including slave children, faced countless situations that could not be avoided. In the face of impossible circumstances, the author offers the promise of judgment. But the exhortation in Col 3:25 introduces seemingly intentional ambiguity, reminding us that the household codes could be applied in a flexible and inconsistent manner. It is not completely clear whether "the wrongdoer" who will be paid back for what was done wrong refers to the master or the slave. The wrongdoer could be a slave who has not been compliant and has not served with the right attitude or possibly a slave who failed to abide by the moral code of life in Christ when it was within his or her capacity.[80] But the wrongdoer could also be the master who has used and abused slaves. In this case, slave members of the household code audience would hear the promise of divine judgment as helpless and otherwise hopeless victims.[81]

A further point needs to be considered with respect to ideologies of slave-holding. The household codes reflect ideologies of masculinity that intersect with ideologies of dominion over slaves. Traditional concepts of male control of paternity, male control of women's sexual experience (developed further in Eph 5:22-33), and male control of slave bodies are intertwined.[82] Such notions also overlap in the ancient agricultural handbooks that dealt with the running of large rural estates and the slave labor thereupon. In these handbooks there is considerable attention given to the role of the *vilicus*, the slave manager, who was normally a slave. Recommending that the *vilicus* would have a wife (*vilica*) and children was a strategy adopted by the head of the household to manage the manager. Particularly intriguing for the present discussion is how the advice given in the second century BCE by Cato the Elder to the *vilicus* echoes conventional notions of household management in which the *pater familias* "rules" his wife: "Make sure that the *vilica* carries out her duties. If the master has given her to you as your wife, be satisfied with her. Make sure she fears you. Do not let her be too extravagant. She should have as little as possible to do with neighbors or other women and never invite them into the house with her. She must not accept invitations to meals or go out all of the time."[83] Again, for the purposes of this study, it is interesting to note how the growth of religious associations among slaves surfaces as a possibility in the instructions given to the slave manager; his efforts to control his wife must include prevention of her participation in unauthorized religious activities. It is the master of the house alone who is to sacrifice on behalf of the whole *familia*. Similarly, the warnings to the *vilicus* not to be too harsh in his treatment of slaves offers another example of household management ideals associated with the *pater familias* applied to the slave manager; at the same time, however, as is revealed by Columella's first-century CE recommendations, the limited capacity of the *vilicus* as a slave himself is proclaimed:

> He should not merely be skilled at agricultural work; he should also have such personal qualities—in so far as this is possible in a slave—that he will exercise his authority neither irresponsibly nor brutally, and should always be giving encouragement to some of the better slaves, and should not be too hard on those who are less good, so that he will be feared for being severe rather than hated for being cruel. He will achieve this if he keeps watch over those under his authority so that they do nothing wrong, instead of finding that he has to punish delinquents as a result of his own incompetence.[84]

One cannot help but notice the resemblance to the advice given to masters in Col 4:1, but also to fathers in Col 3:21.[85]

Concern with slave formation and attitudes runs throughout this Roman agricultural handbook advice: Authors encourage the proper training in agricultural work from childhood into maturity, the winning of the respect of the younger slaves, and the prevention of the older slaves feeling as though they are being commanded by youngsters.[86] Too much education in a slave manager can even be dangerous, as reading and knowledge of figures bring the risk of the slave cooking the books![87] The author of Colossians goes to considerable effort to make sure that the service of believing slaves is complete and wholehearted (Col 3:22-23). Once again we need to include children within the purview of the instructions, for child slaves too could be depicted as serving with the correct attitude or orientation. The slaves of Col 3:22 are warned against mere eye service as people pleasers—probably a reference to a service only provided while the master is watching or to curry favor. In comparison, the *delicium* child Philetus—the slave boy of the learned and wealthy estate owner Flavius Ursus (who died most probably at age 15)—is eulogized for having mastered himself; finding delight in being a slave, the ultimate wholehearted acceptance of his state: "Who liked his pleasant servitude, who felt no gloom, who of his own accord mastered himself."[88]

One final aspect of the overlap between childhood and enslavement needs to be considered with respect to ideologies of masculinity; slaves were excluded from paternity. They were considered as having no legal father and could not legitimately father a child. They were excluded from patrimony or other inheritance and could not transmit the family name. A freeborn man was expected to have mastery over his own body in the way that a slave never could (making Statius' poetic rendering of the attitude of the slave Philetus striking for the way it alludes to the self-mastery usually associated with the freeborn). Male slaves were essentially excluded from the very category of manhood despite physical maturity. In an important sense, they remained perpetual children.[89] The ideological distinction between a freeborn man and an adult slave surfaces plainly and in many different ways in ancient literature. Often comparison between children and slaves plays a key role in conveying the message. Pseudo-Plutarch conveys the ultimate divide between a household slave and legitimate son with an appeal to education: "Wherefore Aristippus not inelegantly, in fact very cleverly, rebuked a father who was devoid both of mind and sense. For when a man asked him what fee he should require for teaching his child, Aristippus replied, 'A thousand drachmas'; but when the other exclaimed, 'Great heavens! What an excessive demand! I can buy a slave for a thousand,' Aristippus retorted, 'Then you will have two slaves, your son and the one you buy.'"[90]

Given the position of *delicia* children and the fact that slaves and freeborn children often shared the same living spaces, Seneca's comparison of an elderly slave with an infant is particularly poignant. The circumstance involves a visit to his country estate, where he encounters a former slave playmate, presumably specially selected to be a family favorite and companion for Seneca.[91] The slave is now elderly and is given a job often reserved for elderly and feeble slaves, that of doorkeeper:

> Then I turned to the door and asked: "Who is that broken-down dotard? You have done well to place him at the entrance; for he is

outward bound. Where did you get him? What pleasure did it give you to take up for burial some other man's dead?"

But the slave said: "Don't you know me, sir? I am Felicio; you used to bring me little images. My father was Philositus the steward, and I am your pet slave (*delicium*)."

"The man is clean crazy," I remarked. "Has my pet slave become a little boy again? But it is quite possible; his teeth are just dropping out."[92]

Elsewhere Seneca is capable of making arguments concerning the humane treatment of slaves, but there is no such sensitivity here. Despite the slave's expectation to the contrary, status as a former "favorite" does not buy the slave respect or tolerance. The line is drawn and maintained, and the old man is caricatured as an infant. There is no shared inheritance to be given despite the shared childhood experience. In the next section, therefore, it will be necessary to probe the significance of the promise of inheritance to slaves in Col 3:24 in light of the fundamental cultural divide between slaves and freeborn children.

Cultural Resistance: Ideologies of Honor and Pseudo-parenting

In the case of *delicia* children, for whom conditions of pseudo-parenting existed, slaves are sometimes described in a manner that blurs the line between the conditions of slavery and freedom. We have already considered an example from Statius' poetry in which the slave boy is described as engaged in a type of self-mastery. In his description of Glaucias, Statius presents the deceased twelve-year-old boy as almost like an indulged and beautiful freeborn child; he lacks only the *toga praetexta* of the freeborn: "No crowd of escorts failed, no presents; what your modest beauty lacked was just the toga freeborn children wear."[93] Although it is quite rare, inscriptional evidence suggests that sometimes slaves were raised with the expectation that they would share completely in the fate of freeborn children; in other words, they would share in the inheritance (cf. Col 3:24). An inscription from Rome makes this clear: "To the gods of the underworld. Aulus Furius Crassus. Aulus Furius, the house-born slave of Festus, has been considered a son. He lived four years, six months, twenty-nine days."[94] But in an even more elaborate inscription from Rome, one hears of a mother's intention to raise a house-born slave and a freeborn child as brothers. The inscription is found on an altar dedicated by Publicia Glypte to her infant son and *verna* (a term that usually refers to house-born slaves) and reads as follows, with the dedication for each child in a column side by side: "To the departed spirits of Nico, her sweet son, who lived 11 months and 8 days and; Eutyches, her home-born slave, who lived for 1 year, 5 months and 10 days; dedicated by Publicia Glypte."[95] The iconography on this altar is particularly striking. Eutyches is clearly a slave, but he is portrayed in a way as to advertise his pseudo-mother's intention to grant the child his freedom. In contrast to the poetic description of Glaucias cited previously, Eutyches is depicted as wearing a toga in the same manner as Nico. There are images of schooling that suggest both boys would be raised as educated citizens; each holds a scroll, with a scroll box between them at their feet. Finally, mythological symbols suggest a fostering relationship and perhaps the almost-twin boys were suckled by the same nurse; the altar contains an image of Telephus, suckled by a hind.[96]

These images, poems, and inscriptions present an optimistic picture in the face of death. Certainly such equalizing practices and aspirations were not the norm. It was, however, legally possible to adopt a freed child after manumission, which would lead to inheritance and the possibility that freedpersons be chosen as heirs.[97] Such occurrences invite us to think about what is actually being promised to the slaves in Col 3:24. Here the promise of inheritance (*klēroma*; cf. 1.12) is fittingly expressed as something that will happen in the future—something associated with the kingdom of God. In the social realm, slaves as slaves were completely barred from inheritance. But there is also something of the present reality experienced by slaves that is expressed in this exhortation. It is intended to shape the behavior of real interactions within the community and is at the heart of the ideological justification for welcoming all—even the slaves of nonbelievers—as God's chosen ones (cf. Col 3:11-12).

The promise of inheritance may offer evidence of a countercultural element in the household codes or even of a "hidden transcript" whereby the community members are receiving a message about the treatment of slaves encoded in discourse that only appears on the surface to match imperial ideals and will, therefore, appease tension with the broader society.[98] The evidence concerning the adoption or quasi-adoption of slave children should raise some caution, however, with respect to reading this material as completely countercultural; nevertheless, it is reasonable to conclude that it represents some level of cultural resistance. With respect to the appeal to the concept of inheritance, the author of Colossians brings a more radical perspective to the concrete situation of slaves than the Paul of the undisputed letters. Paul's metaphorical description of adoption as a child-heir of God (Gal 4:7) demonstrates his familiarity with the process of adoption and probably also with the legal complexities associated with the process (cf. Gal 3–4).[99] In Rom 8, Paul highlights the benefits of divine inheritance by contrasting it with the circumstances of enslavement. But what is so striking about Colossians is that metaphorical language, once applied to describe the changed circumstances of the whole community, is now being brought directly and specifically to bear on the lives of slaves via the household code instructions.

The reference to the promise of inheritance is one of few indications that slaves of the community are being granted honor, a public acknowledgment of worth. Slaves may suffer dishonor now, but this is a temporary state of affairs.[100] Both slaves and masters are reminded of the distinction between the early master (lord) and the master (Lord) in heaven. Slaves and masters ultimately serve the same Lord and may both experience the reward of inheritance or the punishments of final judgment. In comparison, Roman households used various means to draw distinctions between the slave owners' honorable family and honorless slaves. And this was not simply a theoretical concept; various rituals and routines reinforced the honor of the *matrona* (legitimately married wife), found lacking in the *ancilla* (slave girl).[101] The sharp rebuke that Seneca gives to his former slave playmate cited above is fundamentally a proclamation of the slave's lack of honor— the perpetual child who will never be able to defend his honor like a man. Demonstrating a strong awareness of the humiliation of the

slave trade, the author of Colossians allows the experience of slavery—
and lack of honor associated with it—to subtly influence his or her
language and thought. It becomes the backdrop for explaining what
God has accomplished in Christ (Col 2:14-15). Colossians 2:15 speaks
of stripping the "rulers and powers" and "making a public example of
them, boldly triumphing over them" (cf. 2 Cor 2:14; Rev 18:11-13). The
verb "to triumph over" (*thrismbeuō*) was employed to refer to the triumphal procession of military leaders that included enslaved peoples,
including children. Christ's triumph over the powers is a different
conquest indeed. Hearers are to distinguish this cosmic victory from
what they have personally experienced, heard about, or seen displayed
in the monuments of the Roman Empire.[102]

Children were used to great visual effect for purposes of propaganda in the Roman Empire. The columns of Trajan and Marcus
Aurelius depict scenes of children being torn away from foreign mothers to offer symbols of Rome's power and her enemy's humiliation.[103]
But much closer to Colossae and probably familiar to many of the
recipients of Colossians, is the previously discussed temple complex
of Sebasteion at Aphrodisias. Dedicated to Aphrodite and the Julio-
Claudian emperors, this monument features reliefs depicting children
as symbols of pacified peoples. Among the most striking is a relief
wherein an imperial prince holds an orb in one hand and appears to
be crowning a trophy in the other (a cuirass on a pole). Between the
prince and the trophy, one sees a small barbarian boy held captive.
He looks up at his captor, his hands are tied behind his back, and his
tunic appears to have been torn off his shoulder. He is a dishonored
foreigner, now an enslaved boy.[104]

Monuments like the Sebasteion at Aphrodisias are designed to
proclaim how pacified peoples are now assimilated in imperial harmony. The baptismal proclamation of Col 3:11 offers its own vision of
the harmony that has been achieved in Christ, which seems quite contrary to the imperial agenda. As in Gal 3:28, slave and free are listed,
but in keeping with the international flavor of the Sebasteion, there
is explicit reference to "Scythians." In NT times, "Scythian" was a
common label for slaves procured from the many regions of the Black
Sea area, with such cities such as Ephesus offering points of entry and
markets.[105] It is entirely possible that the slave members of Colossian

community included not only house-born slaves or slaves adopted as foundlings, but also slaves who had traveled long distances through the process of trade or as captives of war. While the great wars of expansion were over at the time of Colossians' composition, ongoing conflict at the edges of the Empire continued to produce captives as slaves. The Jewish War of 70 CE also produced captives (Josephus explicitly singles out the sale of women and children who did not bring a good price due to a glut in the market and too few purchasers), and some of these people may have made their way into early church communities.[106] Colossians 3:11 may reflect the suffering slaves endured in traveling long distances, offering them hope and belonging. Once again Statius' poetry offers crucial evidence for slave trade of children, in this case beautiful boys. He writes of the *delicium* child of Flavius Ursus, Philetus: "Will you go off to some Italian fortress-town and Venus not do anything about it? Will you endure a shoddy house, the yoke of common servitude? Heaven Forbid!"[107] The sexual dimension of the enslavement of captives can also be presented as strategy for dishonoring them and as the ruination of familial relations. We see this clearly in one of the speeches that Josephus supplies for Eleazar during the siege of Masada:

> Is a man to see his wife led off to violation, to hear the voice of his child crying "Father!" when his own hands are bound? No, while those hands are free and grasp the sword, let them render an honorable service. Unenslaved by the foe let us die, as free men with our children and wives let us quit this life together! This our laws enjoin, this our wives and children implore of us.[108]

Especially when read in light of the cosmic triumphal procession of Christ over the powers (Col 2:14-15), and when taken together, some type of cultural resistance to the humiliation of slaves seems to be reflected in Col 3:11 and 3:24. There is so much one would like to know about how slaves made their way into early church communities. Even though the patriarchal rhetoric of Col 3:18–4:1 is undeniable (and undeniably dangerous, especially for the legacy it produced well into the twentieth century), it is important to remember there were almost certainly slaves present in the community at Colossae who had taken major risks, both for themselves and for their children. There were almost certainly child slaves who had taken major risks. In a society in which children were often cared for by a much wider group than natural parents, there were almost certainly pseudo-parents who took major risks.

When one considers that the Colossian household code does not state that all the members of the various pairs are Christian, however, there is reason to pay particular attention to the implications. Here one encounters a feature of the code that represents more than cultural resistance, but signifies a countercultural orientation. Some members of the group have broken down their allegiance to their own family units or at least have multiple identities straddling not only familial categories such as slave and parent, but also the believing and the nonbelieving worlds.[109] Once again, it is important to pay attention to what is not being said. Household loyalty and civic loyalty, which include the worship of the gods of city and state, is a typical feature of household management discussions in the ancient world. Instead, the NT household code authors frequently introduce their own style of household management discussions with exhortations to worship the one God (cf. Col 3:17; Eph 5:19-20; 1 Tim 2:1, 5, 8).[110] To imperial ears, these texts would sound like bold defiance, despite the veneer of familial stability and virtues. Community members—slave and free—were casting their allegiance to a new type of familial community in which subordinate members of households were welcome, even if the household head had not approved: the household of God. It was precisely what the authors of the agricultural handbooks had feared; illegitimate religious activities had spread among slaves and they had failed to remember that it is the master who should sacrifice on behalf of the whole *familia*.

The Family Is Watching: Seeking to Understand the Nature of the Community's Cultural Stance

Elements of cultural compliance and cultural resistance are both present in the Colossian household code, raising the question of whether the code simply incorporates contradictory tendencies without an easily identifiable cultural stance. One is struck, for example, by a document that includes "liberating" imagery with respect to Christ's rule of the cosmos and believers' participation in heavenly rule, yet introduces the hierarchical and patriarchal household code into early Christian literature.[111] The author of Colossians is certainly not advocating the abolition of slave-master relations, and the play on the term Lord (*kyrios*), which in Greek is the same term for Master and master, does indisputably give a spiritual justification for ongoing subjection of slave to master. Similarly, the exhortations concerning the parent-child relationship cannot be considered in any way novel; the most that might be said is that the call to fathers not to provoke children has points in common with warnings against excessive severity toward children found in other ancient texts.[112] But there are still many questions remaining about what kind of community this text reflects and the nature of the familial interactions. When we bring slave children to the center of interpretation and consider the overlap between childhood and slavery both in reality and in ideological discourse, we can detect traces of a challenge to the traditional concept of family that did not mean the complete reversal of hierarchical patterns but was lived out in other ways.

The direct appeal to children and the promise of inheritance to slave children offered hope in a world in which life was often brutal for children. The experience of such a utopia is certainly pushed into the future, but the subtext is a message that slave children might share in the destiny of freeborn children, mirroring the relationship between Eutyches and Nico celebrated in the inscription from Rome described previously. The well-established practice of pseudo-parenting discussed above offered early Christians a model of what might be possible. Whether slave caregivers were looking after free and enslaved children or freeborn parents were entering into quasi-adoptive relationships with slave children, there were many examples of children being brought up by people other than their natural parents. The identities of the children addressed in Colossians are unknown, but the group would certainly have included a mixed group of children living in a variety of circumstances. Later church literature identifies the care of orphans as a priority of church groups[113] and even speaks of

Christians rescuing orphans from those who treat them harshly,[114] but such ideals are not made explicit here. Nevertheless, Colossians articulates a vision of a community of belonging; given the atmosphere of ancient neighborhoods (where the street was the playground), children could find plenty of opportunities for association with an ancient house church and to be cared for by believers and/or within a believing household. While it comes from a significantly later era—the third century CE—*The Martyrdom of Perpetua and Felicitas* offers a vivid example of the adoption of a slave child by believers. The infant of the martyred slave Felicitas is said to have been adopted by a Christian woman of the community.[115]

Two further features of the life of slave children need to be brought to bear on the examination of the nature of the cultural stance reflected in the community: the sexual use of slaves and the instability of slave families. In both cases it is useful to recall the community dynamics of the Philadelphian religious/household association described previously.

Given the silence in our sources, it is important to remember that early Christian communities arose in a setting in which the sexual use of slaves was taken for granted. In some instances the Christian communities almost certainly failed to protect children from sexual abuse. However, the inscription for the cultic group from Philadelphia (which seems so close in its inclusive stance to early Christian communities) included a directive to avoid corrupting boys and virgins, suggesting that this expectation was within the scope of sexual ethics propounded by Colossians. Similarly, the prohibition against men having sexual relations with other married women (including slave women) announced on the stele points to an awareness of the need to protect slave families in a familial group. Once again, it seems very unlikely that members of the believing community lived out this ideal at all times. Nevertheless, something specific is being demanded in the call to treat slaves justly and fairly in Col 4:1. Despite the arguments of some commentators to identify elements that counter the prevailing subordination ethos (especially with respect to the use of the term *isotēs*, fairness), the fact that slavery is clearly not completely abolished means that it is difficult to accept that the text refers to a type of equality in slave-master relations.[116] But one may avoid interpretations that render the verse completely countercultural by looking for ways in which just and fair treatment of slaves was lived out within the existing structures; namely via protection of slave families that included limits on sexual relations with slaves. Something has changed within the community, for there is clearly a proclamation of a new identity "according to the image of its creator" (Col 3:10), involving the stripping of old practices (Col 3:10). This new community exhibits such transforming virtues as compassion, forgiveness, and love (Col 3:15-17). While we have no conclusive proof of how this was lived out, it is difficult to harmonize such virtues with the callous disregard for slave families and the dishonoring that was inherent in the sexual use of slaves.

Once again the comparative evidence from the Philadelphian religious/household association may help us to understand how these dynamics played out. The inscription is deliberately framed to include slave and free, reminiscent of the language of mutuality in both the household code and Col 3:11. Participants are instructed that they must expose those who fail to live up to the sexual/moral ideals (cf. Eph 4:11).[117] The expectation of keeping fellow members in check and reporting on them is one that is apparently shared by all. Similar expectations shape the Colossian ethical stance. Accountability is called for in the encouragement of community complaints to be met with forgiveness in Col 3:13-14. Moreover, in an important sense, in Col 3:22–4:1 slaves and masters are reminded of their accountability in a type of "everybody is watching" atmosphere.[118] The parallel between earthly masters and the Lord is undeniably fraught with potential for abuse. Yet, slaves also seem to be recognized as having some type of moral responsibility. The notion of obedience not only when one is being watched (Col 3:22) should be understood in light of the visibility of familial relations in house churches.[119] It is worth reflecting on what this might have meant for familial/sexual ethics. We do not know whether slaves were ever in a position to protest when they were called upon to cross the moral line in family relations. Most of what we know about the structures of ancient society suggests they were never in such a position. But the uniting of slave and free in one household/family community that uses inheritance and transformative language to describe the changed reality of slave existence intimates that slaves could at least hope that fellow believers would act as moral protectors; this hope would extend to slave parents calling upon fellow believers to guard against the abuse of their children. It is important to remember that the reminder to masters of the existence of their heavenly Lord in the midst of the household code teaching was more than a neutral statement about God standing above all in the community. The implication is that masters will be held accountable for their behavior in the family. They may choose to prevent the dishonor and despair that comes from violation of family members before the eyes of children— recalling Eleazar's speech at Masada cited above. Especially given the strong ascetic currents in Colossae, the exhortation to masters (and husbands) most likely includes an emphasis on sexual containment not unlike what we find in 1 Cor 7. Of course, the line between the outside world and the believing community that has been so often identified as central to the background of the NT household codes should not be forgotten here. Outside eyes were watching as well. For slaves and slave children who lived on the borderline between these two worlds by living in domestic settings ruled by nonbelievers, there could be no protest or true moral agency. For these slaves the possibility of moral conundrum or of silently suffering the breakup of one's family was particularly acute. The household code exhortations are almost certainly shaped by "moments of panic" when slaves and women and children were discovered as noncompliant with respect to figures of authority.[120]

The author of Colossians chose to project an image of an obedient household and to preserve the hierarchical order of relations in the church community. Reacting negatively to a false teaching that included strong ascetic tendencies (Col 2:16-23), household management teaching encouraged family life and harmony within the community based on a vision of mutuality within the family. The present life of believers was celebrated as a type of heavenly enthronement (Col 3:1-4) with a promise for all to share in the inheritance.[121] When a group embraces an ethos that combines cultural compliance with cultural resistance, risk, compromise, and silent suffering within community life seem to be inevitable realities. In a place of overlapping identities between parent, child, slave, free, believing, and nonbelieving, ethical directives would inevitably be applied flexibly and inconsistently in relation to the complexities of family life (Col 3:24). But placing slave children at the center of our interpretation enables us to see the house church as a place of belonging. This was a community wherein slave children could be exhorted side by side with free children—some of whom were probably brought to the community by slave caregivers belonging to nonbelievers. In an intimate atmosphere with opportunities for mutual admonition (Col 3:16), free and slave parents alike could serve as advocates and protectors of children; parents were also teachers and disciplinarians who sometimes encouraged the risky membership of children who were not their own in a church group viewed as an illegitimate association by outsiders.

Conclusion: Small, Silent, but Ever Present Slave Children

The most often forgotten members of early church groups are the slave children. Placing children at the center of interpretation of Col 3:18–4:1 offers an opportunity to remember them. An appreciation of the social reality of the presence of slaves in families in the Roman world allows the presence of slave children in the audience of Colossians to emerge boldly. There has been a tendency to draw sharp distinctions between the group categories in household ethics, and this simply distorts the circumstances of overlapping identities in ancient households.

Limited evidence means that conclusions must be somewhat speculative. But informed by research on Roman families, one can be fairly confident of reconstructions. The oppressive and patriarchal legacy of the household codes cannot be denied. Yet it is important to realize that the ethical stance recommended in its own day had both conventional and countercultural elements. A focus on children leads to a more complete vision of what was at stake.

Child slaves were among the most vulnerable members of early church communities. The exhortations in Colossians suggest, however, that they found a place of belonging in early church communities. These communities could strive to overcome the reality of slaves as owned bodies, with the slaves of nonbelievers most vulnerable of all. The threat of the breakup of families and disregard for the sexual commitment of slaves to their partners and for the safety of their children loomed large. But the nature of salvation and community transformation meant that a new morality was adopted by community members. All were re-created in a new image and united in a new type of harmony (Col 3:11). The ideal—even if not always practiced— was a united family wherein parents, husbands, wives, and children could find a place, whether slave or free.

The direct address to children in the household code of Colossians should be read as a statement that free and slave children were exhorted side by side. The common practice of slave and free children sharing household space, often under the supervision of slave caregivers, has enormous implications for a community that promised slaves inheritance. For while typically any childhood comradery between slave and free children would come to an end in adulthood, the members of the Colossian community were given hope for a completely transformed future existence. In the meantime, they would share daily life in house churches, and children—slave and free—were called out by name and taught together. In the next chapters it will be demonstrated that with the passing decades the socialization and education of children will become an explicit priority in communities that combined elements of home and school.

3

SOCIALIZATION AND EDUCATION
The Nurture, Teaching, and Discipline
of Children in Ephesians 5:21–6:4

A quick comparison between the teaching on the child-parent relationship in Colossians and Ephesians reveals that the treatment in Ephesians is significantly longer. Further examination, however, shows a subtle transformation from an emphasis on the socialization of children to the education of children. With reference especially to the educational role of fathers (Eph 6:4), the household code of Ephesians demonstrates more explicit concern for the treatment of children within the family/house church. This concern operates in conjunction with elements of greater "Christianization" of the household management material. But there are also subtle traces of an attitude that leaves room for the children of nonbelievers in the household of God.

The household code in Ephesians calls for careful reflection on the role of parents, especially the role of fathers, who were in a special way responsible for ensuring family memory and continuity. In light of family life in the Roman world, however, it is also important to read the household code with an awareness of the phenomenon of pseudo-parenting. Parental responsibilities and duties could be exercised by a variety of individuals in the Roman world, raising many possibilities with respect to the identity of the parents exhorted in the code and the nature of the relationship with the children. Concepts in Ephesians also point to the significance of investigating childhood in terms of an interest in socialization and education throughout the life course. Here it will be important to consider Jewish texts, especially the writings of Josephus and the Dead Sea Scrolls. A comparison with Jewish sources is helpful in uncovering the emerging role of teacher in Ephesians and its relationship to family leadership and dynamics.

Comparing Ephesians to Colossians:
Further Christianization

In contrast to Colossians, Ephesians does not speak of children obeying their parents "in all things," leaving an opportunity for the kind of disobedience that might result from a child joining a church group without the permission of his or her father. Philosophers, most notably Musonius Rufus, entertained the possibility that under certain circumstances a child might actually disobey his or her father, especially in the interests of philosophy.[1] Furthermore, Ephesians amplifies the call to obey with the phrase "in the Lord," which gives the command an obvious Christian connotation absent from the Colossians reference to obedience in all things.[2] Obedience takes on a new meaning as manifesting the nature of commitment to the Lord and to life in the Lord. The text also raises the possibility that parents "in the Lord" might be distinguished from biological parents.

More subtle evidence of "Christianization" can be found in how the theological justification for obedience of children is conveyed in Eph 6:1 in comparison with Col 3:20. On one level, the statement "this is right" (Ephesians) functions in the same manner as "this is pleasing in the Lord" (Colossians); at first glance, it constitutes an even more forceful appeal to convention and tradition. In essence, it suggests that God has ordained the obedience of children to their parents and that this has been acknowledged as correct down through the ages. Yet English translations mask a verbal parallel with the ethical markers of life as a believer—the fruits of light that set believers apart from nonbelievers in the world. "For this is right" (lit. this is righteous: *dikaion*) calls to mind the previous appeal to live as the children of light dissociated from the disobedient: "for the fruit of the light is in all goodness and righteousness [*dikaiosynē*] and truth" (Eph 5:9).

The most explicit evidence of the greater Christianization of Ephesians' treatment of the child-parent relationship is found, however, in Eph 6:2-4. This text contains material almost completely absent from the Colossian household code, including the citation from the *Decalogue* concerning the honor due to parents and the call for fathers to bring up children "in the discipline and admonition of the Lord." Ephesians marks the beginning of a trend, which gains further visibility in the Pastoral Epistles and various church writings from the second century CE, to view the education of children as church duty and to identify the formation of children as offering the foundation for the development of future teachers and evangelists.[3]

Although slightly different terminology is used, both Colossians and Ephesians exhort fathers not to provoke their children. The specific focus on fathers is quite fitting, as fathers in law and ideology were given extreme authority over their children (the extent of the application in real life is a matter of debate). As has frequently been observed, however, the call for moderation is also in keeping with many ancient texts.[4] Thus there are strong resonances of convention in Ephesians, as in Colossians, in its treatment of the parent-child relationship, despite the more explicit conviction of a distinctly Christian perspective. But as in the case of Colossians, such conventionality needs to be interpreted in light of a thorough understanding of the house-church setting. The house church acts as a locus for the education of children. A look back at Colossians will show the interest in the socialization of children that Colossians and Ephesians share. Moreover, it will reveal the education of children as a feature of Christian identity in Ephesians.

Calling All Children, Including Slave Children; Calling All Parents, Including Pseudo-parents!

A social constructionist perspective can help one to appreciate the significance of the call to children—the direct appeal to children—to obey their parents as an important instrument of socialization.[5] This approach deals with the dialectical interaction between individuals and their social world. The overall dialectical process through which the symbolic universe (a body of language and traditions that encompasses the social order and infuses it with meaning) is both constructed and altered is institutionalization. The introduction of a third party, such as a new generation, is particularly significant for the transformation of interactions, so institutions are experienced as a type of external force having a quality independent of their producers. In a manner similar to the natural world, an objective world confronts the individual: "There we go again" becomes "This is how things are done!"[6] The rule-like statements and the obvious connection to the world of the everyday make the household code an especially good indicator of the process whereby the symbolic universe confronts the individual in a manner similar to the natural world.[7] Family patterns of interaction and regulations are simply taken for granted as the way things are and have always been. It is also important to recognize that this type of exhortation acts as a form of socialization, a means by which the social world is internalized. Most importantly, the code is a means of drawing children into the community and reinforcing a sense of belonging.

Because household code language is so thoroughly rooted in the interactions of the everyday and the traditional interactions of family life, it is perhaps more important to imagine how the taken for granted, symbolic world appears to be altered even in a minor way. The reference to inheritance in the midst of exhortations to slaves who under Roman law had no rights as such (Col 3:24) offers a good example of such an alteration (in this case, perhaps not so minor).[8] The symbolic universe that was being constructed among the first believers developed as a result of communication. Believers were members of many social worlds, including households, associations, and various social communities; with every exchange within the church group there was opportunity for multiple traditions to interact with new forms of expression. The stability and existence of the symbolic universe shared by believers should also be understood as continuously threatened by conflicts between traditions; values and realities shared by a member of the *ekklēsia* might stand in conflict with the realities and values of his or her household, association, or local community. There is always a back-and-forth movement between forces for constancy and forces for change.[9]

It is particularly important to pay close attention to language in the development of how forms of knowledge are achieved by people in interaction. Social constructionist analysis of culture tends to high-light the importance of language as more than a matter of expres-sion; in daily interaction it becomes essentially a form of action and may even be thought of as "performative."[10] From this perspective, the deliberate singling out of children as members present when the community is gathered and the epistle is read out loud takes on new significance. While the Apostle Paul makes extensive use of child-hood and infancy metaphors, there is only one fleeting reference to the presence of children in community life: the puzzling reference to chil-dren of mixed marriage who are now holy (1 Cor 7:14). But in Col 3:20 and Eph 6:1, the "performative" quality of children being called out by name in the midst of the assembly *constructs* a world of belonging.

The social constructionist approach to interpreting the house-hold codes in Colossians and Ephesians invites examination of *pro-cesses* rather than *social structures.*[11] Thus, instead of focusing simply on how the text reflects the structures of the household of antiquity, it is important to contemplate how the oral performance of this exhorta-tion creates and sustains a new social world. In fact, overemphasis on structures can lead us to a misguided vision of single-dimension identities of hearers as children, slaves, masters, or parents governed by straightforward social rules. Instead, one needs to imagine being called out by name as a dynamic and fluctuating social process. It is important to consider what one might hear as a child when one is also a slave. Likewise, it is crucial to think about what one might hear when one is both a master and a parent, or a slave and a parent.[12] Inscrip-tional evidence wherein family terminology was employed freely in slave commemorations erected by freedpersons supports this vision of multidimensional identity and multidimensional social interactions. Slaves were parents; slaves were children living with slave parents or apart from them; and slaves were sometimes the biological children of their owners. Both as children and adults, slaves ultimately owed obedience to the heads of their households with a myriad of potential divided loyalties with respect to the fragile family units they hoped to establish among themselves.[13]

Related to the multidimensional identities of the audience of the household codes was the far-reaching phenomenon of pseudo-parenting. Taking many forms in the Roman world, it might even be said to be so common as to permeate the whole society. One important social factor was a demography in which, broadly speaking, more than 25 percent would have lost their fathers by the age of 15. Another was the dislocation of children and parents caused by divorce and remarriage. More subtly, we must keep in mind that care arrangements were more flexible than most are accustomed to in modern western society. Not only did many children live with stepparents, but they were also fostered by side kin and elder siblings or were even adopted into another family. It might even be appropriate to speak of Roman "patchwork" families.[14] Moreover, even when the law protected the authority of the male line (the *pater familias* if still alive or next male agnate) over the children in the case of divorce or widowhood, in reality a divorced or widowed mother frequently appealed to her natal kin for assistance. This often left paternal authority over the children challenged by potentially dominant surrogate fathers such as maternal uncles, stepfathers, or especially in the case of well-to-do widows, the single mothers themselves.[15] In light of such social realities, it is vital to question the identity of the fathers of Col 3:21 and Eph 6:4 and examine the opportunities for surrogate fatherhood. The possibility of single mothers acting as surrogate fathers is especially intriguing given the sustained references to women named without male counterparts in earliest Christian communities, including Nympha, who has a church in her house (Col 4:15-16).

Given the detailed interest in the slave-master relationship in the Colossian domestic code, however, a final type of pseudo-parenting needs to be considered before dealing with the reference to fathers in Col 3:21: the role of the slave as wet nurse and caregiver.[16] The role of the wet nurse illustrates the sometimes fuzzy distinction between socialization and education. Whereas education involves active and intentional communication of knowledge, socialization should be viewed "as a process in which a child internalized social structures and unconsciously learned the codes and standards of his [or her] social sphere."[17] Ancient authors gave detailed advice on the selection of wet nurses in a manner that makes their importance for the overlapping functions of socialization and education clear.[18] In a housechurch context one should not underestimate the further overlap of these processes with evangelization, even extending to believing slave nurses of nonbelieving children. As was frequently recognized by ancient authors, wet nurses provided formative influence on speech and were the tellers of a child's first stories, which could easily have included abridged gospel stories. The whole domestic context of child rearing, often among slave children as playmates, was recognized as a domain requiring some supervision to produce the desired formative effects.[19]

The socialization and educational influences of slave wet nurses in the Roman world found a complement in the use of slave attendants, the *paedagogi*. Perhaps best known for accompanying children to school and offering rudimentary education, slave attendants also coached children in day-to-day behavior, including expectations for social events. Some social gatherings included readings at which slave attendants shared with parents the task of explaining literary and moral points.[20] Once again, it is important to keep in mind the mixing of free and slave children, for slave children were often servers at dinner parties and thus could witness the elevated dinner conversations or the speeches of learned guests along with their freeborn playmates.[21] The direct address to children in the household codes of Colossians and Ephesians reminds us that children were present when the Epistles were read aloud in the assembly (Col 4:15-16). One should probably imagine also that parents and well-educated slaves (who may even have been parents themselves) would explain the substance of the Letters.[22] The exact nature of house-church meetings are shrouded in mystery, but most likely included scriptural readings, admonitions (Col 3:16), and a ritual meal (cf. 1 Cor 11:17-34). Indeed, in Col 3:16, community members are instructed to admonish one another and to give thanks by singing psalms, hymns, and spiritual songs. Once again, children may well have participated in these activities. The involvement of children in religious rites of various kinds was a prime means of passing on religious knowledge in the Roman world, and the phenomenon of children singing at public feasts is well attested.[23]

In creating this opening for the participation of children, however, it is crucial to not overlook undisputable reinforcement of the authority of fathers in Col 3:21 and in Eph 6:4.[24] The overlap between the Colossian household code and the ideologies and perspectives of slave-holding are unmistakable. As discussed in the previous chapter, the scope of obedience ("in everything") is the same for children and slaves. In the case of Eph 6:4, the ideological links between the ultimate authority of fathers and masters fade from view as greater emphasis is placed on the "Christian" education of children. Yet the warnings about excessive severity are conventional, even if in keeping with more moderate approaches. The net result in both Colossians and Ephesians is that the extreme authority of fathers over their children in the Greco-Roman world is recognized. But when one contemplates the domain of daily interaction in church groups, several questions arise about the identity of the fathers and whether these instructions *merely replicate* cultural ideals.

Virtually no attention has been given to children of nonbelieving parents as members of house-church communities. The lack of explicit treatment of this issue in the sources does not mean that it was not widespread, as mixed marriages existed from the earliest period (1 Cor 7:12-16; 1 Pet 3:1-3). Our knowledge of the domestic/work world of first believers strongly suggests that children may have entered church groups via the networks created by child care, play, and even chance encounters in the workshops and crowded urban streets in a Mediterranean environment. Believing children's (including slave children's) obedience to nonbelieving parents would no doubt "please the Lord" (Col 3:20). But it could be surmised that the Lord would also be pleased if a child made his or her way to the community, perhaps brought by a mother or slave attendant without the knowledge of the *pater familias*. It is also reasonable to wonder (unfortunately without any real possibility of determining a correct answer) how many freeborn believing fathers were actually present in these communities; this question is especially relevant in the case of the Colossian community, in which the slave presence is of obvious concern (Col 3:22–4:1). Of this we may be certain: acting as a surrogate father was a common practice in the Roman world. The reference to the children belonging to believing fathers should perhaps not be taken too literally, allowing for fatherhood authority and protection to extend over children and slave children who in reality belonged to nonbelievers or were orphaned or abandoned.

Even if it is utopian and futuristic, the promise of inheritance to slaves should also again be born in mind. Despite the fact that slave and freeborn children were often nursed and cared for by the same slave caregivers, there is much literary evidence of an ideology that not only reinforced the chasm between slavery and freedom in adulthood but also encompassed differing expectations and treatment from the *pater familias* in childhood. Seneca offers especially important evidence to consider, including the idea that while the *pater familias* must enforce the strongest discipline (or in Seneca's words, be a severe and demanding maestro of virtue) with his own sons, he can afford to be indulgent with the household slaves, having little regard for their education and even taking delight in their vices.[25] Such notions should lead to consideration of how the promise of inheritance in Colossians might challenge traditional notions of paternity and entitlement, especially with respect to the treatment and instruction of children in the community.

The Father as Teacher in Ephesians 6:1-4

Ephesians 6:4 calls for fathers to raise their children "in the discipline (*paideia*) and instruction (*nouthesia*) of the Lord." This verse points to a body of instruction with significant Christian content to be imparted to children in a home setting.[26] Here a concern for socialization has become a deliberate attempt to educate. This deliberate attempt to incorporate the next generation via education is a sign of institutionalization—it is very much a case of "this is how things are done."

The special responsibility of fathers for the education of children is recognized in Scripture: "Listen, children, to a father's instruction and be attentive, that you may gain insight; for I give you good precepts: do not forsake my teaching" (Prov 4:1; cf. 4:1-4). Likewise, fathers were the traditional custodians and disseminators of religious knowledge in the Roman world. Like the earliest collections of Christian teaching, this knowledge was often conveyed orally. Especially with respect to rites associated with the ancestor's tradition, knowledge was passed down from father to son, generation to generation, with a particular attention to the cultivation of a child's memory.[27] As is reflected in the Pastoral Epistles, mothers and grandmothers played an important role in the education of young children and of adolescent girls into adults.²⁸ But the ideological emphasis on the education of sons by their fathers is unmistakable. Plutarch describes how "Cato the Elder took care of his son's education himself when he could have employed one of the best tutors of his time. He taught him literature, law, and gymnastics. He also wrote a history book 'in big letters so that his son would have the means to learn about the ancient traditions of his country at home.'"²⁹ Contact between father and son and even the socialization that occurred through accompanying and observing one's father was prized. Presuming the convention that sons would go along with their fathers to participate in religious rites, the proclamation of the young Greek boy as recorded by Xenophon would be equally at home in the Roman world, "I am not without experience because I continually attended sacrifices."³⁰

While the NT household code has very often been understood as an apologetic text, virtually no attention has been paid to the role of the child-parent and father-child exhortation within that discourse. Yet the ideological importance of the role of fathers in preparing the next generation, preserving tradition, and ensuring continuity invites us to reflect on the possibility that apologetic intent is not confined to teaching on marriage and slavery but extends to parenting. The very public face of the father-son relationship and its significance for family identity can be sensed in the dominant public perception of the son as the living image (*imago, effigies*) of his father. The son could be described both in terms of body and countenance as the image of his father. But it was not so much nature that created this resemblance but socialization within the family and ascription by others. The imitation of the father by the son (*imatatio patri*) was central to the perpetuation of family traditions. Such imitation became an active and dynamic means of living up to the memory of a young man's ancestors and of continuing family identity.³¹ Epictetus, the Stoic philosopher who was a contemporary of the NT authors, spoke forcefully about the line of continuity from father to son and the obligations for obedience so attached. He addresses males directly:

Next bear in mind that you are a son. What is the profession of this character? To treat everything that is his own as belonging to his father, to be obedient to him in all things, never to speak ill of him to anyone else, nor to say or do anything that will harm him, to give way to him in everything and yield to him in precedence, helping him as far as is within his power.[32]

The son's deference to his father was a prime indicator of the son's identity and character, rooted in the very essence and authority of his father.

Such notions were also reflected in the writings of Flavius Josephus, who emphasized the importance of grounding children in tradition in his apologetic discourse in *Against Apion*, appealing to values associated with the firm authority of the *pater familias*. According to Josephus, Jews living under the law are as under a father and master (*hupo patri toutō kai despotē*; cf. Gal 3:24).[33] Jews united under the law are like the family ordered and rendered harmonious by the household head. The subordinate members of Jewish families exhibit piety (*eusebeia*)—a concept typically linked with devotion to matters of state and family, especially the obedience of children.[34] The discipline delivered for disobedience matches the scope of discipline that is the prerogative of the Roman *pater familias*.[35] The education of the next generation on the basis of what has been inherited from the past is, in a remarkable passage, identified by Josephus as the priority of the Jews: "Above all we pride ourselves on the education of our children, and regard as the most essential task in life the observance of our laws and of the pious practices (*eusebeian*), based thereupon, which we have inherited."[36] Such an approach has practical consequences. In keeping with other Hellenistic Jews who sought to distinguish themselves from their Greco-Roman contemporaries with a reputation for practicing abortion, infanticide, and exposure, Josephus states that the law "gave orders to nurture all children."[37] Moreover, the child's upbringing is to be marked by sobriety from the very start (in contrast to the rowdy birth parties of the Romans). Children should be taught to read and become thoroughly familiar with the traditions of the forefathers—deeds that should be imitated and laws in which children should be grounded.[38]

It is precisely for the usurping of the educational authority of the *pater familias* over his children and his influence in the selection of appropriate teachers that Celsus criticized the early Christians.

According to Celsus, in houses (no doubt including house churches) and shops that included a large slave presence, children accompanied by "stupid" women were exposed to a curriculum based on nonsense.[39] The very antitheses of an assembly of honorable and intelligent men, in Celsus' view the gatherings seemed intent on targeting adolescent boys.[40] It is against such a background that one should evaluate the exhortation to fathers to bring up their children in the discipline and instruction of the Lord in Ephesians. The curriculum that Celsus felt should be the subject of ridicule remains unknown to us, although interesting insight into the content might be found in 1 Clement, which uses the same term for discipline or training (*paideia*) with respect to the instruction of children: "Let our children partake of the discipline (*paideias*) that is in Christ, let them learn the strength of humility before God and the power of pure love before God. Let them learn how the reverential awe of him is beautiful and great, and how it saves all those who conduct themselves in it [*Or: in him*] in a holy way, with a clear understanding. For he is the one who explores our understanding and desires. His breath is in us, and when he wishes, he will remove it."[41]

First Clement's notion of the discipline that is in Christ combines concepts of reverential attitude toward the divine with ethical comportment. Such an approach also frames the exhortations in Eph 6:1-4, wherein the call to honor parents in Eph 6:2 is rooted in the command from the Decalogue (LXX Exod 20:12; Deut 5:16). The command to honor parents is frequently discussed in Hellenistic Jewish literature, with topics ranging from the divine authority of parents[42] and the blessings that befall obedient children,[43] to the mortal consequences for crimes against one's parents.[44] New Testament commentators have debated whether the exhortations to children include adult children; the reference here to ancient scriptural traditions does point to a respectful attitude that begins in childhood but ultimately culminates in ongoing care by adult children of parents into old age.[45] The case of the rebellious son in Deut 21:18-21 leads to a long commentary by Josephus that includes what the parents would have said to the son while disciplining him. They remind him of his obligations and press for the most serious consequences only as a last resort:

In cases in which young men disdain their parents and do not grant them honor—whether because of shame or lack of understanding—demeaning them, let the parents first of all warn them with words, for they are autonomous judges over their sons, saying that they came together with each other not for the sake of pleasure, nor of increasing their wealth by placing in common what the two of them had, but in order that they might have children who would tend them in their old age and who would have from them whatever they needed: "When you were born, we raised you with joy, and giving the greatest thanks to God we reared you with devotion, sparing nothing of what seemed to be useful for your well-being and education in the best things. Now, however, for it was necessary to grant pardon for the failings of youth, you have sufficiently disregarded honor toward us. Change to the more reasonable way, considering that God is also annoyed with those who commit outrage against parents, because He Himself is also the father of the whole human race."[46]

Ongoing reverence for parents was a moral ideal that Romans shared with Jews in the ancient world.[47] Seneca speaks of reverence and obedience to parents that has no bounds and includes compliance and submission, even when parents have appeared too harsh or unfair. A lack of compliance, in the end, should only be revealed in the unwillingness to be outdone by one's own parents in providing care (no doubt what is included here is care to aging parents): "In only one respect I was unyielding: in refusing to let them do me more kindness than I did them."[48]

In seeking to understand the social context of the child-parent exhortations in the NT household codes, it is a mistake to exclude ongoing relations between adult children and their parents and to envisage rigid end points for childhood and rigid demarcations between grown and young children.[49] Attitudes toward the end of childhood were markedly different from modern western attitudes in a variety of respects, including the ongoing influence of parents on adult children in definitions of authority (*patria potestas*), the dominance of marriage without *manus* (wherein a woman remained fundamentally linked to her father's line in terms of property and inheritance), and the great flexibility in determining when boys might undergo coming-of-age ceremonies. It is not surprising that 1 Clement makes an easy transition from a focus on specific children to an appeal to believers as children when presenting the call of Christ through the Holy Spirit, which repeats the words of the Psalms: "Come, children and hear me; I will teach you the reverential awe of the Lord" (cf. Ps 34:11).[50] The quotation from the Psalms is followed immediately by a description of God as a beneficent and compassionate father.[51] Similarly, Ephesians appeals to the concept of fatherhood to link God the father with the community in the proclamation that God the father is the one from whom every family (lit. fatherhood: *patria*) on heaven and earth takes its name (Eph 3:14-15), recalling Josephus' previously cited description of God as the father of the whole human race.

The reference to *paideia* (discipline or training) in Eph 6:4 resonates with a concept that has figured prominently in recent discussions of the Roman family: the life course. *Paideia* not only refers to the upbringing of a child in the strict sense but also to the formation of an adult. Josephus refers to the concept in laying out the two schemes of education or training (*paideia*) (by precept and by practical exercising of the character) that are combined in Jewish teaching of the law:

> Our legislator, on the other hand, took great care to combine both systems. He did not leave practical training in morals inarticulate; nor did he permit the letter of the law to remain inoperative. Starting from the very beginning with the food of which we partake from infancy and the private life of the home, he left nothing, however insignificant, to the discretion and caprice of the individual. What meats a man should abstain from, and what he may enjoy; with what persons he should associate; what period should be devoted respectively to strenuous labour and to rest.[52]

This proclamation culminates in the previously cited statement about Jews living under the law as under a father and master.[53] Building upon Jewish concepts, the Pastoral Epistles also envision training from infancy and continuing throughout the life course. For example, in presenting the formation of Timothy, 2 Tim 3:15 describes his education from infancy (*brephos*) in the sacred writings (*hiera grammata*).[54] A second reference to Scripture (*graphē*) occurs in a text that also speaks of discipline or training (*paideia*), in which there is a clear emphasis on teaching; in this case the instruction of adults is envisioned, but the teaching of children is by no means ruled out. Training (*paideia*) in righteousness is the purpose of Scripture according to 2 Tim 3:16-17. One detects in this text the same emphasis on a combination of precepts and the practical application thereof that Josephus identifies as a hallmark of the teaching of the law. In 2 Tim 3:16-17, being grounded in Scripture (training in righteousness) involves teaching (*didaskalia*), reproof (*elegmon*), and correction (*epanorthōsis*).[55] It seems best to understand the instruction delivered by fathers in Eph 6:4 as a similar type of practical instruction that calls for leadership on the part of fathers (they should not provoke their children to anger) that extends into their old age and invites reciprocal reverence and obedience from their children.

Family Socialization, Lifelong Learning, and the Construction of Identity

By far the greatest attention to the household code texts, especially those having to do with the child-parent relationship, has centered on how these exhortations replicate the conventional standards of society. This book challenges a simplistic vision of conventional ethics merely being reproduced in the disputed Pauline literature. One must consider broadly how such teaching might be central to forging a distinct identity in the Roman world. Ephesians is particularly important to consider here. Ephesians displays the most negative and uncompromising attitude to the evil unbelieving world of all the Pauline and deuteropauline works, strongly reinforcing the boundaries of the community (Eph 2:1-3; 4:17–5:20; 6:10-20).[56] This, combined with a virtual lack of dialogue with nonbelievers (cf. Col 3:5-6), suggests that it is useful to think about Ephesians, and its instructions on family life, in terms of "sectarian" identity. In other words, we need to consider the household exhortations in light of the demonstrated conviction of the work to create a community that is markedly set apart from the outside world. All Pauline literature might be said to demonstrate this quality to a certain degree. But the extent of the desire for separation (if not outright withdrawal), admittedly not really possible in the urban environment of Ephesians, is remarkable.[57] This feature of Ephesians is increasingly calling attention to parallels with the strongly sectarian language of the Dead Sea Scrolls.[58] One particular feature of comparison between the scrolls and Ephesians is of particular importance for this study: interest in the education of children.

Although it is just now being recognized, the Dead Sea Scrolls contain fascinating material concerning the education of children presented within the framework of the life course. The two documents that provide rare evidence concerning the education of children in the late Second Temple period are the *Rule of the Congregation* (1QSa) and the *Damascus Document* (CD).[59] Expectations of the teachings of the laws throughout the life course are revealed in 1QSa 1:4-8:

> [4]When they come they shall assemble all those who enter, from children to women, and they shall read in [their] h[earing]
>
> [5] [al]l the statues of the covenant, and instruct them in all [th]eir regul[ations] lest they stray in their errors.
>
> [6] And this is the rule for all the hosts of the congregation, for all born in Israel. From his youth
>
> [7] they shall [ins]truct him in the Book of Hagu, and according to his age, they shall enlighten him in the statute[s of] the covenant, and acc[ording to his understanding]
>
> [8] [they shall] teach (him) their regulations.[60]

The immediate context of this proclamation is the important annual Renewal of the Covenant ceremony, which involved the renewal of allegiance of the whole group. As in the covenantal ceremony described in Deut 31:10-13, the presence of the children is significant (Deut 31:12-13). The learning described as taking place during the Renewal of the

Covenant ceremony appears to be based on listening to statutes of the covenant (commandments) and regulations (cf. Deut 6:4-9; 11:18-19); the oral setting calls to mind the house-church context, wherein children are singled out for instruction (cf. Col 3:20-21; Eph 6:1-2). But it is also clear that the ceremony serves to remind the participants of knowledge they have already acquired. This is made clear by the repetition of the term "statutes of the covenant" and "regulations," as the text of 1QSa 1:4-8 shifts from the ceremony (lines 4-5) to consideration of regulations for the sectarians in general as they move through various stages of the life course (lines 6-8). Lines 6-8 are actually followed by reference to various stages of life by which a man acquires further responsibilities, beginning with marriage (lines 9-10).[61] But despite the awareness of life stages, these exhortations display evidence of the flexibility that we have seen was part of the approach to dealing with the transitions of childhood in the Roman world. There is an awareness of progression according to maturity and, if the reconstruction of the fragmentary text above is correct, the notion of "according to his understanding" suggests attentiveness to differences of learning in relation to ability and pace.[62]

"Statutes" and "covenants" are typical expressions used by Moses when he instructs the Israelites (e.g., Deut 4:1, 5, 8, 14, 45; 5:1, 31; 6:1, 20; 7:11). In the Hebrew Bible, Deuteronomy is notable for the importance it places on the instruction of children: "Keep these words that I am commanding you today in your heart. Recite them to your children and talk about them when you are at home and when you are away, when you lie down and when you rise" (Deut 6:6-7). The sectarian community reflected in 1QSa appears to be fulfilling the laws concerning the teaching of children.[63] In the instructions to children in Eph 6:1-3, it is not surprising to find an appeal to Deut 5:16, with its promise of well-being and long life to children who honor their parents. Ethics are imbued with traditional notions of community and familial identity and continuity, as we also find in Deut 6:2-3: "So that you and your children and your children's children may fear the Lord your God all the days of your life, and keep his decrees and his commandments that I am commanding you, so that your days may be long. Hear therefore, O Israel, and observe them diligently, so that it may go well with you, and so that you may multiply greatly in a land

flowing with milk and honey, as the Lord, the God of your ancestors, has promised you." Ephesians is very close to the world of the
Dead Sea Scrolls in calling upon these ideas to define the interaction
between parents and children in the house-church community. The
fulfillment of commandments and instruction of children (Eph 6:4)
becomes a means of daily affirmation of commitment to the Lord and
articulating the parameters of the community.

In envisioning the education of children in the ancient world, it
is important not to overplay the focus on what we would consider
the fundamentals of early childhood education, especially reading and
writing. 1QSa 4–5 appears to point, rather, to listening to the reading of the laws following the example of Deut 6:6-7. While reading
and writing may well be presumed by some of the texts dealing with
children from Qumran, even references to specific works such as the
mysterious book of Hagu (CD 10:6; 13:2; 14:7-8) might refer to content
intended to be learned through memorization, followed by gradual
introduction of deeper insights. Jewish sources from this period reveal
the importance of memorization and recitation and often link such
practices to the formation given by parents; once again, we detect the
close relationship between socialization in the family and education.
In 4 Maccabees, the mother of the seven sons who are about to be
killed recalls the role of their father as teacher of the Law and the
Prophets, framed as stories and sayings of Scripture that could be
recounted aloud:

> While he was still with you, he taught you the law and the prophets.
> He read to you about Abel slain by Cain, and Isaac who was offered
> as a burnt offering, and about Joseph in prison. He told you of the
> zeal of Phinehas, and he taught you about Hananiah, Azariah, and
> Mishael in the fire. He praised Daniel in the den of the lions and
> blessed him. He reminded you of the scripture of Isaiah, which
> says, "Even though you go through the fire, the flame shall not
> consume you." He sang to you songs of the psalmist David, who
> said, "Many are the afflictions of the righteous." He recounted to
> you Solomon's proverb, "There is a tree of life for those who do his
> will." He confirmed the query of Ezekiel, "Shall these dry bones
> live?" For he did not forget to teach you the song that Moses taught,

which says, "I kill and I make alive: this is your life and the length of your days." (4 Macc 18:10-19)

Among widespread evidence for the teaching of Scripture and laws to children from infancy, Josephus makes specific reference to memorization of the laws, which finds its grounding in childhood and sets Jews apart from other nations, who are often ignorant of their own laws:

> But, should anyone of our nation be questioned about the laws, he would repeat them all more readily than his own name. The result, then, of our thorough grounding in the laws from the first dawn of intelligence is that we have them, as it were, engraven on our souls. A transgressor is a rarity; evasion of punishment by excuses an impossibility.[64]

Josephus here reveals a commitment to what modern people would term a "lifelong learning" approach; this passage is preceded by a description of the weekly gathering at which Jews listen to the Law and endeavor to gain a thorough knowledge of it.[65]

Once again one is invited to think about how the ethical teaching of Ephesians might incorporate teaching materials introduced during childhood with the expectation of heightened understanding as one matures. There is clearly a communal teaching function implied in the command in Eph 5:18 that community members are to speak to one another using songs, hymns, and spiritual songs, but this text is preceded by ethical instructions that incorporate several wisdom sayings and baptismal recollections that might be easily learned orally and memorized. These display considerable overlap with Colossians and the undisputed Letters of Paul, as well as with Greco-Roman ethical codes and Jewish ethical teaching, including the Qumran literature.[66] A few examples illustrate the point. Ephesians 4:26, which acknowledges the existence of anger and calls for people not to go to bed angry, seems at once to reflect the language of Ps 4:4 and a traditional Greco-Roman maxim.[67] Ephesians 5:13 cites an early Christian hymn that draws upon the light/darkness motif that figures prominently in the chapter and may allude to Isa 60:1. Emphasizing the priority of heightened knowledge and discernment, the text shifts from this motif to consider the unwise/wise contrast in Eph 5:15-17, echoing an approach commonly seen in Jewish ethical teaching.[68]

The long passage of Eph 4:17–5:20 is heavily dependent upon traditional material and sometimes seems like a disjointed collection of sayings. But it is actually structured according to the traditional notion of the "two ways"—alternating catalogues of virtue and vice—found in other early Christian texts and the Dead Sea Scrolls.[69] Such an organizational structure might be somewhat tedious to read, but it is well suited to oral learning. It is particularly striking that Eph 4:20 conveys the transition from a description of the state of unbelievers to the reality of the existence of believers as that of having "learned Christ." This expression refers to learning traditions about Christ (cf. Acts 5:42; Col 1:6-7), as is made clear in the following verse, which speaks of "hearing of him" and "having been taught in him, as truth is in Jesus."[70] Only here in Ephesians (and it is fairly rare in the undisputed Letters of Paul) does the name of Jesus appear alone, and it may well refer to the teachings of the historical Jesus that are taught in the community.[71] But even if the expression is only a stylistic variation of "in Christ," clearly some type of prior instruction about Christ is presumed, and from the context we may surmise that it includes active devotion to a way of life. For many members of the audience, such prior instruction would have been received from the fathers (and mothers) in the community (Eph 6:4).

While it may not be immediately obvious, concepts of the family run under the surface in Eph 4:17–5:20, the text leading into household code teaching. Most obviously, there is a sustained interest in sexuality and sexual morality, with references to the impurity and immorality of nonbelievers (e.g., Eph 4:19; 5:3, 5). The mention of shameful acts performed in secret likely points to sexual indecency and immorality (Eph 5:12)—the very antithesis of the community envisioned as a pure bride joined to Christ in Eph 5:26-27.[72] Believers are to shun the sexual practices of the Gentile, nonbelieving world. We cannot know precisely what kind of acts are in view, but the reference to secrecy might point to adultery or even the sexual use of slaves and general debauchery that does not reflect the honor of the family and the fidelity of marriage.[73] Most striking, however, is the manner in which the life of believers is described in Eph 5:1. They are to be imitators of God (the more usual expression being "imitators of Christ") as beloved children. This is the only place in the whole of the NT that believers are called to imitate God. But given what we have seen about the importance of the concept of children (especially sons) imitating their fathers in the formation of identity in the Roman world, it is likely that such notions underlie the proclamation in Eph 5:1. According to Eph 3:14-15, the Father is from whom every family in heaven and on earth is named—human or angelic. The Father exercises his authority over all, leads all, and unites all (cf. Eph 1:2, 3, 17; 2:18; 4:6; 5:20; 6:23).

Fathers, Teachers, and Community Leaders

With rich metaphors and practical ethical instructions, Ephesians leaves much unsaid about the socialization of children into adults in the Lord. But the comparative Jewish material in particular helps to identify the importance of this agenda, which can be detected through careful analysis of the text. With various theological concepts, ethical norms, and (often conventional) cultural values, Ephesians subtly reinforces the role of teacher and of the teaching potential of familial relationships. Once again, comparison with the Dead Sea Scrolls is instructive.

In the Dead Sea Scrolls, teaching is clearly presented as communal responsibility, entrusted especially to the men of the community. The relationship of this communal scope to the traditional locus of education of children in the home invites further exploration. Proverbs 4:1-4 captures the home-based educational approach of Jews in this era, with special attention to the role of the father. But what is especially intriguing is that the Dead Sea Scrolls appear to offer the first example of *mandatory* communal education for children. Schools were widespread in the Greco-Roman world, but the emphasis on the teaching of Scripture in Ephesians invites us to look to Jewish models first in seeking to understand the educational character of house churches.[74] The house-church atmosphere seems to have combined the close association of education and family life with the communal dimensions of the Dead Sea Scrolls. If we imagine fathers being called out in the assembly of the house church as in Eph 6:4, we sense a merging of the communal responsibility of the men of the community with home-based expectations. This dual communal/household dimension of the responsibility of fathers emerges even more clearly when we consider the relationship between teaching and leadership in Ephesians.

The *Damascus Document* presents further evidence of the juxtaposition of fatherhood and the communal responsibilities of the teacher in its characterization of "the examiner" (the *mebaqqer*). In a very fragmentary text that forms part of "the rule for the Examiner of the camp" (CD 13:7-19), there is a very brief reference to the role of the examiner in instructing children (4Q266 9 iii 6-9/CD 13:17-20):

> [6] He (the Examiner) shall instruct their sons [and their daughters]
> [7] and their little children [in a spi]rit of hu[mi]lity and lov[ing-kindness.]
> [8] Let him (the Examiner) not keep a grudge against th[em] with wrathful an[ger]
> [9] [be]cause of their failings, and against one who is not.[75]

The metaphorical association between fathers and teachers is brought out in CD 13:9, in which the examiner is to teach the whole congregation ("the many") and is to "pity them as a father does his children." A similar attitude is displayed in the above excerpt in relation to the teaching of young children. Along the same lines, Ephesians calls fathers not to provoke their children to anger (Eph 6:4; Col 3:21). All of these texts stand at some distance from calls for harsh discipline, emphasizing the extreme authority of fathers in other ancient sources. They are not completely countercultural, for warnings against extreme severity are by no means unknown.[76] Nevertheless, evidence from both the Dead Sea Scrolls and Ephesians points to practices involving nurturing and encouragement in education.[77]

According to the *Damascus Document*, the examiner also plays a role in the initiation of new members, which involves teaching and examining components in relation to living according to the laws (CD 15:5-15). Of particular interest is the text dealing with the initiation of the children of adult members: "And all who have entered the covenant for all of Israel as an eternal statute shall let their children, who have reached (the age) to cross over into those who are enrolled, take the oath of the covenant" (CD 15:5-6).[78] It appears that the "oath of the covenant" includes the promise to live according to the correct interpretation of the laws in keeping with what the children have learned until this point within the community and within the context of their own families. What seems to be in view here is the taking on of full responsibility for living according to the received knowledge of the laws. There are suggestions of a type of automatic acceptance of the children of adult members that calls to mind Paul's description of the children of believers as holy in 1 Cor 7:14, even though there is a recognition of the possibility of newcomers making mistakes, with the potential for ongoing instruction by the examiner for a further year.[79] But there is also an acknowledged process of transition from childhood to adulthood as children are initiated as full members.

The connotations of lifelong learning in the evidence from the Dead Sea Scrolls and the role of the examiner in relation to family structure and organization invite one to rethink the implication of the subtle reinforcement of the role of teacher in Ephesians. The reference to fathers raising their children in the discipline/training (*paideia*) and instruction of the Lord in Eph 6:4 resonates with concepts associated with the life course, ultimately leading to the formation of an adult. There are indications in the text of an underlying notion of the perfecting of this grounding in the family by community teachers, revealed especially in the nature of the emphasis on the role of teacher. The depiction of unity in the spirit in Eph 4:1-16 is especially significant. In describing Christ's role in the giving of gifts, the author of Ephesians strings together several leadership roles that have teaching and/or preaching components: the apostles, the prophets, the evangelists, the pastors, and the teachers (4:11). The apostles and prophets are mentioned twice previously in Ephesians (2:20; 3:5) in a way indicating they represent a type of charismatic teaching authority that laid the foundation of the community.[80] In contrast, the evangelists (cf. Acts 21:8; 2 Tim 4:1-4), pastors (cf. Acts 20:28-31; 1 Pet 5:2; John

21:16), and teachers (1 Cor 12:28; Rom 12:7; Acts 13:1; 1 Tim 3:2; 5:17; Titus 1:9) seem to be more current to the situation of the time of the composition of Ephesians, perhaps representing a shift from the itinerant leadership of Paul's day to a more residential leadership.[81] The connection of the teacher-preachers of the community to the apostles and prophets of an earlier era clearly reinforces the legitimacy of the current leadership, although it is impossible to distinguish precisely between the functions. All of the related ministerial roles, however, contribute to the growth, nurturing, and knowledge of the church, the body of Christ. In fact, it may well be the case that the author envisions the ministers in Eph 4:11 as the ligaments holding the body together, providing the connection between the parts of the body, allowing it to move and grow.[82]

Once again, it is important to take account of the interweaving of family and education metaphors. Emphasis on the role of teacher is brought out with childhood and life-course metaphors. The ultimate goal of the work of the teacher-preachers is to bring the members of the congregation to maturity, to the measure of the full stature of Christ. The Greek text literally refers to the mature man (*anēr*; cf. Col 1:28). The construction of gender here invites comment. The mature man is one who emulates his father, becomes the image of his father. This was a standard way of representing the continuity between father and son in the Greco-Roman world. The purpose here is to measure up to the Son of God, specifically expressed in terms of knowledge of the Son of God (Eph 4:13). There is no doubt that conventional ideals about male perfection underlie this verse, but the metaphorical contrast with children generally suggests the whole community of persons—male and female—is in view. The implications of this inclusivity framed in terms of male, Christlike perfection (cf. Eph 2:15) is difficult to discern. Yet, because of the underlying theme of education, it is not an overstatement to suggest that both men and women, male and female children, are potentially capable of sharing in this life-giving knowledge. The mature person refers to a corporate entity, the one who stands in contrast to the children, who are vulnerable to being led astray (Eph 4:14). A similar contrast is found in 1 Cor 14:20, but in Ephesians the emphasis is specifically upon teaching and false teaching. By implication, the important role of the teacher is reinforced. Ultimately, the role of the teacher is to reveal something more than can be grasped in childhood, calling to mind the emphasis on initiation and transition in the Dead Sea Scrolls.[83]

The move from such metaphorical language of Eph 4:14-15 to the concrete world of teaching, including the teaching of boys and girls is inevitably speculative. But a focus on the familial context of education in the Roman world and the house-church setting does bring certain elements to light. First of all, it is important to remember that by the second century, early Christians were accused of not respecting familial boundaries closely associated with educational practices. From the words of the pagan critic Celsus cited above, it is clear that early Christians were charged with ignoring the prerogatives of legitimate teachers and heads of households and targeting vulnerable children, especially adolescent boys. On the cusp of maturity, these boys were, instead, duped by disrespectful Christian evangelists. Perhaps as response to such accusations against believers, the author of Ephesians uses highly stereotypical categories to describe how children (here symbols for how believers should not behave) might be carried away by human trickery (*kybeia*).[84] In contrast, in the vision of community presented here, members are nurtured and perfected until they attain maturity. In many respects, the author presents a vision of the community that is closely tied to the ideal family. The overall emphasis on unity in Eph 4:16 is supported by a repeated call for love between members, with the term repeated on three separate occasions (Eph 4:2, 15, 16). Love is a central theme in Ephesians (e.g., 1:4, 15; 2:4; 3:18-19; 4:2, 15); it is that which ensures the proper growth of the community.[85] Love is central to the characterization of the marital relationship both in its earthly manifestation (husbands are to love their wives) and as a metaphor for the union of Christ and the community (Eph 5:25-29).

As is the case frequently with both Colossians and Ephesians, however, there is a countercultural twist that becomes readily apparent when one imagines the educational features of the house church. Ephesians 4:2 deserves comment irrespective of its close resemblance to Col 3:12-13, wherein the same list of virtues is found. In Eph 4:2 we have one of the many references to love found in this text; in contrast to Colossians, the emphasis is on bearing with one another "in love"—that is, the love shared between believers. The other virtues also take on new significance in light of what is said within the context of Ephesians. The call for humility (*tapeinophrosynē*), a term typically associated with servility in the Roman world,[86] takes place in the midst of exhortations concerning unity in light of a diversity of gifts associated especially with teaching/preaching ministries. In the context of Ephesians, humility is clearly intended to defuse the competition. Ephesians 2:11-22 describes the unity of Jew and Gentile as the pinnacle of God's accomplishment in Christ. As a prelude to the focus on unity in Eph 4:11-16, the text leads us to consider how differences based on status and ethnic diversity must be alleviated.

In envisioning the house church as a locus for socialization and education, one should consider what this would mean for both how teaching should be conducted and who might be counted as the learner. There is much about the perspective and values promulgated in Ephesians to suggest that preachers entered houses and shops ignoring the proprieties of convention. They would be subject to hostility from those who live "in the futility of their minds . . . darkened in their understanding, alienated from the life of God because of their ignorance and hardness of heart" (Eph 4:17-18). Slaves and the children of slaves would be told that they were equal beneficiaries of salvation, coming to "the unity of the faith and of the knowledge of the Son of God, to maturity, to the measure of the full stature of Christ" (Eph 4:13). Societal norms dictated that slaves perpetually retained the qualities of a child, but in this context slaves would be granted maturity. There is much about the worldview of Ephesians to suggest that teachers acted like pseudo-fathers, imparting scriptural traditions potentially at odds with the traditional instructions that should be imparted from father to son among the Gentiles; these teachers would have little regard for the line separating the potential of the slave child from the potential of the free child. Ephesians 6:1-4 represents a call to all children, including slave children, and a call to all parents, including pseudo-parents.

The image of the house church as school does not emerge as clearly in Ephesians as in the Pastoral Epistles, and a good deal of uncertainty remains about social practices. Nevertheless, there is much that points to a heightened interest in socialization and education going forward into the next generation. The emphasis on knowledge (cf. Eph 1:9, 17; 3:4-5; 4:13, 18-19) in particular points to the role of education in the formation of distinct identity. The vision propounded in Ephesians is that powerful experiences of the Spirit lead to enlightenment and a type of knowing (Eph 3:16-18). This involves an awareness of the vastness of the love of Christ, which transforms the universe (Eph 3:17, 10), and of the fullness of God (Eph 3:19). The reference to comprehending with all the saints reinforces the idea that this knowledge is available to the whole community and is not some type of esoteric speculation.[87] Yet this knowledge is special in the sense that it is at the heart of what is setting the community apart from the broader social order—it is at the heart of identity. Of particular significance for the focus on children in this book, however, is the fact that the doxology of Eph 3:20-23 is the only doxology in the NT that refers to generations (*genea*): "To him be glory in the church to Christ and in Christ Jesus to all generations, forever and ever" (Eph 3:21). These generations stand in contrast to previous generations, for whom insight into the mystery of Christ was not made known (Eph 3:5).

There is a definite link between the reference to generations in Eph 3:21 and the reference to the dominion of God the Father, from whom every family in heaven and on earth is named, in Eph 3:15. This language serves to reassure hearers that they have a place of belonging that transcends the earthly world and offers assurance against any societal or cosmic threat. But its full force can be appreciated more readily when one recognizes that family memory and insolubility were one of the most important components of Greco-Roman culture.[88] The importance of the family name for survival and continuity of reputation is well attested in ancient sources.[89] The Greek play on words in Eph 3:15, which is masked by English translations, establishes the family name, giving identity and securing the reputation of the group. Believers belong to the *patria* (family) of the Father (*pater*). Children propagated continuity and lineage in the Roman world.[90] Believers now belonged to a spiritual family that did not require the continuity of legitimate heirs.[91]

Like much of later early Christian literature, Ephesians both absorbs and stands apart from dominant social values concerning family continuity and lineage and the significance attached to children.[92] There is certainly a type of continuity encoded within a vision of the *ekklēsia* as a family community that will extend into the future for generations. With explicit appeal for the education of children (Eph 6:4) by their fathers, Ephesians displays explicit interest in the socialization of the next generation. Comparison with Jewish evidence, especially from the Dead Sea Scrolls, points to an interest in ongoing educational practices within the communal house-church setting that build upon household-based initiatives. The interweaving of familial and educational metaphors shares points in common with much evidence from Jewish and Roman sources. But as will emerge even more clearly in the next section, Ephesians is critical of efforts to limit those who belong to this family, this household of God, based on ethnicity and social status. It challenges the connection between family, public honor, and societal welfare that was integral to imperial ideologies. The emphasis on universality and unity is tied to perceptions of who may claim access to fatherhood. In particular, openness to all children and all parents defies many dominant views concerning the significance of patrimony and inheritance that were viewed as central to carrying on family and individual identity and traditions.[93]

Silent Children in a New Family

The multiple identities of community members must be borne in mind when envisioning the audience of the household codes. Moreover, the household codes are ideological pronouncements that stand in some tension with the shape of social reality. The latter has long been acknowledged—especially with respect to the apologetic dimensions of the household codes—but what this might mean for the impact of the codes in communities that include children has not been considered. While it does not refer directly to real children in the manner of the household codes of Colossians and Ephesians, it is valuable to consider the household ethics of 1 Peter, a document that has much in common with Ephesians, particularly in its use of images of dislocation for the lives of believers.

First Peter encourages cohesion in the face of some external threat and pressures to conform to societal standards; it offers a home for strangers and aliens (1 Pet 1:1, 17; 2:11).[94] With its explicit reference to relations with nonbelievers within the code (1 Pet 3:1-6), First Peter has seemed to some to offer much more obvious material for an apologetic argument than the other codes. The instruction to wives includes the command to be subject to their husbands (as we also find in Colossians and Ephesians), but 1 Peter explicitly includes a reference to some who "do not obey the word," but who may be "won over without a word by their wives' conduct" (1 Pet 3:1). Exemplifying the virtues of the dutiful and modest wife, the wife here is recognized for her potential as a "quiet evangelist."[95] Given the pervasive expectation that loyalty to a husband meant loyalty to the gods of his household, the subversive presence of these women in church groups is unmistakable.[96] There may well have been instances in which women were able to join multiple associations and their allegiance to new religious groups was not noticed or problematic; indeed the numerous references to women without male counterparts in the Letters of Paul may point to such a phenomenon.[97] But the call for silence in 1 Peter, coupled with the reference to the example of holy biblical women (including Sarah, who offers the comfort of spiritual motherhood in the face of fear; 1 Pet 3:5-6), suggests a context of potential family violence.[98] First Peter holds out the hope that the family relations will contribute to growth and the ultimate stability of the community, but it is markedly cautious, combining both conformist and more radical elements.[99]

Suggestions of family violence may also underlie the instruction on slaves in 1 Pet 2:18-25. The author calls on household slaves (*hoiketai*) to obey masters both good and bad. Bad masters are described as those who are crooked (unfair or perverse: *skokliois*), which probably implies harsh treatment of slaves at the hands of unbelieving masters.[100] The context suggests the physical beating of slaves—a commonplace punishment in the Roman world—that slaves are encouraged to endure by remembering the example of the sufferings of Christ.[101]

First Peter does not explicitly refer to child members of the community, but the presence of children would have been presumed by ancient listeners. Household slaves were generally born and bred within the household and would have included children. In the context of 1 Peter, these household slaves seem to have included children whose masters were unbelievers. Similarly, it is safe to assume that the wives of unbelievers brought children with them into the community; the presence of children of mixed marriage is already a subject of Paul's concern in 1 Cor 7:12-16. The dual loyalties of subordinate household members who joined church groups without the head of the household, and often without the head of the household's approval or knowledge, is a fascinating but little understood subject. In part, this has to do with how little we know about the domestic rites of the slave population. Although the cultural expectation of slave and wifely observance of household gods is clear, early Christian evidence suggests that women, slaves, and inevitably children were not always compliant. The archaeological evidence for worship practices of the slave *familia*, however, is not straightforward; niches that would have contained statuettes of gods and goddesses have been found in kitchens and in other service areas where slaves would have worked, but scholars are divided as to whether such evidence should be read as indicating autonomous worship activities.[102]

What is evident, and until recently has not been fully appreciated by interpreters of NT texts, is that the domestic cult permeated domestic life; the domestic cult involved worship practices associated with everyday household activities such as dining and even coming and going from the house or events such as birthdays.[103] It is difficult to know whether refusal to participate in these everyday practices led to strain between believers and nonbelievers or even the type of slave beatings mentioned in 1 Peter. Shrines dedicated to the divine spirit or personification of the *pater familias* (his *genius*) and household gods often associated with the ancestors of the *pater familias* (*Lari familiari*) were at the heart of ancient houses. Often found in ancient atria or gardens, these shrines offered a mini-version of a more elaborate sanctuary. Members of the household, including slaves, had duties to perform. In Cato the Elder's agricultural handbook (an example of an ancient guide on agricultural practices and the management of estates), we find clear evidence of this: one duty of the male slave overseer is to supervise the religious activities of the female slave he has as his "wife." These activities include decorating the hearth and offering prayers to the Lares on holy days. These religious activities, however, are to be clearly distinguished from those of the head of the household and his wife. Cato reveals a general fear that the slave wife might go astray in her religious observances and initiate her own type of rites, in clear violation of household loyalty.[104] In a frequently quoted passage, Plutarch expresses this fear of women being drawn to superstitions and going against the religious authority of the head of the household, phrasing it in terms of protecting the boundaries of the house: "shutting the front door tight" against them.[105]

Children too would have been involved in the domestic cult in various ways, including the adornment of shrines for birthday celebrations and, in the case of older girls/young women, prayers for good marriages and fecundity. A precious window into the shared ritual activities of mother and daughter comes from the first-century BCE poet Tibullus, who describes the birthday of a daughter, Sulpicia:

> Juno of the birthday, receive the holy piles of incense which the accomplished maid's soft hand now offers you. Today she has bathed for you; most joyfully she has decked herself for you, to stand before your altar a sight for all to see . . . She is making an offering to you, holy goddess, three times with cake and three times with wine, and the mother eagerly enjoins upon her child what she must pray for.[106]

We can by no means be sure that these practices stopped among believers, especially those involved in the delicate dance of multiple loyalties to family members both inside and outside church groups. The second-century critics of early Christianity included children in their depictions of the family strife and violation that resulted from church membership. A direct focus on children's involvement in suspicious rites can be found, for example, in the highly polemical remarks of Marcus Cornelius Fronto, who accused Christians of participating in incestuous feasts with "children, sisters, mothers—all sexes and all ages."[107] Fronto's remarks presume a context of clandestine activities in the household. As was warned of by Plutarch, the boundaries of the house have been violated—the very place that should protect women and children from destructive forces has become the site of their undoing.[108]

Like Ephesians, 1 Peter makes use of familial metaphors and concepts in order to articulate the boundaries of identity. The merging of house church with family life left plenty of chance for observing infancy and nursing, and engaging in theological reflection based on such observations: "Like newborn infants, long for the pure, spiritual milk, so that by it you may grow into salvation—if indeed you have tasted that the Lord is good" (1 Pet 2:2-3). Slave members of the audience would surely have related particularly well to such metaphors, as slave women were used extensively as wet nurses. The house slaves of 1 Pet 2:18-25 would likely have included young women who were brought up in the household specifically to act as wet nurses and nannies. At the other end of the spectrum, the author of 1 Peter appeals to traditional notions of reverence toward parents and grandparents (1 Pet 5:1-5). Senior members of the family community are to lay out basic authority structures. Recalling the traditional concepts of Eph 6:1-3 about honoring mothers and fathers, those who are younger must accept the authority of the elders (1 Pet 5:5).

Perhaps nowhere does 1 Peter appear more accommodating to an imperial ideology encompassing a basic conviction of the household as the microcosm of the state, however, than in 1 Pet 2:16-17, in which the slaves of God are instructed: "Honor everyone. Love the family of believers (lit. the brotherhood: *adelphotēta*). Fear God. Honor the emperor." Like many early Christian texts of the late first century and early second century, 1 Peter calls believers to live peaceably within the Empire and even to acknowledge the authority of the emperor. But it is evident at the same time that the church community underlying the text is challenging the *ultimate* authority of the head of the household and, by implication, the *ultimate* authority of the emperor. The family of believers claims ultimate allegiance, as members are to fear God. Given that these exhortations addressed to the whole community as slaves of God serve as the bridge to the specific exhortations to slaves that begin at 2:18ff (there are no parallel exhortations to masters as in Colossians and Ephesians), the message would not have been lost on an ancient audience: this is a family (the household of God: 1 Pet 4:17;

2:5) of a different kind, wherein the silence of slaves, wives, and children might not really mean acceptance of subordination at all, even if beatings and maligning must be endured.

Ephesians contains no direct reference to the line between believers and nonbelievers cutting across families in the same way as 1 Peter, which contains references to mixed marriages and to brutal (probably nonbelieving) masters of slave members of the community. Yet there is much at an ideological level to suggest the same worldview. An examination of the household ethics in 1 Peter is helpful in highlighting the idealistic nature of Ephesians, pointing to scenarios that were probably also shared by the audience of Ephesians, including the presence of children of nonbelievers.[109] Bringing this together with the clear emphasis on the socialization of children and educational motifs in Ephesians, we are left to think carefully about the possible identities of the children addressed in the household code and the motives behind the exhortations. Not only should we envision members of believing families, but also children of mixed marriage with one parent as a believer, neglected children who made their way into meetings without parents, and slave children. The emphasis on the role of teacher-preacher combined with remarks from the second-century critics of early Christianity points to the very real possibility of children being recruited from neighborhood children who were otherwise abandoned or neglected.

Remembering the Mothers

In laying out the complexities of family life that underlie the context of the household codes, both the realities of a demography in which many adolescents in any community would be without their biological fathers and the pervasive existence of surrogate fathers have been considered. This has opened up various possible scenarios concerning the identity of the fathers in Eph 6:1-4, extending beyond biological fathers. But in seeking to understand how a focus on the socialization and education of children changes the meaning of Eph 5:21–6:4, it is crucial to reflect upon the influence of mothers. The Pastoral Epistles are much more revealing here, but the celebration of the wife in Ephesians as the pure bride does take on new meaning if the role of mothers is remembered.

One of the most important insights that has emerged from work on women and gender in the Roman world is that idealized proclamations of authority by no means tell the whole story, whether we are talking about the world of business and trade, politics, or the life of the household. When it comes to hierarchical rules such as we find in the household codes, we must recognize that they functioned in relation to informal conventions and exercises of authority of which we can only catch a glimpse but ancient audiences would have understood de facto.[110] We have enough evidence to know that despite the ongoing conviction that wives should obey husbands, they were given considerable authority in household management and considerable leeway in the overseeing of the affairs of their children. In the next chapter the educational influences of mothers upon children will be discussed in depth, but here it is important to consider their influence in the arrangement of marriage matches.[111] Behind the highly symbolic depiction of the presentation of pure bride to her one true husband in Eph 5:21-33 is the cultural reality of the parents, especially the mother, presenting her daughter to the prospective husband. Although Ambrose's comments are from a significantly later period and deal with the sacrifice parents make in committing their daughters to ascetic life, the traditional norms, including the ancient Mediterranean value placed on the virginity of the girl, fit also with the world of Ephesians: "A virgin is a gift of the parents to God, holding a priesthood of chastity. The virgin is an offering from her mother, by whose daily sacrifice the divine power is appeased. A virgin is the inseparable pledge of her parents."[112] The parents (and prospective grandparents) of the husband and wife of Ephesians 5 are usually never considered in commentary on the text but are nevertheless part of the background, especially in the symbolic marriage between Christ and the church.

There is an interesting twist on the accepted practice of parents presenting the bride in Eph 5:26-27; although the bride remains the passive participant, it is the bridegroom Christ himself who initiates the prenuptial bath. There is even a suggestion of a purity inspection conducted by the bridegroom.[113] All of this imagery is informed by the scriptural notion of the preparation for marriage by washing (Ezek 16:9; cf. 16:8-14), wherein the washed woman ultimately becomes a metaphor for the community faithful to the gospel message. There are connotations of independence in the manner in which the bridegroom takes the lead and the manner in which the couple together stand apart from the corruption of the world. Later early Christian literature offers some memorable examples of Christian young people—especially women—breaking with their pagan parents to join church groups. The hostility that Thecla experiences from her mother and Perpetua experiences from her father are notorious.[114] It is perhaps no coincidence that the author of Ephesians draws upon the scriptural tradition (Eph 5:31), which celebrates the unity of the couple with reference to distance from parents: "For this reason a man will leave his father and mother and be joined to his wife, and the two will become one flesh" (Gen 2:24).

It is important to remember, also, that the bride in the metaphorical sacred marriage of Eph 5:26-27 is clearly a virgin—a young bride, in modern terms, essentially an adolescent girl. This is a world in which girls married in their teens, whether in early (12–15) or late teens is a matter of debate, but there is general agreement that it was usually to men between 25 and 30 years of age. The initiative of the bridegroom in Ephesians fits with a society in which men were expected to be more experienced sexually, and young girls were often suddenly confronted with sexuality upon marriage.[115] In fact, marriage was the main indicator of adulthood in women. The expression *nupta verba* (married words) to refer to the words that could be spoken only in front of matrons (and not unmarried girls), who had been exposed to the secrets of sexuality, makes this point forcefully.[116] Grandmothers undoubtedly played a key role in the education of girls through the course of the marriage and the birth of the first child. This role, in fact, becomes a Christian duty in the Pastoral Epistles.[117] When believing girls lacked their mothers as teachers and advocates, they seemingly turned to other older women in the community, especially widows. There is not a word about any of this in Ephesians, of course, despite the fact that such relations were integral to daily life and survival in the ancient world; where biological parents and grandparents were lacking, pseudo-parents and grandparents would need to be found. What remains unsaid in the Ephesians household code, but would have been abundantly clear to any ancient audience, is that in celebrating the life of the married couple within the *ekklēsia*, the author of Ephesians was celebrating the transition of the child/virgin/bride into a mother.

In reflecting on the significance of mothers in the community and their influence upon children, we must once again keep in mind that many members of the audience of Ephesians were probably slaves, freed slaves, and widows, or somehow did not reflect the ideal of the believing family that the text celebrates so powerfully. Most recipients of early Christian texts lived daily lives far removed from the world of the sophisticated Roman matron. In a context of great uncertainty from day to day, mothers no doubt often acted as anchors, replacing husbands in reality if not in ideological discourse.[118] Moreover, it is important to note that despite their indisputable patriarchal tenor and reinforcement of the father's authority, both Colossians and Ephesians include mothers in the direct address to children. Children are to obey both their parents (Col 3:20; Eph 6:1) and in Ephesians there is an appeal to children to honor both their fathers and their mothers (Eph 6:2-3).

The Ideal Unified Couple, Children, and Empire

In Ephesians we find many political concepts, such as notions of citizenship and membership in the household of God (Eph 2:19), and remembrances of dislocation (Eph 2:11-22), not unlike the social dynamics of 1 Peter. These ideas gain new relevance against a background of imperial ideology.[119] Of special significance to the Ephesians household code is the depiction, at both a symbolic and historical level, of the ideal unified couple. There are unmistakable resonances of a trend that swept the Roman world from Rome into the eastern provinces and was approaching its height within the decades leading to the second century: the tendency to use images of harmonious couples and families for purposes of political propaganda (the stability of the Roman fabric, the *Pax Romana*) and social commentary. The proclivity to demonstrate the ideal of the Roman family can be observed from art (especially funerary art), inscriptions, coin issues, and literature from the late Republic onward.[120]

A few comments are in order about how children figured in imperial ideology that have particular relevance for Ephesians. Children appeared as emblems of identity in a variety of ways in the Empire. They were frequently employed in rites and ceremonies and could serve equally as communicators of triumph and or poignant symbols of defeat and dislocation. There was a long history of generals using their children in celebratory parades, just as there was a long history of defeated kings being paraded with their children to illustrate the humiliating defeat of nations.[121] Children should be included as part of the image of triumphal procession that is meant to underscore Christ's victory in Col 2:15, which may well include an ironic jab at the powers of Rome.

Art, including funerary art, makes the propaganda value of children stand out sharply. Imperial children were made to serve dynastic purposes. Emperor Augustus, for example, made use of his own family members to demonstrate imperial stability and continuity. Not only were his grandsons Gaius and Lucius seen at public festivals, with Gaius being sent on campaign to the provinces at a young age, but busts and statues of them were widely circulated in Italy and beyond, frequently copied in depictions of private children. Their depiction on coins as future heirs further added to their high degree of visibility.[122] Of the famous monuments erected by Augustus, the *Ara Pacis* is notable for its imagery of parents and children both in realistic terms and symbolically. Augustus' own family, as well as the children of one of the senators, is depicted in a ceremonial procession. Two boys are clothed in a manner suggesting a ceremonial role. But there is also a female figure holding infants at the breast, apparently acting as an image of fertility or some type of continuity between past, present, and future.[123] Especially relevant for the setting of Ephesians, is that Augustus' successors took the dynastic messages associated with monuments like the *Ara Pacis* eastward. Travel of imperial family members to the east, often including young children; the use of children in ceremonies involving the emperor or his representatives; and depictions of children on coins and monuments all point to a growing recognition of the importance of partnership with the east. Children were central in winning the favor of the inhabitants of the east and their conviction in the saving power of the peace of Rome.[124]

Two aspects of the narrative associated with the display of children seem particularly relevant to the context of Ephesians (and Colossians). First, it was copied in the funerary monuments associated with freedpersons. A tomb erected by people of servile origin that advertises the freeborn status of a son with his image set apart from the couple is a sure representation of the family's upward mobility. Stability and integration into Roman society are the subtext of this monument.[125] In celebrating the unity of the family in the Lord, the author of Ephesians was communicating messages to believers and (indirectly) to outsiders about the place of the *ekklēsia* in the world—seeking to demonstrate an inner harmony, even if Christians often engendered hostility from the broader society. Second, the audience of the household codes probably identified with many of the foreign children who are frequently the subject of commemorative monuments and triumphal arches celebrating the defeat of Rome's enemies. These children are often depicted in pitiful scenes, being torn away from their foreign-born mothers or humiliated in a way as to imply servility. Just as the childhood symbolism of the *Ara Pacis* symbolized the future, the childhood imagery on these monuments symbolized the loss of an independent future for nations. For inhabitants of the provinces, who included captive slaves, they were powerful symbols of dislocation and the consequences of disrupting the Roman peace.[126]

Ephesians reflects an awareness of isolation, disenfranchisement, and foreign and alien status in the manner in which it describes the new unity between Jew and Gentile that has been achieved in Christ: "Remember that you were at that time without Christ, being aliens from the commonwealth of Israel, and strangers to the covenants of promise, having no hope and without God in the world" (Eph 2:12). Linked together by the core theme of unity, Eph 2:11-22 represents the macrovision of heavenly citizenship, and Eph 5:21–6:4 represents the microvision of household holiness and loyalty.[127] The relationship between the two texts recalls the notion of the household as the microcosm of the state, a fundamental theme in household management discussions from the time of Aristotle's *Politics*.[128] Ephesians 2:11-22 makes extensive use of civic terminology, but links with the micro-setting of household holiness and loyalty are revealed, with believers described in Eph 2:19 as "fellow-citizens with the saints and members of the household of God." As can also be seen in 1 Peter (cf. 1 Pet 2:5; 4:17), household language is used in a manner to describe the believers' new relationship with God, the Father (cf. Eph 1:5; 3:14-15), ultimately challenging imperial ideology despite its appropriation of conventional motifs and associations; for this is a new entity wherein those previously alienated have found a home and identity. Perhaps the strongest echoes of a challenge to imperial ideology are found in the fourfold repetition of the term "peace" in Eph 2:13-18, referring to the peace that comes from the blood of Christ, bringing those near who were once far off. Through their presence at ceremonies, journeys with the imperial parents, and representations in various types of iconography, children were frequently used as instruments to communicate the *Pax Romana*. The role of children should be taken seriously in assessing how Ephesians is responding to imperial ideology. As slaves and members of families who normally stood outside the realm of citizenship, often displaced from one household to another or from one city to another, they found a place of belonging as those who had been brought near.

Discussion of the apologetic functions of the NT household codes has frequently led to consideration of how the codes may be framing messages intended to be communicated directly or indirectly to the neighbors of believers who are wondering what exactly is going on in these household cells. An awareness of points of contact with imperial ideology, however, opens up new possibilities for the types of messages being communicated.[129] What is emerging especially clearly is not simply the accommodating nature of the household codes, but elements of resistance that stand out more sharply when ideological correlations are noted (such as those between Eph 2:11-22 and 5:21–6:4). To date, however, the role of children and the child-parent relationship in household code discourse has not been examined from this angle.

Yet it is evident that emphasis on the unity of the married couple in Eph 5:22-33 is rooted in notions of familial harmony that encompass children. This idea is at play in the apologetic discourse of Josephus, in which he states that Jews living under the law are as under a father and master (*hupo patri toutō kai despotē*; cf. Gal 3.24).[130] Jews united under the law are like the family ordered and rendered harmonious by the household head. The subordinate members of Jewish families exhibit piety (*eusebeia*)—a concept typically linked with devotion to matters of state and family, especially the obedience of children.[131] This familial loyalty cuts across generations, as the use of the Latin equivalent of *eusebia*, *pietas*, in Virgil's epic poem the *Aeneid* illustrates so well; family devotion is symbolized by the image of Aeneas rescuing his father Anchises and son Ascanius from the burning city of Troy.[132] The description of the role of the father as educator in Eph 6:4 and the lifelong loyalty children owed to parents that is implied by Eph 6:1-3 reflect many of these traditional notions. But it is also the case that interpretation of the evidence becomes less straightforward when one recalls the limited capacity of many members of the audience of Ephesians to display their loyalty to members of their households. They simply lacked the freedom and resources to do so in the manner endorsed by Roman, Jewish, and early church authors (including the author of Ephesians) as the ideal. There is a very real possibility that few children in the community—whether because they were abandoned orphans, slave children present without the permission of their masters, or the offspring of women involved in mixed marriages—had their biological fathers present. Instead, many would have been subject to the authority of various surrogate fathers, influential men in the community or even their own mothers or well-respected widows.

Conclusion: Children Must Be Nurtured, Taught, and Disciplined

There is no doubt that the relationship between ideology and reality in Eph 5:21–6:4 is complex. Especially in the treatment of marriage, the use of christological language that infuses the exhortations, and stands in sharp contrast to the brevity of the exhortation in Col 3:18-19, represents a move in the direction of idealizing marriage between believers (even though mixed marriages clearly continued in this era).[133] The teaching on the parent-child relationship in Ephesians is likewise expanded in relation to Colossians, even if to a lesser extent. Ephesians promulgates a vision of the unified family that serves as the perfect representation of the setting for bringing up children in the instruction and discipline of the Lord.

Not unlike Josephus, the author of Ephesians sees this unity and traditional family hierarchy as fundamental to identity. Social structures are emerging that suggest a shift from mere socialization to concern with education in the community and the growing importance of the role of teachers. It is the very communal nature of this enterprise within the familial setting of the house church that points to efforts, not unlike those revealed by the Dead Sea Scrolls, to employ the education of children as the beginning of a life course set apart from the dominant culture. Children, including slave children and the children of nonbelievers, may be instructed to obey their "fathers," who will teach them Scripture and traditions about Jesus but by no means have their paternal authority sanctioned by Roman imperial society.

The various possibilities for surrogate parenting in the Roman world must be borne in mind with the interpretation of household code in Ephesians, paying special attention to the teaching authority of fathers in line with the conventional emphasis on the role of fathers in guaranteeing family continuity and memory. In a world in which mothers, slave caregivers, and various relatives often exercised parental duties, the author of Ephesians nevertheless seeks to interact with the dominant cultural value placed on the example and authority of fathers. Yet the reference to the children of believing fathers should perhaps not be taken too literally, allowing for fatherhood authority and protection to extend over children and slave children who in reality belonged to nonbelievers or were orphaned or abandoned. Moreover, the notion of re-created family inherent especially in the reference to the dominion of God the Father, from whom every family in heaven and on earth is named (Eph 3:15), alerts us to the redefinition of the meaning of fatherhood, especially in terms of lineage and, ultimately, who might be counted as worthy of instruction. Hearers, no matter how small, silent, or marginalized, are reassured that they have a place of belonging.

4

THE HOUSE CHURCH AS HOME SCHOOL
The Christian Assembly and Family in the Pastorals

E phesians 6:1-4 reveals increasing emphasis on the education of children operating within the broader framework of the socialization that occurs through daily interactions. This emphasis on education becomes more pronounced in the Pastoral Epistles. When one approaches 1 and 2 Timothy and Titus with a focus on children, the house-church context emerges as a home-school context.

The Pastoral Epistles do not contain the concise type of mutual teaching concerning the three relationships (wives-husbands, children-parents, slaves-masters) that we find in Colossians and Ephesians. But these works nevertheless display interest in all three relationships. There is more fluidity in discussions of the household management theme, and household code traditions are incorporated more loosely in the Pastorals. Most significantly, the domestic traditions are integrated within exhortations concerning burgeoning church offices, and they help to shape the vision of the ideal teacher—a role shared by men and women, even if heavily influenced by traditional gender constructions. The Pastoral Epistles acknowledge the presence of children and the significance of their behavior in a new way.

The effort to integrate new generations combined with a heightening concern to respond to the problems of apostasy and false teaching is leading to a new stage of institutionalization. There are at least three identifiable components: (1) a program of educational content combining scriptural, doctrinal, ethical, and domestic elements, sometimes including differing roles and responsibilities for men and women; (2) a heightened importance and responsibility being assigned to the role of teacher; and (3) evolving leadership criteria and guidelines anchored in the traditional organization of the household and values of family life. The Pastoral Epistles reveal the existence of educational infrastructure within a domestic setting. More than any other Pauline works, they display an interest in the education of the child that continues throughout the life course.

My Children, Timothy and Titus

The Pastoral Epistles are addressed to communities in Ephesus and Crete, via Paul's delegates Titus and Timothy, respectively.[1] Timothy is called Paul's beloved child (2 Tim 1:2) and a true child in the faith (1 Tim 1:2). Titus is also called Paul's true child in the faith he shares with the apostle (Titus 1:4). The Pauline example offered by Timothy and Titus to the community is a central element of these texts, calling for examination of the role of teacher in the familial setting of the house church and in the broader context of the Roman imperial world. In particular, Timothy serves as an example in a second important sense: the process of maturing in faith that develops throughout the life course.

The close relationships between Paul and Timothy, and Paul and Titus, is well known. Timothy, for example, is the coauthor of several Letters (cf. 2 Cor 1:1; Phil 1:1; Col 1:1; 1 Thess 1:1; 2 Thess 1:1; Phlm 1). In both the undisputed Letters and the Pastoral Epistles, family dynamics shape the narratives concerning Timothy and Titus.[2] In 2 Corinthians, Titus plays a key role in facilitating dealings with the Corinthians, including arrangements for the collection; he has an intimate relationship with the apostle as his "brother," providing him with encouragement, relieving him of anxiety, and sharing his concern for the welfare of the community (2 Cor 2:13; 7:6-7, 13-16; 8:6, 16-17, 23; 12:18).[3] References to Timothy in Paul's Letters abound with the use of childhood and father/son metaphors. The call for the Corinthians to imitate Paul, for example, is followed by the statement that he has sent Timothy, his "beloved and faithful child," to remind them of his ways in Christ (1 Cor 4:16-17). Timothy's worth to Paul

is described as being that of a father to a son in Phil 2:19-23.[4] There
is also a sense that Timothy's youth might be held against him and
that he needs encouragement (1 Cor 16:10-11). Timothy is called (along
with Paul) a slave (*doulos*) of Christ in Phil 1:1. The same picture of a
youthful, timid, and potentially subject to ridicule figure appears in
the Pastorals (1 Tim 4:12; 2 Tim 1:7).[5] While it is not as forceful, something of the same sentiment is expressed with respect to Titus, who is
to let no one look down upon him (Titus 2:15).

According to Acts 16:1, Timothy had a Greek father, but his
mother was a Jew who was a believer in Christ. Even less is known
about Titus, who is never mentioned in Acts but is presented in Gal
2:3 simply as a Greek who accompanied Paul to his famous meeting
with the Jerusalem apostles; Paul emphasized in Galatians that at the
meeting Titus was not required to be circumcised (Gal 2:3).[6] The Pastorals leave any trace of the hereditary male ancestry of Timothy and
Titus behind, however, and present Paul as a "fictive" father of both
(1 Tim 1:2; 2 Tim 1:2; Titus 1:4). The appeal to the family structures
of parenting on a symbolic level works closely with the notion of Paul
as the teacher of his delegate apprentices. Paul, the fictive father, is
ultimately Timothy's teacher and calls Timothy to follow the pattern
of "sound words" that he has heard from Paul (2 Tim 1:13). The role
of Titus as teacher (and combatant of false teaching) permeates the
entire letter to Titus; the letter begins with an elaborate introduction
of Paul, however, that reinforces his apostleship and Titus' concomi-
tant authority in the strongest possible terms. Paul is placed at the
center of all revelation as the recipient of "the hope of eternal life that
God, who never lies, promised before the ages began" (Titus 1:1-3).[7]
Paul has been entrusted with a proclamation, but he shares the faith
with Titus. The ultimate task of Paul's faithful child is to teach and
to convey Paul's memory and example. Paul instructs Titus to teach
what is consistent with sound doctrine (Titus 2:1).

The presentation of Paul as the fictive father of Timothy and Titus
reflects one of the most common images of the teacher in antiquity:
the surrogate father who nurtures his students, whom he describes as
his children. The grammarian, for example, might aptly be described
as a child's "father in letters." [8] The frequent presentation of teachers in
quasi-parental roles reminds us that an ancient audience would have

heard the descriptions of Timothy and Titus in imitating and representing Paul as being akin to a father molding his sons. The Roman
satirist Juvenal, writing about the same time as the author of Pastoral Epistles, makes this point clearly—although sarcastically—by
the manner in which he complains about teachers being underpaid
and parents having high expectations that children be shaped in their
image: "Require that the teacher shape their tender characters as if he
were molding a face from wax with his thumb. Require that he take
the father's role in that scrum . . . 'That's your job,' says the father,
but at the turnaround of the year, you get the same gold as the crowd
demands for their winning fighter."[9]

If Paul provides the male example in the fictive fathering and
teaching of Timothy and Titus, however, this does preclude the influence of female members of the immediate family. It is the example
of women—a mother and a grandmother—that anchors Timothy in
faith according to 2 Tim 1:5 (cf. 3:15). Real flesh and blood familial
influences are presented here as setting the stage for Timothy's ongoing formation under the guidance of Paul. From childhood, and as a
youthful and perhaps easily ridiculed figure on account of his youth,
Timothy matures in faith throughout the life course. The familial
atmosphere of the house church also offers much of the foundation
for patterns of community interaction between Paul the teacher-
evangelist and his delegates as teacher-evangelists. In 2 Tim 2:24,
Timothy is called a slave of the Lord who must not be quarrelsome,
but a teacher who is kindly and forbearing with his charges. Real
slave tutors and childminders might have offered the model here, for
in ancient society they often had more direct and formative influence
on children and children's early education than the children's parents.[10] Regardless of whether parents, teachers, nurses, or attendants
were the educators, the consensus that emerges from ancient literature
is that children were the products of their education. In the modern nature versus nurture debate over the intellectual development
of children, the ancient voice would have come down on the side of
nurture. What might count as educational theory viewed children as
passive beings to be worked on, baby birds to be coaxed out of the nest
and taught to spread their wings in imitation of their parents.[11]

The dominant view—that children were empty buckets waiting to be filled by various educational influences—means that frequent allusions to the setting of examples must be taken very seriously in the Pastoral Epistles. The setting of examples and the reality of leaders (especially teachers) representing others is one of the main social constructs in the Pastoral Epistles. Often memory and representation lay the groundwork for independence and communal acknowledgment of authority. For example, Timothy's connection to Paul is certainly celebrated, but Timothy's own (and perhaps even independent) role as a teacher is crucial. Timothy is to emulate Paul's example (2 Tim 1:13), and Timothy is also to remind the churches of Paul's teaching (2 Tim 2:2). But Timothy's own teaching mandate as a preacher and a teacher is also expressed very forcefully; he is to exhort others constantly and relentlessly (2 Tim 4:1-2). Timothy appears to be a teacher of teachers, ensuring that house churches have a teacher prepared to challenge false teachers. He is also a fearless evangelist, ready to preach the gospel everywhere and to confront any opposition. Timothy imitates his "father" to the end, as he also endures suffering in doing the work of an evangelist and in fulfilling his ministry (*diakonia*; 4:5).

Much the same can be said about Paul's child, Titus. It is on the basis of the shared faith between Titus and Paul that Titus appoints presbyter/overseers in Crete (Titus 1:5) who in turn are to teach the true message, exhorting with sound doctrine and refuting opponents (false teaching is a major concern in Titus [Titus 1:9]). Titus himself is reminded that he is to teach what is consistent with sound doctrine (Titus 2:1). Like Timothy, sometimes he must adopt a bold and forceful approach, exhorting and reproving with all authority (Titus 2:15), insisting to the point where opponents reveal recalcitrance.

The Pastorals reflect a chain of memory and representation that extends from Paul, to his delegates Timothy and Titus, to leaders in the community. The interest in established church offices has often been recognized, but little attention has been paid to how parenting metaphors are used to convey organizational structures. This takes place in multifaceted ways. In a manner that recalls Paul's final speech to the Ephesian elders in Acts 20:17-38, in 1 Tim 1:3 the youthful Timothy is instructed by his "fictive father" to remain in Ephesus and seemingly sets in motion a type of leadership structure involving the local supervisor (overseer: *episcopos*).[12] He will go on to instruct the local overseers to be ideal fathers (1 Tim 3:4). Such linkages are even more explicit in Titus, in which Titus is to appoint presbyters/ elders whose "children are believers, not accused of debauchery and not rebellious" (Titus 1:6).[13] While 2 Timothy pays no explicit attention to church offices per se, it does reveal a great deal of interest in the role of teacher through both internal and outreach functions.[14] Moreover, it is 2 Timothy that displays the greatest interest in the process of formation, using Timothy himself as the prime example and harkening back to his infancy and the important influence of the women in his life.

The Influence of Mothers: Educating Sons and Daughters

Mothers are instrumental in the education of both sons and daughters in the Pastoral Epistles. Their educational influence often surfaces in texts unmistakably patriarchal and restrictive. Yet at the same time, the manner in which gender is delineated in the text contains some surprising elements.

The initial formation of Timothy's faith by his grandmother Lois and mother Eunice, described in 2 Tim 1:5, deserves careful attention within the broader context of 2 Timothy, which otherwise refers to specific women only in the final greetings (Prisca and Claudia). The childhood instruction of Timothy prepares the way for the solemn instruction to Timothy as a model teacher and evangelist who is sharply distinguished from his adversaries in 2 Tim 4:1-8.[15] Paul, the suffering and persecuted apostle, is clearly Timothy's role model par excellence (2 Tim 3:10). But Timothy has also received formation within the context of family life through the initiative of grandmother and mother—there is no reference to Timothy's actual father, who has been metaphorically replaced by Paul. This is a presentation of an initial formation on the knees of women. The language chosen to describe Timothy's education makes this clear. Paul's delegate has been instructed from infancy (*brephos*; 2 Tim 3:15). The agency of women in the education of children is also reflected in the household code traditions found in Polycarp's *Letter to the Philippians* from the first part of the second century CE, in which wives are exhorted to discipline/educate their children in the fear of God.[16] In Polycarp's teaching, as in Eph 6:4, there is use of the well-attested educational notion of *paideia*, but rather than it being the purview of fathers as in Ephesians, in Polycarp's correspondence it concerns the duty of wives.[17] The same terminology also occurs in 1 Tim 3:16, often translated as "training."

The reference to Timothy's instruction by women might seem surprising given the specific attention given to the preparation of Timothy for his important ministerial task. The educational activities of women were controversial in the Roman world. The literate education of elite women is well documented in the sources with famous examples of women who studied rhetoric and philosophy. The case of Hortensia, the daughter of a Roman orator from the Republican era offers a good example; according to Valerius Maximus, Hortensia made a speech to Octavian when he was triumvir that was said to be so impressive it was used as an example for at least a century in schools.[18] But the comments of the Roman satirist Juvenal offer evidence in the distinctly opposite direction:

> But she's much worse, the woman who as soon as she's taken her place at dinner is praising Virgil and forgiving Elissa on her death-bed, who pits the poets against one another and assesses them, weighing in her scales Maro [Publius Vergilus Maro, i.e., Virgil] on this side and Homer on the other. The schoolteachers give way, the teachers of rhetoric are beaten, the whole party falls silent, there'll not be a word from any lawyer or auctioneer—and not even from another woman. Such vigorous verbiage pours from her, you'd say it was the sound of people bashing all their bowls and bells at once. . . . Don't let the lady reclining next to you have her own rhetorical style or brandish phrases before hurling her rounded syllogism at you. . . . I loathe the woman who is forever referring to Palaemon's Grammar and thumbing through it, observing all the laws and rules of speech, or who quotes lines I've never heard, a female scholar.[19]

Juvenal offers a satirical attack on the increasing presence and public visibility of women at dinner parties. Not only were the women promiscuous and self-indulgent, the semblance of education that such wives received made them pretentious and tedious—noisy bores.[20] Such perceptions are part of the societal background to the restrictive comments in the Pastoral Epistles, as in 1 Tim 2:11-15, which seek to move women away from public visibility into the more traditional domestic settings.[21] The publicly visible matron who attends the dinner parties is, inevitably, also a married woman or a widow, and usually a mother (cf. 1 Tim 2:15).

The acceptability of the educated woman increased the more closely it was associated with familial life, ranging from the use of literacy in managing a large household to musical skill in setting one's husband's verses to the lyre and performing them for him.[22] But the clearest illustration of this point comes in the form of a sustained celebration of the heroic educational achievements of mothers in relation to sons. The influence of mothers on the education of sons among the elite—although presented in the form of unique stellar examples—seems to know no bounds, ranging from the development of character, to curriculum, and even to speech. Sometimes there is specific mention of mothers filling in the educational gaps for dead or absent fathers. Pseudo-Plutarch describes the efforts of Eurydice (b. ca. 410 BCE), the Illyrian mother of Philip II of Macedon and grandmother of Alexander the Great; she is described as one who successfully taught her children self-control, having only begun her Greek education late in life, specifically so she could pass it on to her son.[23] In speaking of the Roman era, Plutarch praises the dedication and also the educational formation delivered by Cornelia, the mother of the Gracchi (Tiberius and Gaius) and often depicted as the ideal Roman matron, who took charge of the household and children upon the death of her husband. She is depicted as essentially making them into the men they became: "Although there is general agreement that her sons displayed the best natural aptitude in all of Rome, it was believed that their preeminent qualities were more the product of their education than of their natural disposition."[24] According to Cicero, Cornelia's responsibility for the tutelage of Tiberius Gracchus (b. ca. 163 BCE) ensured that he was educated in Greek literature.[25] Cicero emphasizes that Cornelia's role was by no means limited to traditional maternal responsibilities: "I have read the letters of Cornelia, the mother of the Gracchi, and it would appear that her sons were actually raised not so much in their mother's bosom as in her language!"[26] Cornelia's example proved to be so laudatory that Quintilian used it to back up his argument that both parents, mothers and fathers, are central to the transmission of oratorical style.[27] Virtue, language, and learning all emerge in these texts as within the purview of a mother's educational impact. In considering the role of parental influence on learning, it is striking that the problems and the solutions in the Pastoral Epistles are often represented in terms of speech (that which corrupts and that which instructs leading to an identity as a man or woman of God).

These ancient sources can help assess the significance of this representation of Timothy as being formed by the influence of his mother and grandmother. Likewise, they invite us to consider 2 Tim 3:15, which describes Timothy's education from infancy in the sacred writings or Scriptures (*hiera grammata*).[28] The reference to infancy clearly suggests the instructional influence of women. The value attributed to this education is indisputable. Such formation and ongoing learning had the effect of making Timothy wise.[29] There is a second reference to Scripture (*graphē*) that occurs in 2 Tim 3:16-17, verses replete with educational concepts. The emphasis is on the practical function of Scripture for teaching (*didaskalia*), reproof (*elegmos*), correction (*epanorthōsis*), and training (*paideia*) in righteousness.[30] *Paideia* is associated with the family life of the house church and the educational influence of parents (Eph 6:4; 2 Tim 3:15; Pol. *Phil.* 4.2). It is a correcting word, with the verb (*paideuō*) finding its root in the classical Greek word for child (*pais*). Rather than having a narrow focus on the education of the child, however, it is associated with broader goals of education that include the upbringing of the child: the discipline, instruction, and direction that bring the child to maturity.[31] Thus, the term is ultimately associated with the formation of an adult and reflects ancient notions of lifelong learning extending indefinitely from early childhood.[32] The author is instructing Timothy to continue in what he has already learned, including his study of the sacred writings he has known from childhood. Moreover, despite the exceptional nature of his youthful leadership, Timothy's ongoing maturation is implied by the plea to leave behind youthful passions in 2 Tim 2:22.[33]

Taken together, 2 Tim 1:5 and 3:15 clearly place women in the position of teachers of the youthful Timothy. Yet it is important to recognize the many conventional features of the presentation. Eunice and Lois are model believing women. They are like the noble widows of ancient literature who make sacrifices to ensure the education of their sons, passing on valued traditions and learning. Ultimately, they enhance Timothy's prestige in both the worldly and church contexts. The grounding of Timothy in the Scriptures from infancy leads to a statement about the completeness of the man of God (*ho tou theou anthrōpos*) that reflects standard notions of masculinity.[34] But such reinforcement of traditional masculinity receives an unexpected twist. The conventional formation within the family that Timothy has received provides the basis and preparation for recommendations to defy convention within the patterns of his own ministry. In 2 Tim 4:1-2, Timothy is solemnly charged to preach the word and be urgent (or be prepared) "in opportune time and in inopportune time" (in season and out of season: *eukaipōs akaipōs*). The shock value of this phrase, while usually not apparent to modern readers, would have reverberated with an ancient audience. Timothy is being urged to forgo the judgment and discretion of public speakers who couched their discourse to suit the circumstances of a particular audience, including emotional state and moral conditions. These speakers discerned when or when not to speak to maximize persuasiveness and effect. Instead—whether because the audience is insensitive to such finesse or, more likely, because the crisis requires truthful speech in whatever circumstances—Timothy is instructed to bypass normal conventional approaches.[35]

The crisis before Timothy clearly involves some type of opposition. But whatever the precise circumstances, this man of God is being urged to forgo one of the most important signs of masculinity: the poise and erudition of the rhetorician.[36] In the face of a dangerous and growing opposition, Timothy must be prepared (be alert to all opportunities) to stand apart from such rhetorical standards given the crisis before him. Such considerations provide new significance to the presentation of Timothy in the early chapters of 2 Timothy as an honorable man, schooled by honorable women. This mother and grandmother have prepared their charge for a challenging vocation: Timothy must be prepared to relinquish the qualities of an honorable man by the world's standards and to adopt tactics that might compromise his reputation in the public arena.

The effect of this crisscrossing of conventional and counter-cultural gender expectation is to create potential tension between women, perhaps especially older women (mothers and grandmothers) and younger women/girls. The opponents (whose specific identity remains unknown) are said to deceive people in 2 Tim 3:13 (cf. 2 Tim 3:6). They are engaging in teaching both in church meetings and in private conversations in people's homes.[37] Their teaching is said to be particularly attractive to women, as the opponents creep into houses and capture silly women, weakened by sin and desire (2 Tim 3:6). Gender stereotypes are unmistakable, but the efforts to control the activities of women, especially young widows who are inclined to be "gossips and busybodies," points to an atmosphere wherein women hold various interpretations of the gospel (1 Tim 5:13).[38] The consequences of the endorsement of Eunice and Lois as ideal maternal figures may have the effect of setting church women against other church women as they prepare their sons (understanding Timothy here as an example to other men) to combat teaching that is popular among women. Yet there is another aspect of the child-care example set by Lois and Eunice that should not be overlooked. There is no reference to a believing father in Timothy's case (Paul is Timothy's fictive father), and ideal motherhood certainly includes the possibility that only the mother is a believer. Thus, as perfectly as the example of Lois and Eunice might seem to match ancient conventional motifs, the representation of these women certainly leaves open the possibility of women defying their husbands and joining church groups without their spouses' permission and teaching children Scripture and church traditions from infancy.

Various twists on traditional gender expectations and constructions also characterize the relationship between mothers and daughters in the Pastoral Epistles. Once again a focus on the education of children brings out new ways of understanding exhortations. The Pastoral Epistles reveal a sustained interest in intergenerational connections between women for teaching purposes. Rarely, however, have modern readers grasped that the links extend from the childhood of women into old age.[39]

At the outset, it is important to keep in mind the fuzzy distinction between girlhood and womanhood in the Roman world. With girls marrying in their mid- to late teens (often to significantly older men), girls' outward transitions into adulthood could be sudden and dramatic, brought on by marriage and the first child. The death of young women in childbirth meant that the transition could be sudden, dramatic, and tragic, as the following first-century inscription documenting the risks of early motherhood, in this case of a slave who may have become pregnant by her master, reveals: "My name was Calliste—befitting my appearance (Calliste, in Greek, meaning very beautiful one). As for my age, I was fifteen years old. I was charming to my master and loved by both my parents. I had become weak and ill: the seventh day of my illness was the last. The cause of my death is unknown. They say it was childbirth. But whatever it was, I did not deserve to perish so soon."[40] The ongoing attachment of the young mother to her parents is reflected in this inscription. Assuming a young woman survived the birth of the first child, in practical reality the transition from girl to wife and mother took time to evolve. Mothers continued to educate their daughters in household management as they attained greater maturity and independence. Symbolic household ceremonies involving the bride's offering of her dolls and toys to the household gods or to Venus on her wedding day stand in tension to the ongoing involvement of mothers in the lives of their married adolescent/young adult daughters.[41] The ceremonies suggest an immediate transition from childhood to adulthood, but the reality was far more complex.

It is precisely this need for ongoing transition and education that forms the background of Titus 2:3-5, in which older women are instructed to encourage younger women to be good wives, mothers, and household managers. Children are specifically mentioned in the reference to teaching young women to love husbands and children. The ideal younger woman in this passage is undoubtedly the mother with children.

Older women were expected to be role models for younger women in the ancient Mediterranean world and could be presented as strong advocates, as in the following episode from the first half of the second century CE: A mother assisted her daughter through a very difficult first delivery and was subsequently very vocal during a birth celebration held with the father's friends, insisting that a wet nurse be hired for her too-exhausted daughter. The protests of the male group, which were characterized by strong philosophical interests, remind us that the merit of mothers nursing babies themselves versus the hiring of wet nurses could be a subject of intellectual debate.[42] Likewise, within the home-based atmosphere of these early communities, doctrinal, ethical, and domestic elements might easily become interwoven within the conversation. At the same time, it is important to keep in mind that the author of Titus clearly does not consider the influence of the older women on the younger women as narrowly restricted to domestic concerns, for it extends to the priority of preventing the word of God from being discredited (Titus 2:5). Most significantly, the recognized word for teacher (*didaskalos*) is used for this intergenerational instruction of women in Titus 2:3; the older women are to teach the younger women what is good. This is striking, given the prohibition of women teaching in 1 Tim 2:12, but it begs the question of whether this wisdom imparted by women to the next generation of women was considered of equal significance with the instruction they received from men on other topics.[43]

There is no question that the model behavior of the older women in these texts is seen as central to the formation of the younger women. The corollary here is that bad mothering leads to bad daughters, as expressed so colorfully by the Roman satirist Juvenal in his stereotypical critique of the troublesome and debauched mother-in-law:

> There's no hope of harmony if your mother-in-law is alive. She'll train her daughter to reply in no simple or straightforward way to the letters sent by her seducer. She'll outwit your chaperones or buy them with a bribe. . . . You don't really expect a mother to pass on respectable behavior, so different from your own, do you? Besides, it profits the disgusting old woman to bring up her little daughter to be disgusting.[44]

The older women of Titus 2:3-5 are encouraged to emulate the opposite of such debauchery, being told to be reverent in behavior, not to be slanderers or slaves to drink. The relationship envisioned in Titus is not restricted to that between mother and daughter, but in the domestic setting of the house church—the household of God—the relationship between these groupings takes on familial coloring. This can also be seen in the directives to Timothy, who is to speak to older women as mothers and younger women as sisters (with parallels for men; 1 Tim 5:1-2). Moreover, in the biblical text, as in Juvenal's satirical discourse, the premise is the same: the older woman is the moral guide.

The presence of older women in the church community is not surprising given the demographic trends in the Roman world. Because women married at an earlier age than men, children were much more likely to have living mothers and grandmothers than fathers and grandfathers. It is estimated that by age fifteen, only 10 percent of children had a living grandfather. Almost a quarter of Roman children had lost their fathers by age ten, and less than half had a living father by the time they reached twenty years of age.[45] It is especially in considering the detailed treatment of the lives of widows, which explicitly distinguishes between older and younger widows (1 Tim 5:3-16), that we sense the influence of older women in the community. The influence of widows young and old clearly underlies 1 Tim 5:3-16; this text includes a call to assist widows, seeks to describe and circumscribe the activities of certain widows, and encourages young widows to give up widowhood altogether in favor of household management, so they will have less opportunity for the kind of wandering of which the Pastoral Paul clearly disapproves. As in Titus 2:3-5, children are specifically mentioned in the recommendations concerning the young widows. They are to marry, bear children, and manage their households—they are to forgo early widowhood and become mothers fully engaged in the work of running the household (1 Tim 5:14). The stereotypical nature of the warning against gossip and busybody behavior and generally overly public and wandering behavior (1 Tim 5:13) stands out especially plainly when one considers Juvenal's sarcasm about the bold and promiscuous wife:

But it's better for her to be musical than to go brazenly racing all over Rome, the sort of woman who can attend men-only meetings and actually converse with the generals in their uniforms in her husband's presence with her face unflinching and her nipples dry. This is the woman who knows everything that's happening throughout the world—what the Chinese and Thracians are up to, the secrets of the stepmother and the boy, who's in love, and which Casenova they're fighting over. She'll tell you who got the widow pregnant and in which month. She'll tell you the words each woman uses in bed and how many positions she knows. She is the first to see the comet that's bad news for the king of Armenia and Parthia. She picks up the latest tales and rumours at the city gates and she even invents some herself.[46]

The relationship between public behavior, promiscuity, and the abandonment of motherhood is especially striking in this text—precisely the type of behavior the author of 1 Timothy wished young widows to avoid in favor of respectable motherhood.

Despite the gender stereotypes that color much of the Pastorals' teaching on widows and women more generally, however, what is said about the potential influence of older women fits with what we know of the life course of women in the Roman world. With respect to the older widows, a simulation of the life course of the imaginary Tatia (based on a simulation of the life course of a model family), reads like a blueprint for the context of 1 Tim 5:3-16: "By age 60 Tatia is perhaps a widow living alone; her two surviving children (aged in their 20s or 30s) have left home and she has three living grandchildren, as well as two nieces and a nephew. She has attended many family funerals over the years, of parents, of a husband or two, of a number of her own children, including those of half of her siblings. She herself has only a few years left."[47] The author of 1 Timothy deals with the issue of the widow left alone. This author would indeed expect Tatia's own children or grandchildren to look after her (1 Tim 5:4). But there are many scenarios left unspoken by the author in which this would not be possible, including the refusal of the children and grandchildren, who would not be inclined to look after a relative who has become involved in a strange new religious group. The strong warning to believers that they are worse than unbelievers if they forgo their responsibilities to family members provides a hint of the suffering of older women that could occur. Almost as if admitting that the ideal familial support often does not exist, the author of 1 Timothy sets out to describe the circumstances of the real widow who in many ways resembles the imaginary Tatia—a widow, left alone, who can continue in prayer and supplication, night and day (1 Tim 5:5). The enrolled widow (probably terminology referring to an emerging order of older ascetic women) of 1 Tim 5:9-10 is like Tatia as well when it comes to her age of sixty (or more) and her history of child rearing, family duties, and commitment.[48]

In his description of widows the author of 1 Timothy relates celibate life to family life. Motherhood remains closely linked to the life of the older ascetic—a reality that is also hinted at in other early church texts from about the same period. The greeting to the orphans and widows that Grapte is to instruct in the *Shepherd of Hermas* points to the existence of a household group in which celibate women are caring for orphaned children and may apply to widows living together with their own children and/or abandoned children they have taken into their households.[49] The mention of the believing woman who "has widows" (often translated as relatives who are widows, but the more literal translation better communicates the various possible scenarios) in 1 Tim 5:16 likewise suggests this type of household setting. The puzzling reference to "virgins called widows" in the writings of Ignatius points to existence of older ascetic women living with younger women—perhaps adolescents of marriage age or very young widows.[50] Older women become models for younger women in these texts. The author of the Pastoral Epistles seems more intent than some other early Christian authors in ensuring that young women (in whatever circumstance) married. Older women were to act as models or even assistants in child rearing and the education of young women in the early stages of married life. And in a context wherein Christianity is looking increasingly suspicious in the eyes of outsiders, it is important to remember that even the call for young widows to marry and rule their households has two important dimensions; it is both an apologetic defense against those who would slander the community for violating familial and political norms and an opportunity to establish new family units that can provide the infrastructure for house churches—all under the tutelage of older women acting as wise guides.

If we approach the Pastoral Epistles, including the texts on widowhood, with a focus on children, we sense an increasing acknowledgment of their place within the community. From the association of salvation with childbearing (1 Tim 2:15),[51] to the formative value associated with motherhood (1 Tim 5:2, 10; 2 Tim 1:5; Titus 2:3-5), to the encouragement to embrace motherhood (1 Tim 5:14; Titus 3:4), to the duty to parents (1 Tim 5:1-2, 3-8, 16; 2 Tim 3:2), the child-parent-grandparent bond is strongly reinforced. Such interests characterize all three of the Pastoral Epistles. Moreover, in many of the texts, this bond is envisioned as one of crucial educational value.

The Influence of Fathers: Educating Sons and Daughters

The relationship between older and younger men is less straightforward in the Pastoral Epistles than the relationship between older and younger women. On the one hand, Timothy is not to speak harshly to older men but to treat them as fathers, whereas younger men are to be treated as brothers (1 Tim 5:1-2). On the other hand, one would expect older men to be given pride of place, yet there is evident reservation about establishing the type of hierarchical teaching relationship between older and younger men that seems to exist for women. In part, this might have to do with the demographic realities of the Roman world, where few adult men would have fathers living. But there is a sense that the Pastorals leave room for younger men exercising authority in surprising ways. Titus 2:2 exhorts older men only very briefly in comparison with the attention given to older women in Titus 2:3-5. Younger men, in fact, are given much more cautionary advice, including with respect to their role in teaching, their display of sound speech, providing a model that will defy any opponent; all of this suggests that the youth of men in the community might be of some concern both within the community and in relations with outsiders. In 1 Tim 4:12, in the midst of discussion of Timothy's teaching role, Timothy's youthfulness is addressed head on; given the exhortation that youthfulness should not lead to anyone despising him, it is probably best to understand it as challenging the cultural norms.[52]

The cautionary attitude with respect to young men and direct treatment of Timothy's youthful leadership, combined with the realities of ancient demography, raise the question of whether male leadership was often exercised by men who might otherwise often be considered too young. In other words, one might consider whether the elders were actually juniors. Moreover, the demographic realities and the effort to control older women found in 1 Tim 5:3-16 lead one to ask whether young men were being confronted by wise older women on a fairly regular basis. It is striking that this text is followed immediately (1 Tim 5:17-22) by a reinforcement of the authority of presbyters/elders, who are said to deserve double honor—especially those engaged in preaching and teaching.

In 1 Timothy and Titus we find a definite attempt to reinforce the authority of elders/presbyters (*presbyteros*). There are many problems of interpretation related to the identity of these people, which is caused by the fact that in both Jewish and early Christian sources the term can both be a designation for age and also a title for a church office. Sometimes it is obvious that the terminology refers to older men, as in Titus 2:2 and 1 Tim 5:1-2, but in other instances in which the terminology seems to have a more titular meaning, such as 1 Tim 5:17-22, there nevertheless remain connotations of authority associated with fatherhood and heads of households.[53] The matter is further complicated by the interchangeability of the titles overseer/bishop (*episcopos*) and elder/presbyter (*presbyteros*), especially in Titus 1:5-7. But there seems to be little interest in the Pastoral Epistles in distinguishing precisely between officeholders or even in reinforcing a particular structure of church governance. The approach is more reactive, making sure leaders emulate the right virtues and gender roles remain appropriate.[54]

Exhortations concerning offices and leadership roles for both men and women in the Pastoral Epistles, however, have one definite thing in common: they are all concerned at one level with deportment within the family and relations with family members. As was the case with the teaching concerning mothers and grandmothers, children emerge as a key concern. This can be seen especially clearly in Titus 1:6, in which the children of elders/presbyters are required to be believers and not accused of debauchery and not rebellious. In the context of the Pastoral Epistles, Titus 1:6 constitutes a strong reinforcement of the authority of elders/fathers and strong endorsement of their leadership that is reminiscent of Eph 6:4: The elders/presbyters are being held accountable for the religious training of their children.[55] Leadership is tied to the ability of the head of the household to teach sound doctrine and refute those who contradict it. These leaders stand ready to challenge opponents who upset whole families by teaching what is not right to teach (Titus 1:11).

The teaching role being assigned to the elders/fathers is in actual fact not terribly different from that assigned to older women, who must teach younger women, which no doubt included girls, what is good (Titus 2:3-5). While it is expressed more indirectly (older women teach younger women to be model wives and mothers), the teaching role for women is also linked with household management, the significance of which in a house-based movement should not be underestimated. There is clearly a hierarchy of teaching/managing functions based on gender in the Pastoral Epistles, however, that should also not be overlooked. This is especially apparent in the close relationship between the emerging leadership structures for men and the household structures; it becomes almost impossible at times to distinguish between titular offices and familial assertions of authority.

The criteria for the selection of male officers essentially function as prime assertions of masculinity. In addition to the directive concerning the responsibility of elders/presbyters to ensure the loyalty of believing children, it is important to consider the overseer's responsibility to manage his household well; he would keep his children submissive and respectful (1 Tim 3:4-5). Similarly, the deacon has a mandate to manage his children and household (1 Tim 3:12). According to the author of 1 Timothy and ancient authors generally, paternity was a fundamental facet of the honorable male and the public assessment of his worth (1 Tim 3:5, 7). We might compare, for example, Plutarch's second-century observation, "A man therefore ought to have his household well harmonized who is going to harmonize state, forum, and friends," to 1 Timothy's directive, "If someone does not know how to manage his own household, how can he take care of God's church?"[56] In 1 Timothy, it is the display of submissive and respectful children that is a particularly potent sign of suitability for office (1 Tim 3:4-5). In contrast to 1 Timothy and Titus, 2 Timothy pays no explicit attention to criteria for officeholders, but it is not surprising to find disobedience to parents as one of the characteristics of enemies of the church (2 Tim 3:2).

Like much ancient literature, the Pastoral Epistles present coordinating authority and responsibilities for mothers and fathers in the household. In comparing the Pastoral Epistles with conventional descriptions of male heads of the household such as Plutarch's observation, however, there is a certain irony and a certain contravening of the standards of an honorable male. For it is not the city, state, or public space of the forum that the male leaders of the Pastoral Epistles will oversee, but the *oikos* (household) of God that meets in their own homes! In the Roman world, much authority in the household was delegated for practical purposes to women, so men could be free to attend to more public affairs. The establishment of church offices is clearly a sign of the institutional growth and visibility of church groups, with an acknowledgment of risks of public scrutiny surfacing in the criteria.[57] But in the Pastorals the emerging male leadership is asked to look inward as much as it is bidden to look outward. Deacons, elders/presbyters, and bishops/overseers are instructed to become fully implicated in the community as fathers. Especially in the teaching concerning widows, but also in 1 Tim 2:8-15, in which women are silenced and told they will be saved by childbearing, we sense tension between male and female authority in a community that meets in the domain traditionally ruled by the male head of the household, the *pater familias*, but managed by his wife. In the *ekklēsia*, with the Pastoral Epistles as guide, the balance of power appears to be shifting, with divisions of labor solidifying along gender lines.

It is instructive to compare the similar use of household management language for both men and women in these works. According to 1 Tim 5:14, young widows should marry and rule the house (*oikodespotein*), forgoing the potential official status as enrolled widows, which is reserved for older women. Likewise, younger women are to be instructed by their elders to be good household managers (*oikourgous*) in Titus 2:5. The bishop/overseer is one who rules his own house well (*oikou kalōs proistamenon*; 1 Tim 3:4) and the deacon is one who rules both his children and household well (*teknōn kalōs proistamenoi kai tōn idiōn oikōn*; 1 Tim 3:12). Perhaps the strongest reinforcement of authority, however, comes in the assertion that the bishop is God's steward (*oikonomon*) in Titus 1:7. The steward is the slave manager of the household who typically represents and is charged with enforcing the authority of the *pater familias* in all matters of the daily running of the household, including discipline and the overseeing of the family lives of other slaves. While the two figures remained distinct, in a very real sense, the voice of the household manager was the voice of the ultimate lord.[58]

It is especially in the instructions concerning the overseer/bishop that we sense the reinforcement of supreme jurisdiction in household affairs of the male leadership. But behind the directives, there is good reason to suspect that a lot of butting of heads was actually taking place. For lack of better words, the experience must often have been one of too many cooks in the kitchen! At first glance, the instructions might seem like a recommendation of offices for men and home-based responsibilities for women. But such a characterization oversimplifies the situation. Household management for both men and women always involves a type of parenting or pseudo-parenting. Both mothers and fathers are to foster obedience in and reverence from their children, and both older men and women are to mentor young people.[59] Moreover, both men and women might be said to occupy church offices. Even if the capacity for women to hold offices is circumscribed, there is clearly an office of widows reflected in 1 Tim 5:3-16, and many commentators are in favor of reading the reference to the women of 1 Tim 3:11 as a reference to female deacons and not to wives of deacons.[60] One gets the best glimpse into the capacity for real tension and conflicted roles, however, in imagining what was actually going on within the house church whose meeting place was a family space where women typically had enormous influence and—albeit delegated—authority. As much as women's influence in the domestic sphere is celebrated in the Pastoral Epistles, in a real sense women are being asked to make way for the growing presence and influence of fathers or their representatives. These male figures are to be fully engaged in household affairs and are not to exercise their rule indirectly.

The perspective of the Pastoral Epistles is one in which male offices should gain new ground and hierarchies should be established. In part, this has to do with the increasing importance attributed to teaching and teachers. Once again, paying close attention to familial relations, and to parenting in particular, can help identify new associations. Developments often seen as independent from one another need to be brought together. On the one hand, the connection between emerging leadership structures and household code material has long been recognized, and such linkages (also detectable in the writings of the Apostolic Fathers) have been investigated in light of the house-church setting.[61] The content of the exhortations, however, has meant that the focus has naturally been on criteria for selection (e.g., the qualities of a good householder), rather than on duties such as teaching and evangelizing, which largely seem to be ignored in these texts. On the other hand, while the role of teacher and evangelist is clearly prized in the Pastoral Epistles (as is especially evident in the depictions of the roles of Timothy and Titus), at first glance there appears to be very little concern with teaching associated with the emerging offices. Yet there has not been due attention paid to the implicit teaching function of *pater familias*/overseer/bishop. These instructions presume the ideological importance of the role of fathers in preparing the next generation (most especially sons), preserving tradition, and ensuring continuity in the family.[62]

It is probably not too much of a stretch to read into the command that the overseer/bishop should not be a recent convert, that he himself should be educated in the traditions by his own parents or pseudo-parents (1 Tim 3:6). After all, it is Timothy, who has been educated within the family (2 Tim 1:5; 3:15) and in the Scriptures (from infancy), as well as by his fictive father, Paul himself, who provides such a strong role model. In 2 Tim 2:2, Timothy is told that what he has heard from Paul before many witnesses he is to entrust to faithful people (overseers/bishops?) who will be able to teach others also. This suggests an interest in succession—preparing the next generation—that fits the context of the late first century/early second century CE. Timothy and the ideal teachers/preachers who succeed him must conduct their duties out in public for all to see (e.g., 1 Tim 4:12-15; 5:19-21, 24-25; 2 Tim 2:2; cf. Titus 2:7-8).[63] Once again, there are connotations of the honorable male who, like the overseers/bishops (*episcopoi*), will be assessed according to the determinants of public reputation (1 Tim 3:7).

There are three instances, however, in which teaching terminology does occur with respect to the duties of leaders. The role of the father/elder as teacher is implied by the statement in Titus 1:6 that his children should be believers. Even more significantly, 1 Tim 5:17 states that elders/presbyters who rule well are worthy of double honor (perhaps some kind of payment), especially those who labor in preaching and teaching (*en logō kai didaskalia*). One of the attributes of the overseer/bishop is that he is an apt teacher (*didakiton*; 1 Tim 3:2). This is an indication of the familial teaching authority tied to fatherhood; household leadership is expanding into a communal teaching role. The house church is becoming a type of home school.

Education in the Roman world is closely tied to the authority of fathers. Probably the most important writer on the nature and significance of education in the Roman world, Quintilian, in his *Institutio Oratoria* (The Orator's Education) begins with the hope that as soon as his son is born the father "should form the highest expectations of him," as such aspirations will guarantee careful attention to his son's education.[64] Parents and caregivers are seen as fundamental to the child's early education in speech and even in reading and writing, but fatherly authority extends to the choice of the right schooling for the child. Parenthood (especially fatherhood) is often used as an analogy for the relationship between teacher and pupil in ancient sources.[65] Images stress the fact that parents know what is best for the child and exert authority while inspiring devotion. The dominant model is one of education as formation, wherein children have no independent position as children. The uneducated are to be memorizers and imitators, receivers of orders and information.[66] Often agricultural images are used, suggesting the teacher's relationship to the pupil is like that of the farmer who must get the most out his land or the pupil is soil that must be sown with the seeds of knowledge. In Pseudo-Plutarch's thought, farming and parenting images are combined, so the teacher is presented as breaking animals: "The impulses of young men should be kept fettered and restrained by careful supervision. For life's prime is prodigal in its pleasures, restive, and in need of a curb, so that parents who do not take hold of the reins . . . are . . . giving their sons license for wrongdoing."[67] Parents should maintain firm reins and yoke children in marriage if necessary to quiet them down.[68] The perspective calls to mind the attitude of the author of 1 Timothy, who would see young widows married, apparently to quiet them down (1 Tim 5:11-15). It is very much in keeping with the pro-marriage for young people position that permeates these Epistles.

The household structures, which merge with the criteria for offices in Pastoral Epistles, have often been recognized as boosting the authority of the officeholders, especially the male householders. The authority of teachers, which sometimes seems to stand apart from the exhortations concerning church offices, is also rooted in *patria potestas*—the authority of fathers. Already in the classic statement on household management by Aristotle one sees a presentation of the natural capacity of the male head of the household to rule over his wife, children, and slaves.[69] Roman law preserved this notion of dealing with wards with respect to the father's authority (*patria potestas*) and guardianship (*tutela*). The guardian as an adult male has a better informed mind and capacity for judgment, and this basic idea is exploited in educational ideals. The role of the educated man in society is naturally to impose on the uneducated the discipline that they cannot achieve on their own and that is required for the good of all.[70] Writers on education such as Quintilian, the Senecas, Plutarch, and Philo talked about education on a very large scale, creating ideals for the good of society and its stratification and reproduction. Their idealizing language tended to depict matters in very black-and-white terms, such that "the gap between the educated and the uneducated, particularly the literate and illiterate, is inflated until it appears as the difference between power, status and authority and the complete absence of those qualities."[71] The *episcopos* in 1 Timothy is presented in conventional terms as bearing the qualities of a good citizen, including the capacity to educate. He is a model householder with resources to bestow. The endorsement of the overseer/bishop, which begins at 1 Tim 3:1, makes these conventional associations clear.[72] The one who desires the role desires a noble task (NRSV biblical translation), or more literally, a good work (*kalon ergon*). By analogy, this is the role of the richer citizen making benefaction in service to the city. It is the property-owning church member—the very concept of *patria potestas* is related to ownership of property—who is to serve the household of God (1 Tim 3:15).[73]

On Educating Wives

The most obvious connection between *patria potestas* and teaching authority can be sensed in the most highly controversial text in all of the Pastoral Epistles, 1 Tim 2:9-15. In this passage women are silenced with an appeal to the meaning of the creation of Adam and Eve in Genesis and promised salvation through childbearing. There are many complex theological (including the meaning of salvation) and textual problems related to this text that cannot be considered here, but a focus on children and education does offer a window into certain aspects of the text that might otherwise be neglected.[74]

First, it is important to recognize the emphasis on teaching and learning. Women are to learn in silence, but they are nevertheless to learn. The implication is that they are to be educated within the community, perhaps taught by their own husbands or, more likely, by other men in the community who are assuming positions of leadership. The idea of a husband "teaching" his wife can be found in the household management material in Xenophon's *Oeconomicus*, wherein a husband is presented as teaching a skill-less young wife virtually everything involved in the running of the household.[75] The husband teaching his own wife may serve as the ultimate idealization of the hierarchical relationship of marriage, but that substantial teaching really happened this way is most unlikely.[76] There is much more extensive and believable evidence that young women learned the skills of household management from other women, including their own mothers and female relatives. In fact, this is the role that the author of Titus authorizes for older women with the recognized word for teacher (*didaskalos*) occurring in the instruction for older women to teach younger women in Titus 2:3-5.

It does not appear that the goal of the Pastoral Epistles is to ban women from all teaching roles. Even the reference to women being saved by childbearing (*teknogonias*) in 1 Tim 2:15, a concept that fits very well with the dominant concern throughout the Pastorals that

women should marry and manage households, implies the obligation to raise and educate children—to follow the example of Lois and
Eunice (2 Tim 1:5).[77] Moreover, the particular shift from the singular
(referring to the wife or woman) to the plural in 1 Tim 2:15 may mean
that "provided that they continue in faith and love and holiness, with
modesty" refers to the children of the woman.[78] To tie the salvation
of women to the behavior of children may seem incompatible with a
community stance wherein people were clearly welcomed who had
broken with their families. But it is important to remember that this
is idealizing discourse, standing in inevitable tension with the messy
realities of real families. Moreover, having believing children of a certain moral standard is presented as a requirement for elders/presbyters
in Titus 1:6. What we can say for certain is what the author of 1 Timothy desires for women is motherhood.

The operative concept in 1 Tim 2:9-15 is, as in Xenophon's idealization, hierarchy. The educational influence of women is explicitly
acknowledged in the endorsement of motherhood and by the approval
of learning for women. There is an important distinction to be made
between learning in silence and keeping silent. The voices and activities of women are reinforced in the address to women who profess
reverence for God by means of good works (1 Tim 2:10). But in a
world in which the order of the household reflects the order of the
community, women are neither to teach nor have authority over any
man. Because women played a major part in the education of their
own sons (cf. 2 Tim 1:5), what is in view here is a type of communal
teaching responsibility that is seen to be reserved for men only.[79] The
appeal to the scriptural traditions from Genesis 3, including the fact
that Adam was formed first and reference to his initial innocence, is
meant first and foremost to reinforce this hierarchy. This approach is
in keeping with the traditional order of the household. Emphasis on
the role of Eve as the transgressor is to make the point forcefully that
disaster will ensue if this proper order is reversed. The implication is
that Adam eventually obeyed Eve, and there will be similar negative consequences if women are to teach and have authority over men
(1 Tim 2:12).[80]

Once again we sense the tension that must have resulted from
the merger of home and school contexts, as house churches began to

develop institutional features that emphasized their public and visible dimensions, such as criteria for officeholders and concepts guiding the education of the next generation. It is important not to lose sight of the fact, however, that this was a domain where women were being educated and seen as contributing in valuable ways to the formation of children, including in Scripture (2 Tim 3:15), implying some type of literacy. The education of women was controversial, with its acceptability increasing the more closely it was associated with family life. When the education of women became linked with a role in society, such as making presentations at law courts or becoming a philosopher, it became problematic.[81] The silencing of women in 1 Tim 2:9-15 needs to be read against this background. It reinforces the traditional place of women within the family, ensures the hierarchy is maintained, and seeks to prevent educated women from speaking in public.

In many respects 1 Tim 2:9-15 simply repeats highly conventional concepts concerning the education of women. This can be seen especially clearly when one considers the writings on literate education in the Roman world (roughly what we would consider schooling, involving such subjects as reading, writing, grammar, literature, arithmetic, geometry, and music, and usually excluding higher education in rhetoric and philosophy, which was accessible only by the wealthiest).[82] The evidence includes both literary texts and especially numerous forms of papyri that have been preserved in the dry climates of Egypt. School text papyri from Greco-Roman Egypt offer some of the most important evidence for the process of educating children in the Roman world.[83] Among them can be found school exercises involving the memorization and reproduction of wisdom sayings or general principles (*gnomai*) from various poets or literary authors; these wisdom sayings conveyed a range of social attitudes and behaviors on a variety of themes, including respect for the gods, friendship, and the desire for wealth. A significant number of these concern women (especially wives), who are generally treated negatively (though mothers more favorably). Often the need for the silence of women is emphasized and their consultations with one another (by implication of gossip) are not to be trusted: "Seeing one woman talking to another," Diogenes said, "the asp is getting poison from the viper."[84] In various texts women are viewed as dangerous, associated with error, and needing to be ruled—concepts that also appear in one form or another in the Pastoral Epistles.[85] It is striking how power, speech, and education converge as the prerogative of men along with the denial of these to women.[86] It is also amazing to think that these kinds of texts would be taught to children who had many adult women influencing their lives. But the educational goal here is to imbue children, especially sons, with the perspective of the older male. The standpoint is that of the husband who must rule his household.[87] This is the standpoint that Pseudo-Paul the teacher (*didaskalos*; 1 Tim 2:7; 2 Tim 1:11) and fictive father seeks to impart to his child Timothy, who in turn will impart it to the children of the church community, especially the young men.

The House Church as Home School

Recipients of the Pastoral Epistles with even the most basic education were probably familiar from childhood with maxims that called for the silence of women and highlighted the dangers of women's speech. Be they Jewish or Gentile, members would have brought into these communities varying levels of education or literacy, including varying amounts of exposure to Scripture and the content of ancient literature. What is clear, however, is that the first Christians did not set up separate and distinct institutions for schooling and seemingly continued to make use of existing organizations, despite their sometimes critical attitudes of the content of pagan education (from the latter decades of the second century CE) and their deep commitment to teaching in various forms.[88] This state of affairs naturally raises the question of the relationship between the *ekklēsia* and the school.

Of all the types of institutions found in the Roman world (e.g., synagogues, households, cultic entities such as mystery religions, voluntary associations), some historians have been convinced that early Christian communities most closely resembled a type of "scholastic" community (not to be confused with the Scholasticism of the medieval period).[89] What has been largely in view here is the existence of philosophical schools that, like church groups, valued the student/disciple relationship, wisdom, and various intellectual activities, and linked learning with an ethical stance.[90] Comparisons of church groups with philosophical schools have largely concentrated on "adult education."[91] Not all have been convinced by the usefulness of viewing philosophical schools as the closest analogy to early Christianity, however, since this fails to account for certain features of early church life, most notably the interest in rituals, perhaps most especially baptism.[92] The best approach is probably to consider how early church groups emulated various models from the environment and to see how these models functioned in tandem, creating new types of social entities by combining elements from existing forms.

With a focus on children, this study has naturally been concerned with familial relations and the familial atmosphere of the house church. An examination of the evidence has uncovered a frequent concern with education that surfaces in texts dealing both directly and indirectly with children. Thus, it makes sense to evaluate the interaction between the church as a household and the church as a type of school. An examination of this interaction reveals not so much a community devoted to adult education, but a community devoted to education throughout the life course. A failure to recognize the presence of children, the value attached to the formation of children, and the lack of rigid demarcation between childhood and adulthood has led to a neglect of educational efforts that were closely tied to the familial life of the house church. There were certainly some initiatives in church groups that resembled the activities of philosophical schools, but others resembled more elementary aspects of education. Church teaching should by no means be equated with schooling for children, but probably incorporated methods that were often part of childhood education.

The Pastoral Epistles are rich in terminology associated with teaching, including references to speech, preaching, discipline, correction, knowledge of Scripture, and so on.[93] But even if one concentrates on the main word for teaching or instructing (the verb *didaskō* and its derivatives), one can detect the close relationship between home and school. In the ancient world, references to teaching implied recognition of the authority of the teacher. Moreover, the etymology suggests repeated activities during which learning takes place in increments, much as a child learns by observation and imitation, and as one would expect in a life-course approach. In fact, the student was to learn from the example of the teacher.[94] It is not surprising that teachers were often depicted in parental roles.

The very first instance of the term occurs in 1 Tim 2:12, in which women are prohibited from teaching men. Instead, women are to learn in silence. This first mention of teaching makes the association of the activity with the exercising of authority abundantly clear. It also asserts from the outset that the space of the gathering *ekklēsia* for worship is one where traditional familial hierarchies are in place. So whatever is said about teaching or teachers henceforth must be faithful to this household foundation. In fact, the formulaic statement, "the saying is sure," which follows the teaching with respect to women in 1 Tim 3:1, serves to bolster this foundation.[95] Here the author, as in Aristotle's classic delineation of the order of the household, is presenting the household as a microcosm of the broader social entity, not society in general as in the case of Aristotle, but the *ekklēsia*.[96]

Defined by constructions of gender, the reference to teaching in 1 Tim 2:12 refers to the gathering of the community of both men and women wherein worship takes place and which is understood as having educational elements. There are other instances of the use of the term teaching (*didaskō*) where community gatherings have educational purposes (e.g., 1 Tim 4:13, 16; 5:17). Timothy, for example, is told to pay close attention to his teaching, for it is a source of his own salvation and that of his hearers (1 Tim 4:16). The elders/presbyters/older men who labor in teaching (1 Tim 5:17) seem to have exerted their influence in a gathered community setting (cf. 1 Tim 5:20). These texts lend support to the notion of the emergence of a "public" teaching function reserved for men only (cf. 1 Tim 3:1-8) or at least the intent of the author of 1 Timothy to encourage such limitations on the teaching roles of women.[97] But it is in the passage on older women teaching other women (Titus 2:3-5) that one is introduced to the fact that this teaching occurring in the midst of the gathered *ekklēsia* is only one type of teaching; the texts points to the existence of other types of instruction occurring in other settings or configurations.

In Titus 2:3 we find a derivative of the recognized word for teacher (*kalodidaskalos*), a compound word that refers to the teaching of what is good. It is also the clearest and most detailed reference to the content of teaching in the Pastoral Epistles, a feature of the works that is quite nebulous.[98] Many aspects of this teaching involve domestic duties and virtues, the kind of teaching that needed to take place through mentoring and active learning (older women are to train [*sōphronizōsin*] younger women). This was instruction that young women (in our terms, including adolescent girls) received from mothers and female relatives. Yet, lest one think that it is only domestic concerns women were charged to impart, the mention of the "word of God" in Titus 2:5 suggests that this teaching, like the teaching seemingly reserved for the efforts of men, is imbued with authority.[99] In other words, domestic apprenticeship was combined with doctrinal and scriptural elements. The description of the formation in the faith of Timothy by his grandmother Lois and his mother Eunice (2 Tim 1:5) and his exposure to Scripture from infancy (2 Tim 3:15) suggests that domestic activities were combined with the teaching of Christian content. Taken together, these references suggest that women taught others in a variety of settings linked to church communities. In the case of Timothy, the implication is one of family ties linked to church communities. But in Titus 2:3 the reference to teaching is broader than the reference to women teaching members of their own families. In a context in which various houses acted as bases for the movement, women gathered together for teaching purposes. One needs to imagine a type of apprenticeship, in which groups of female believers—no doubt accompanied by boys and girls—not only discussed what constitutes a holy life (Titus 2:3) but also various domestic duties. A list of possible issues is endless, but could include how to treat slaves (a central part of household management; cf. Titus 2:5), how to nurse children, how to encourage faithfulness in their husbands. By necessity, much teaching would have gone on at times and in spaces other than when and where the community gathered for worship.

One must be cautious even where one might be tempted to assume some type of public gathering; the household setting points to a more flexible approach. In 1 Tim 3:2, for example, the description of the ideal bishop/overseer as an apt teacher comes at the end of a list of virtues befitting a respectable householder. In an era in which infidelity on the part of married men was often tolerated unless it involved a respectable unmarried daughter or a married woman, the householder is to be faithful to his one wife.[100] Responsibility for keeping his children submissive (1 Tim 3:4) includes responsibility for ensuring his children's education. Clearly, however, this father has communal responsibilities, including the virtue of hospitality. Teaching was an extension of the fatherhood role, which might include opening his house for the teaching of believing children (slave and free) along with the children of his own household. For if communities prized doctrinal teachings, gospel traditions, and Scriptures, spaces needed to be found to undertake this teaching task beyond larger gatherings of the *ekklēsia* for worship. Colossians 3:16 speaks of the community members teaching and admonishing one another and singing psalms, hymns, and spiritual songs (cf. Eph 5:19).[101] But in an environment with mixed levels of literacy and virtually no capacity to duplicate texts, these teachings and expressions of praise needed to be memorized and practiced. The educational requirements of church groups meant that many more types of gatherings were taking place than our texts wish to reveal. It is important to recognize that church members would have naturally made use of the resources and structures available to accomplish their goals. The bishop/overseer might well, for example, have a literate slave who could serve as a teacher of young children, thereby partaking in an extension of the master's ministerial responsibilities. First Timothy 6:1-2 offers instructions concerning the slaves of the community, paying special attention to the circumstances of slaves with believing masters. Greater service is expected from these slaves, because they are serving those who are both believers and beloved. In the Roman context, this group of believers and beloved should not be taken in a narrow sense as a reference only to the masters themselves, but should be understood as including all the masters oversee.

The exhortations concerning slaves in 1 Tim 6:2 conclude with the global command to Timothy to "teach and exhort these things." Whether this refers only specifically to the content of 1 Tim 6:1-2 cannot be determined with certainty, but it is in keeping with a tendency to refer to the content of teaching in general terms in the Pastorals (cf. 1 Tim 4:11; 2 Tim 2:2).[102] Sometimes reference is made to teaching without any information about content (1 Tim 2:12; 4:13, 16; 5:17). There are, however, a few guiding principles: conformity to apostolic teaching (Titus 2:8) and rooted in Scripture (1 Tim 4:13; 2 Tim 3:15-16), with God as the ultimate source (2 Tim 3:16; cf. Titus 2:12, in which the related term training, *paideuō*, occurs). As in texts such as Titus 2:3 and 1 Tim 6:2, the content of teaching is not limited to belief, but includes ethics and order within the family and the *ekklēsia*. Teachers—male and female—are to display virtues (e.g., 1 Tim 3:2; 2 Tim 2:24; Titus 2:3, 7). All of these texts point to a body of educational content and the need to deliver what it is taken for granted in the Pastoral Epistles.[103] Making more than an effort to socialize members, communities are putting in place structures to educate. The structures create and reinforce both equalizing relationships (e.g., brothers and sisters ultimately are taught content originating from God and communicating the salvation of all; children are instructed together by mothers, fathers, and pseudo-parents) and hierarchical relations (e.g., men are to teach women in the assembly; older women are to teach younger women; elder/presbyter men [possibly equated with the bishops/overseers] are to be recognized for their teaching authority). Likewise, these structures of education are both related to, but to some degree stand apart from, worship activities.

There are many unanswered questions about the content and the methods of teaching employed by the communities reflected in the Pastoral Epistles. But a focus on children can make us aware of the approaches that were available in the environment beyond parallels that have been recognized with the higher literary approaches of philosophical schools. It is important to investigate how church communities may have made use of the techniques of more elementary forms of education that were often tied to the home. One of the most important findings of recent research on the education of children, which has a bearing on this study, has to do with flexibility when it came to space and arrangements. In part, this has to do with the remarkable (from a modern perspective) lack of evidence for centralized oversight or organization of schools or teachers in the Roman world. State intervention amounted to small measures such as tax exemptions for some teachers under Emperor Vespasian and reports that he paid annual sums to some rhetors (whether this was for actual teaching or just performance of their skill is unclear).[104] Occasionally, public patronage of schools was initiated by an individual, such as is indicated in a letter from Pliny to Tacitus; he reports he has contributed a third of the money and convinced some of the citizens of his native Como also to contribute to the hiring of a teacher for the local children, so they do not need to be sent away to school. Unfortunately, Pliny does not provide any information about the type of teacher who should be engaged or other expectations.[105] But the letter does provide evidence of teachers not only being paid by individual parents, but also as a result of benefaction. Patronage was very important in the life of early church communities and, thus, it is wise not to rule out similar measures being undertaken to hire the services of a Christian teacher. Indeed 1 Tim 6:17-19 encourages the rich to be rich in good works, ready to share. Given the familial priorities in these works, children are no doubt intended to share in this benevolence in one way or another.

Official interest in what teachers taught, their qualifications, and their methods are for the most part absent from ancient records.[106] But even more intriguing for the present study is the almost complete lack of archaeological evidence for the existence of schoolrooms. Fragmentary evidence suggests schools took place wherever a teacher set himself up based upon convenience, and could be found in a variety of locales, including auditoriums (which may have been used for other purposes as well), gymnasiums, wrestling grounds, and homes.[107] It has already been suggested that it is important to be open to various possibilities of believers gathering for educational purposes. The fragmentary literary and archaeological evidence for places of education in the Roman world fits with flexible and changing arrangements for educating believers in the Lord throughout the life course. It is also important to recognize that hiring a teacher to educate children at home (perhaps with other children of the neighborhood) was an accepted cultural practice. It was probably more common for girls, although some girls did go out to school.[108] Quintilian indicates that homeschooling versus sending out a child to school was a matter of intellectual debate. He comes down in favor of sending the child out to school because of the benefits associated with what we would call "socialization."[109] In response to the argument that the child's morals will be corrupted in school, he points out that children have ample opportunity to observe the debauched morals of their parents during dinner parties, often involving dalliances with slaves, including child slaves.[110] For better or worse, dinner parties were a venue of impressionability. They were also a home-based activity with potential for education. Visiting intellectuals present in the homes of leading citizens meant elevated dinner conversations, offering opportunities for learning for children free and slave alike.[111]

Conclusion: Children Are Definitely Listening, the *Ekklēsia* Is Definitely Growing, and Neighbors Are Definitely Noticing

The second-century critics of early Christianity drew attention to corrupt and irreverent activities that took place within the *ekklēsia* space. The texts pay rarely noticed and surprising attention to children. The most graphic and condemning account is that by Marcus Cornelius Fronto, who describes the immoral banquets of Christians involving children, who along with other brothers and sisters are involved in incestuous and orgiastic rituals. The clandestine locations are never specified, but are shrouded in secrecy and the very antithesis of the public gathering of respectable men.[112] Although Fronto's speech is highly polemical, the presence of children at gatherings of Christians and, more generally, at banquets in the Roman world suggests an element of truth behind the scandalous rumors. Children were being socialized, learning rites, and listening to after-dinner conversations.

The description of Christianity by Lucian of Samosata (115–200 CE) is less colorful, but nevertheless intended to condemn. Teaching and education are listed as priorities of the group that gathers to offer support and listen to the imprisoned Christian philosopher Peregrinus (also known as Proteus), who is presented as a charlatan. But particularly suggestive for the purposes of this book is that he is visited by groups of believers who include widows and orphans. The crowd brings in succulent meals and their sacred books. No doubt the hope is for enlightened teaching from the imprisoned philosopher whom they call "the new Socrates."[113]

The education of children figures most directly, however, in the work of the pagan intellectual Celsus, who penned *The True Doctrine*, written in about 170 CE and known to us today only through the rebuttal composed by Origen. In his work, Celsus accuses Christians of operating a home-based movement that targets children and is organized by slaves and women, the most despicable and uneducated. In one remarkable passage, Celsus seems to present Christians as targeting schools and leading children to participate in some type of alternate educational milieu:

> And if just as if they are speaking they see one of the school-teachers coming, or some intelligent person, or even the father himself, the more cautious of them flee in all directions; but the more reckless urge the children on to rebel. They whisper to them that in the presence of their father and their schoolmasters they do not feel able to explain anything to the children. But, if they like, they should leave father and their school masters, and go along with the women and little children who are playfellows to the wooldresser's shop, or the cobbler's or the washerwoman's shop, that they may learn perfection. And by saying this they persuade them.[114]

As in the Pastoral Epistles, proper education is connected with assertions of authority, although in this case with the defiance of authority. In addition, both the accounts of Lucian of Samosata and Celsus confirm the impression gained from the Pastorals that educational gatherings involving children took place away from the public gathering of the *ekklēsia*. Celsus presents workshops as possible loci of education—shops that were often attached to houses where other types of meetings may have taken place.

There has not been enough attention given to the extent to which the educational motives of early church communities intersected with and sometimes came into conflict with those of the dominant Roman imperial world. Ancient authors explicitly discuss the educational features of home life and even engage in debates as to whether it is best to educate a child at home or to send him or her out to school. Household life can be presented as an opportunity to instill life-forming virtues from infancy or as a source of corruption, as children so easily witness immoral acts. It was in this world that early church groups had to negotiate the construction of identity. In so doing they made use of the mechanisms of socialization employed throughout society, involving home and school. In acknowledging the complex exchanges of household and house-church life, in which socialization and education often overlapped, the practical education of children and the progress and training from childhood to adulthood were central features of the social construction of reality.

More than any other NT works, the Pastoral Epistles attach value to the progress and training of believers from childhood to adulthood. The very presentation of Timothy and Titus as Paul's delegates and children sets the stage. As faithful children they are to convey Paul's memory and example especially to future teachers. But Timothy in particular serves as an example in a second important sense: the process of maturing in faith that develops throughout the life course. Here the teaching of women is highly valued, as revealed in his formation in the faith by Eunice and Lois (2 Tim 1:5). Understanding the significance of Timothy's formation in the faith within a familial context alerts us to the significance of other passages in which the teaching of children is implied. Interpreters have not paid due attention to the implicit teaching function of *pater familias*/overseer/ bishop. The ideological importance of the role of fathers in preparing the next generation (most especially sons), preserving tradition, and ensuring continuity is presumed in these instructions. Intergenerational teaching among women is also prized in the Pastoral Epistles. The emphasis on young women being taught by older women implies the conveying of knowledge that allowed girls to make the transition into marriage and motherhood. But in this environment it would be a mistake to draw sharp boundaries between domestic and other types of learning, including the teaching of Scripture.

At several points, however, this study has drawn attention to a crisscrossing of conventional and countercultural gender expectations. Schooled by honorable women, Timothy must be prepared to relinquish the qualities of an honorable man as defined by the world's standards and adopt tactics that might compromise his reputation in the public arena. Moreover, there is a sense that the Pastorals leave room for younger men exercising authority in surprising ways; the emerging male leadership is asked to look inward toward household responsibilities as much as it is bidden to look outward. But there are also signs of conflict with respect to gender roles and the teaching influence of women. The best view of the capacity for real tension and conflicted roles can be glimpsed if one imagines what was actually going on within the house church, whose meeting place was a family space wherein women typically had enormous influence and—albeit delegated—authority. In response, a hierarchy of teaching/managing functions based on gender is being set in motion in the Pastoral Epistles that should also not be overlooked. The silencing of women in 1 Tim 2:9-15 reinforces the traditional place of women within the family, ensures that the hierarchy is maintained, and seeks to prevent educated women from speaking in public. The reinforcement of a type of contained teaching authority assigned to older women that forms part of the hierarchical vision has the potential to create tension between women, especially between older women (mothers and grandmothers) and younger women/girls.

On issues of gender and the family, the Pastoral Epistles reflect much conventional thinking, but a focus on children helps us to understand a dimension of engagement with the Roman world that has often been overlooked. In several texts motherhood is encouraged (1 Tim 5:14; Titus 3:4) as well as being associated with salvation (1 Tim 2:15) and formation (1 Tim 5:2, 10; 2 Tim 1:5; Titus 2:3-5). Community members are reminded of their duty to parents, including older parents (1 Tim 5:1-2, 3-8, 16; 2 Tim 3:2) and the child-parent-grandparent bond is strongly reinforced in many different ways. Such interests characterize all three of the Pastoral Epistles. Moreover, in many of the texts this bond is envisioned as one of crucial educational value. The Pastoral Epistles provide solid evidence that as early Christianity developed, it combined features of the household and school. This combination was central to the treatment of young people and the growth of the movement.

Whether we consider the act of welcoming a teacher into the home to teach a group of children or the educational potential of dinner parties, the Roman world provided precedence for the merging of household space and school space that also at times took place in some *ekklēsia* gatherings. It is important to keep the apparent flexibility associated with teaching arrangements in mind, however, when one considers how the house church may have sometimes functioned as a type of home school. While the NT provides ample evidence that these first believers met in houses, debate continues as to what other kinds of spaces might have been used.[115] Children or adolescents congregating with an older, more experienced teacher of the gospel in a variety of settings may have transformed that space into an *ekklēsia* space.[116] The great interest in family relations with respect to leadership and teaching roles in the Pastoral Epistles, along with the sustained teaching vocabulary, however, suggest that the *ekklēsia* space reflected in these documents often reflects the merging of the household and the school. The household of God is the church instructed by God.

5

CONCLUSION

How Remembering the Little Ones
Changes Things

Bringing the experience of children to the center of interpretation of the NT household codes changes our understanding of these texts. The household codes are among the most controversial passages in the NT on account of their undeniable patriarchal and oppressive legacy. But if one is truly interested in recovering as much as possible about what this familial teaching meant within its own context, it is essential to remember the presence of children.

Across disciplines the study of children and childhood is increasingly recognized as a vital component of investigating the human experience, past and present. In the study of NT communities, there are great advances to be made in seeking to understand the life of Roman families, based not only on ancient literary documents but also on the vast array of material remains, including housing, burial inscriptions, iconography, and monuments—all of which offer evidence of the lives of children. There is also important insight to be gained in approaching the evidence with an awareness of the use of children in imperial ideologies and propaganda. Thus, in reading the NT texts that endorse the traditional duties of children to obey their parents, one must be alert to the messages that might be encoded concerning the interaction between church groups and the dominant culture. If one pays careful attention to what is actually being said both at the level of community ethics and in the theological justifications concerning family relations, there are strong hints that the endorsements of traditional arrangements mask significant departures from the status quo in family life.

In considering the NT evidence as a whole, three facts are especially significant. First, it is beyond dispute that children were ever present in domestic settings. The very reality of Pauline Christianity adopting the house church as a base of operation means that children were always witnesses, whether they are explicitly mentioned or not. The ongoing debate concerning the social status of the first Christians makes no difference here; from the simplest two-room apartment to the most elaborate villa, children found their way into every space, seemingly with much less segregation than we might expect in modern western society.

Second, any attempt to analyze the family relations revealed by the household codes will be far off the mark if it takes the categories of parents, slaves, wives, and others at face value and as singular descriptions of identity. In reality, these categories were overlapping. Parents, for example, could be slave or free and could well be the children of older parents (especially of widowed mothers). Recognizing overlapping categories of identity is crucial to how one hears the household codes. Related to the issue of overlapping identity is the need to acknowledge that some of the children, wives, and slaves exhorted in the household codes were subject to nonbelieving parents, husbands, and masters. This plurality of circumstances and the moral tensions and compromises that might result from such complexities are also crucial to how one hears the household codes.

Third, while there is no doubt that there were ascetic currents in early Christianity, they did not eradicate the presence of children. One can trace a trajectory of welcoming children from the teaching of Jesus in the Gospels to the Pastoral Epistles in which instruction of children is being framed by more formal structures and is tied to leadership roles. Even Paul's eschatological vision and preference for celibacy does not prevent the need to deal with issues related to the presence and status of children in church groups (1 Cor 7:14). Those authors who kept Paul's legacy alive in the latter decades of the first century acknowledged the significance of children by addressing them directly (Col 3:20; Eph 6:1) and calling for them to be instructed in the Lord by their parents (Eph 6:4). What might be quickly skipped over as hardly significant by modern readers was of crucial importance in the NT world and in all likelihood a determinative factor in the shape and growth of early Christianity.

Turning specifically to the content of particular documents, consideration of the perspective and circumstances of slave children changes our understanding of Col 3:18–4:1. The longer treatment of the slave-master relationship in this text has meant that the relationship has received a good deal of attention, but virtually no consideration has been given to the presence of slave children and slave parents. In trying to understand how the institution of slavery can be supported by the author of Colossians who is at the same time presenting a community vision of unity and the breaking down of barriers (Col 3:11), it is helpful to be aware of the circumstances of slaves within the family.

Slaves acted in several pseudo-parenting roles as wet nurses, caregivers, and attendants to and from school—all of these roles should be kept in mind in analyses of the slave constituency of early Christianity. Slaves were involved in the child care of free children together with the care of slave children, raising questions about the evangelical influence of slaves as well the implication of slave children being called out side by side with free children for instruction in the Lord. Temporary membership in the slave community for the purposes of child care was commonplace in the Roman world, but the consensus was that any semblance of equality between playmates would end definitively in adulthood. Slave children were barred from inheriting, and slaves had no rights to patrimony. Such considerations give new meaning to the promise of inheritance to slaves in Col 3:24.

There is no doubt that the promise of inheritance refers to future salvation and ultimate status before God. Yet in a Roman context, it nevertheless stands out as a shocking promise. These early communities were clearly not eliminating the structures of slavery and, in many respects, they reinforced the structures with appeals to the relationship between Lord (master) and the community. But placing children at the center of the investigation suggests how community interaction nevertheless could have been transformed in significant ways.

Colossians 2:15 illustrates that its author was aware of the imperial practice of parading the booty of battle, including enslaved peoples; the author appeals to this public humiliation to refer to what Christ accomplished in triumphing over powers and principalities. The audience listening would have heard such proclamations in light of the iconography of Rome, which included images of conquered women and children to advertise imperial might. The separation of children from their mothers, whether on account of military victory or the slave trade, was a central part of the slave experience, and monuments erected by freedpersons point to the longing for continuity and stability in slave families. If the dishonoring and humiliation of slaves was to be avoided in early church communities, then the protection of slave families would be essential.

A second source of humiliation of slaves, including slave children, that has considerable relevance for our own day was their use as sexual objects. The focus on sexual ethics in Colossians (esp. Col 3:5-7), which includes many general terms for sexual vice, raises numerous questions about how moral standards could be applied in a mixed community of slave and free members found in a society that simply accepted the rights of masters to make sexual use of their slaves. Slave children might even be adopted as favorites, with their "pet" status sometimes referring their use for sexual gratification. There is no explicit treatment of the sexual use of slaves in the NT, including Colossians. But the theological implications of the promise of inheritance to slaves (Col 3:24) coupled with the definition of a baptismal status involving a newly transformed identity (Col 3:9-11) implies an ethical imperative that warns against believing masters making sexual use of slaves of the community. The sexual violation of enslaved peoples was a prime means of demonstrating their dishonor. One could not bestow the slaves of the community with honor as being renewed in the image of God (Col 3:11) and continue to support their sexual use.

This is not to suggest that all sexual use of slaves stopped in these early church communities—the cultural expectations were far too pervasive, and society bestowed far too much power upon slave owners. Moreover, the command for slaves to obey their masters in all things means that slaves were being encouraged to be compliant; here the powerlessness of the slaves of nonbelieving masters comes to mind, including the powerlessness of child slaves and slave parents over the fate of their children. But read in the context of Colossians as a whole, the call for masters to treat their slaves justly and fairly

(Col 4:1) should be understood in relation to the infrequent evidence from the Roman world encouraging the protection of slave families from violation, including respect for slave marriages.

The promise of inheritance to slaves in Col 3:24 has rarely, if ever, been examined from the perspective of childhood. Admittedly, there is inscriptional evidence indicating the uncommon expectation that a slave child reared with a freeborn child as a playmate would share in benefits that were owed to the freeborn child, including education. Such exceptional evidence stands in tension, however, to the general consensus that slave children were barred from all such benefits, and slaves in general never attained the status of freeborn adults—retaining the status of perpetual children. Exhorted side by side with free children in the community, the slave children who were promised inheritance were promised a future with hope. In terms of family life, it was a promise of family continuity, stability, and protection from sexual exploitation (to use modern terminology). It is important to keep in mind that the slave children addressed in Col 3:18–4:1, however, would in all likelihood have included children whose masters and/or parents were nonbelievers and even children who made their way somehow into meetings without adult approval outside of church leadership. These children would find a very uncertain and tenuous place of belonging in church groups, but the promises and fellowship among friends might well have been irresistible.

While it may seem more obvious in Ephesians because of the references to Scripture and the teaching of Christian content (Eph 6:1-4), Colossians and Ephesians share an interest in the socialization of children. In Col 3:20 and Eph 6:1, the "performative" quality of children being called out by name in the midst of the assembly *constructs* a world of belonging: children are drawn into the community and a sense of membership and allegiance is reinforced. In Eph 6:4 fathers are assigned a special role in this process, but the widespread phenomenon of pseudo-parenting needs to be considered for a realistic view of how the socialization of children took place in early church communities.

Pseudo-parenting took on many forms in the Roman world and permeated society at all social levels. In part, this phenomenon was fueled by demographic trends in Roman society that point to approximately 25 percent of children being fatherless by the age of ten. Deaths of parents and frequent divorce not only meant that many children lived with stepparents, but they were also fostered by elder siblings or other relatives, or perhaps even adopted into another family. The lived experience of Roman families might aptly be described as that of "patchwork" families. Such experience was a fundamental part of the identity of the members of early church groups, who contributed to the patchwork quality of their lives by aligning themselves with a new family of brothers and sisters in Christ. Several challenges to parental authority (especially paternal authority) might flow from new arrangements and allegiances. Already in widowhood and divorce, the efforts to protect the father's authority by means of guardianship through the father's line was eroded by potentially dominant surrogate fathers such as maternal uncles, stepfathers, or especially in the case of well-to-do widows (cf. Col 4:15), the single mothers themselves.

In considering the identity of the fathers of Col 3:21 and Eph 6:4, it is important to keep in mind the well-established practice of engaging in various forms of surrogate fatherhood. Be they slave or free, the children of the community may have attached themselves to surrogate fathers, even if their own biological fathers were alive. Especially in the case of children whose fathers were nonbelievers, there was real potential for conflicts over loyalty and authority (cf. 1 Pet 3:1-6). Conflict concerning the legitimacy of paternal authority was at the heart of Celsus' accusations that Christians taught children to ignore established figures of authority such as fathers and schoolteachers.

Thus, when examining socialization in early Christian families and house churches, it is vital to remember that parental roles were undertaken by a much wider group than biological parents. Moreover, it was acknowledged that slave childminders filled in the gaps of parental influences, and it was the duty of parents to choose wet nurses and slave caregivers carefully in order that they might offer the proper educational models, including with respect to speech. The direct address to children in the household codes of Colossians and Ephesians points to the socializing impact of children being present when the Epistles were read aloud in the assembly (Col 4:15-16). The process of explaining the substance of the letter is one that parents would have shared with well-educated slaves (who may even have been parents themselves). The link between socialization and education is, in fact, indirectly acknowledged in Col 3:16, wherein community members are instructed to admonish one another and to give thanks by singing psalms, hymns, and spiritual songs. Children sang at public feasts in the Roman world, and there is no reason to assume children were excluded from the worship activities described in Col 3:16; in fact children may sometimes have learned these songs and performed them alone. It was well accepted that the involvement of children in religious rites of various kinds was a prime means of passing on religious knowledge.

Pseudo-parenting was a pervasive reality in the Roman world. But in familial and political ideologies fathers were consistently presented as the traditional custodians and disseminators of religious knowledge. The role of fathers as educators of their children presented in Eph 6:4 fits with this traditional view. The household codes have long been recognized as containing ideological components, especially apologetic nuances, as communities sought to stabilize their place in society. Usually such nuances have been identified in the teaching on marriage and slavery. Yet an understanding of the ideological importance of the role of fathers in preparing the next generation (especially sons), preserving tradition, and ensuring continuity, points to apologetic intent in the way parenting is being presented in the household codes. The apologetic potential of the depiction of the child-parent relationship in the Ephesians household code emerges even more clearly when it is compared with Josephus' apologetic work, *Against Apion*. Josephus emphasized the importance of rooting children in tradition and teaching them from infancy and continuing throughout the life course, appealing to values associated with the firm authority of the *pater familias*.

In comparison with Colossians, Ephesians moves from a concern for socialization to a deliberate attempt to educate rooted in the traditional authority of fathers (Eph 6:4) that becomes even more pronounced in the Pastoral Epistles. The reference to *paideia* (discipline or training) in Eph 6:4 resonates with a concept that has figured prominently in recent discussions of the Roman family: the life course. *Paideia* refers not only to the upbringing of a child in the strict

sense but also to the formation of an adult. Flexible concepts of maturation and ongoing relations between adult children and their parents are presumed. The Dead Sea Scrolls contain fascinating material
concerning the education of children presented within the framework
of the life course. While it is to be lived out in different ways, both
the Dead Sea Scroll and Ephesians are intent on setting in motion a
distinct, or what might be called "sectarian," identity in the Roman
world. In a manner that resonates with the approach in the Dead Sea
Scrolls, the fulfillment of commandments (Eph 6:1-3; cf. Deut 5:16)
and instruction of children (Eph 6:4) becomes a means of daily affirmation of commitment to the Lord and of articulating the parameters
of the community.

The comparative Jewish material also invites a new approach to
the ethical teaching found in long passages such as Eph 4:17–5:20; this
text incorporates teaching materials that could be introduced during
childhood and that were suitable for oral learning, but with the expectation of heightened understanding with increasing maturity. The
Damascus Document presents intriguing evidence of the juxtaposition
between fatherhood and the communal responsibilities of the teacher
in its characterization of the examiner. Comparison can help one to
understand the relationship between family ethics and metaphors in
Ephesians and the increasing emphasis on the role of teacher. The
agenda for learning is built upon an underlying notion of the perfecting by community teachers of the grounding in faith received in the
family. The ultimate goal of the work of teacher-preachers is arrival at
maturity, to the measure of the full stature of Christ (Eph 4:13).

With various theological concepts, ethical norms, and (often
conventional) cultural values, Ephesians subtly reinforces the role
of teacher and of the teaching potential of familial relationships. In
keeping with what has been observed in studying groups dominated
by colonial powers across history, the marginalized group appeals to
concepts endorsed by the dominant society (in this case, Roman imperial society), but also transforms and subverts them to some degree.
Ephesians 3:14-15 offers a very good example of this phenomenon.
On the one hand, the Greek play on words establishes the family name
through the male line, giving identity and securing the reputation of
the group: believers belong to the *patria* (family) of the Father (*pater*).

Children propagated continuity and lineage in the Roman world, and this cultural reality is reflected in Ephesians. But on the other hand, believers as children of God now belong to a new family that in reality does not require the continuity of legitimate heirs, leaving inheritance open to slaves.

What this means for flesh-and-blood children is that Eph 6:1-4 represents a call for membership of all children, including slave children, and all parents, including pseudo-parents. There is much about the worldview of Ephesians to suggest that teachers acted like pseudo-parents, imparting scriptural traditions potentially at odds with the traditional instructions that should be imparted from father to son among the Gentiles; these church teachers would have little regard for the line separating the potential of the slave child from the potential of the free child.

In understanding the implications of Ephesians for the lives of children one must consider the complex interaction between historical reality and familial representation. The role of children should be taken seriously in assessing how Ephesians is responding to imperial ideology. The direct address to children and instructions concerning the child-parent relationship need to be understood within a societal context wherein children were used to communicate social and political messages. Children were used to communicate the *Pax Romana* in variety of ways, including the presence of children at ceremonies, journeys with the imperial parents, and representations in various types of iconography, often involving displays of the unity of the family. Members of early church groups frequently led lives that were a significant departure from imperial ideals and were subject to the winds of change and whims of the powerful and domineering. As slaves and members of families who normally stood outside the realm of citizenship, frequently displaced from one household to another, or from one city to another, children found a place of belonging as those who had been brought near as members of the household of God (Eph 2:17-19).

With many points of continuity with Ephesians, the Pastoral Epistles acknowledge the presence of children more boldly and attribute greater significance to their behavior. The emphasis on education of children, which is linked to family relations in Eph 6:1-4, becomes more pronounced in the Pastoral Epistles. Much more explicitly than in Ephesians, the education of children is surfacing as a communal responsibility. The education of children is tied to leadership structures, including the burgeoning church offices and depictions of the ideal teacher. The teaching of children is a role shared by both men and women in the Pastorals, however, even if heavily influenced by traditional gender expectations.

The blueprint for this state of affairs can be detected in the manner in which the authority of Paul's delegates Timothy and Titus is constructed. Paul bestows authority upon Timothy and Titus as his heirs; he is their fictive father and they are his children. No mention is made of "real" fathers of these figures. However, female members of the immediate family are clearly important. It is the example of women—a grandmother and a mother—that anchors Timothy in faith according to 2 Tim 1:5 (cf. 3:15). Lois and Eunice are presented here as setting the stage for Timothy's ongoing formation under the guidance of Paul. As in Ephesians, maturing in faith throughout the life course is highlighted. The significance of motherhood is presumed in Ephesians in the celebration of the life of the married couple (Eph 5:21-33). But in the Pastorals, motherhood (and grandmotherhood) is recognized for its educational potential. Together, mothers and the fictive father Paul prepare the delegates to represent Paul and to teach his message. In turn, the delegates set in motion leadership structures that embrace the educational potential of parental relationships. Timothy, for example, will go on to instruct the local overseers to be ideal fathers (1 Tim 3:4-5).

The presentation of the teaching capacity of women is one of the most fascinating features of the Pastoral Epistles, especially given the unmistakable attempt to circumvent certain teaching roles for women (1 Tim 2:11-15). Mothers are instrumental in the education of both sons and daughters. The educational activities of women were controversial in the Roman world, but the acceptability of the educated woman increased the more closely it was associated with familial life. Thus, for example, there is a sustained celebration of the heroic educational achievements of elite mothers in relation to sons, often as a result of widowhood. Taken together, 2 Tim 1:5 and 3:15 (he has been introduced to Scriptures from infancy) clearly place women in the position of teachers of the youthful Timothy, but it is important to recognize the many conventional features of the presentation. Lois and Eunice are like the noble widows of ancient literature who make sacrifices to ensure the education of their sons, passing on valued traditions and learning. At the same time, however, an appeal to ancient conventional motifs masks elements of countercultural reality. Lois and Eunice are presented as having prepared their young charge for a role in a suspicious religious group, which ultimately does not match ideals about the role of the erudite male. Moreover, the lack of references to husbands and fathers in the case of these women leaves open the possibility of women defying their husbands and joining church groups without permission and teaching the children Scripture and church traditions from infancy.

The Pastoral Epistles reveal a sustained interest in intergenerational connections between women for teaching purposes. In a society in which women married young—often to older men—mothers assisted their daughters in making the transition from daughter to wife and mother, and acted as advocates for their daughters as they adjusted to new arrangements. It is precisely this need for education that forms the background of Titus 2:3-5, in which older women are instructed to encourage younger women to be good wives, mothers, and household managers. Children are specifically mentioned in the reference to teaching young women. The ideal younger woman in this passage is undoubtedly the mother with children. It is important to recognize, however, that the relationship envisioned in Titus is not restricted to that between mother and daughter, but in the domestic setting of the house church—the household of God—the relationship between groupings of female believers takes on familial coloring.

To approach the Pastoral Epistles, including the passages on widowhood (1 Tim 5:3-16), with a focus on children is to sense an increasing acknowledgment of the place of mothers within the community. With reference to childbearing, motherhood is associated with salvation (1 Tim 2:15) and recognized as crucial for the teaching of community members (1 Tim 5:2, 10; 2 Tim 1:5; Titus 2:3-5). Both the encouragement to embrace motherhood (1 Tim 5:14; Titus 3:4) and the duty to parents (1 Tim 5:1-2, 3-8, 16; 2 Tim 3:2) throughout the life course are central to the reinforcement of the child-parent-grandparent bond in this literature. This bond is of crucial educational value.

Comparison with Ephesians, however, can help us to sense some of the challenge to conventional expectations inherent in this familial communal setting where the mentoring of younger women by older women is by no means restricted to family members. The presentation of pure bride to her one true husband in Eph 5:21-33 sets aside the cultural reality of the parents, especially the mother, presenting her daughter to the prospective husband. Instead there is a symbolic depiction of the bridegroom taking the lead, with the couple together standing apart from the corruption of the world. In a church setting where people were breaking with family members and joining the church, one cannot assume that mothers were always present in assisting their daughters in making the transitions into their lives as wives and mothers. In the world of the Pastoral Epistles, this role could be undertaken by fellow community members who were older women and widows. The somewhat convoluted teaching on widows in 1 Tim 5:3-16 certainly supports the notion of women helping other women who might otherwise be abandoned (1 Tim 5:16).

Like mothers, the educational influence of fathers is also reinforced both within the immediate family and within the house-church community. In the case of fathers, this educational influence is linked more directly to emerging church offices. As with the teaching concerning mothers and grandmothers, however, children emerge as a key concern. According to Titus 1:6, for example, the children of elders/presbyters are to be believers, not accused of debauchery, and not rebellious. The text constitutes a strong reinforcement of the authority of elders/fathers and a strong endorsement of their leadership that is reminiscent of Eph 6:4 but demonstrates further evidence of institutionalization: the elders/presbyters are being held accountable for the religious training of their children. Similarly, it is important to recognize the implicit teaching function of *pater familias/* overseer/bishop. The instructions concerning the overseer as a model householder in 1 Tim 3:1-7 presume the ideological importance of the role of fathers in preparing the next generation. One of the attributes of the overseer/bishop is that he is an apt teacher (*didakiton*; 1 Tim 3:2). This is an indication of the familial teaching authority tied to fatherhood; household leadership is expanding into a communal teaching role. In comparison with Colossians and Ephesians, in the Pastorals one finds definite evidence of the house church becoming a type of home school.

Like much ancient literature, the Pastoral Epistles present coordinating authority and responsibilities for mothers and fathers. But there also is clearly a hierarchy of teaching/managing functions based on gender that should not be overlooked. Especially in the teaching concerning widows in 1 Tim 5:3-16, but also in 1 Tim 2:8-15, wherein women are silenced and told they will be saved by childbearing, we sense tension between male and female authority in a community that meets in the domain traditionally ruled by the male head of the household, the *pater familias*, but managed by his wife. As much as women's influence in the domestic sphere is celebrated in the Pastoral Epistles, in a real sense women are being asked to make way for the growing presence and influence of fathers or their representatives. These male figures are to be fully engaged in household affairs and are not to exercise their rule indirectly. In the complex gender constructions of the Pastorals, there is a surprising pressure on the male leadership of the church groups to define their identities in terms of household/house-church life that seems to stand at some distance from the honorable Roman male fully engaged in public affairs. There is no question that a hierarchy of men over women, especially with respect to teaching, is being established, but it retains some countercultural elements even as it embraces traditional values.

The authority of teachers, which sometimes seems to stand apart from the exhortations concerning church offices in the Pastoral Epistles, is also rooted in *patria potestas*—the authority of fathers. It appears that whatever teaching authority women possess as mothers, it must be endorsed/delegated by the fathers of the community. The hierarchy is established early in 1 Timothy, with its instruction that women are to learn in silence (1 Tim 2:11). Recalling the idealized household management material found in Xenophon's *Oeconomicus*, with the husband presented as teaching his own wife to run the household, the implication is that they are to be educated within the community, perhaps taught by their own husbands or, more likely, by other men in the community who are assuming positions of leadership.

Much can be gleaned about the community life underlying the Pastoral Epistles by examining the intersection between family life and teaching, the interaction between the church as household and church as a type of school devoted to education throughout the life course. A failure to recognize both the value attached to the formation of children and the lack of rigid demarcation between childhood and adulthood in the Roman world has led to a neglect in examining educational efforts that were closely tied to the familial life of the house church. In contrast, a child-focused perspective allows us to recognize that the teaching occurring in the midst of the *ekklēsia* gathered for worship (1 Tim 2:8-15) was only one type of teaching, with other types of instruction occurring in other settings or configurations.

In the directives to older women to teach younger women, for example, we find a derivative of the recognized word for teacher (*kalodidaskalos*), a compound word that refers to the teaching of what is good (Titus 2:3). Titus 2:3-5 offers the clearest and most detailed reference to the content of teaching in Pastoral Epistles, a feature of the works that is quite nebulous. It is evident that many aspects of the instruction involved domestic duties and virtues, the kind of teaching that needed to take place through mentoring and active learning of the type that young women (in our terms, including adolescent girls) learned from mothers and female relatives. But mention of the "word of God" in Titus 2:5, suggests that this teaching was imbued with authority and linked domestic apprenticeship with doctrinal and scriptural elements. Likewise, the overseer's teaching role could have multiple dimensions. Responsibility for keeping his children submissive (1 Tim 3:4) included responsibility for ensuring his children's education. Given the value attached to hospitality (1 Tim 3:2), however, an extension of the fatherhood role might well have included opening his house for the teaching of believing children (slave and free) along with the children of his own household.

To a greater extent than Colossians and Ephesians, the Pastorals presume a body of educational content and the need to deliver it. Making more than an effort to socialize members, communities are putting in place structures to educate. The significant interest in family relations with respect to leadership and teaching roles, along with the sustained teaching vocabulary, suggest that the *ekklēsia* space reflected in these documents often reflects the merging of the household and the school.

The expansion of early Christianity continues to be a subject of great interest and debate. A focus on children sheds light upon a dimension of engagement with the Roman world that has often been overlooked. Small, silent, but listening, children were absorbing the content of the Gospels, and they would deepen their understanding of the traditions throughout their lives. The Roman world set the stage for the flexible approach to the teaching of children in church groups, both through the variety of possible physical arrangements for teaching children and because of the pervasive presence of children in houses both modest and grand. In the midst of the gathered *ekklēsia*, children were called forth together and promised the rich rewards of inheritance. At home they were instructed in the Scriptures by parents, grandparents, and pseudo-parents. In the houses of leading women they were taught doctrines and household management. In the houses of hospitable overseers, they were taught how to pray to the one God (1 Tim 2:5).

Notes

Chapter 1

1   See comments of Celsus as recorded in Origen, *Cels.* 3.55, discussed later in this chapter.

2   A minority of scholars argue that the term *household code* only properly applies to material in Colossians and Ephesians. See, e.g., Jürgen Becker and Ulrich Luz, *Die Briefer und die Galater, Epheser und Kolosser* (NTD 8/1; Göttingen: Vandenhoeck & Ruprecht, 1998), 234; Peter Balla, *The Child-Parent Relationship in the New Testament and Its Environment* (Tübingen: Mohr Siebeck, 2003), 168.

3   Scholars have speculated as to whether issues having to do with women (e.g., heightened visibility at a time when the insubordination of women was associated with superstitions and illegitimate religious groups) and slaves (e.g., appeals for manumission perhaps inspired by baptismal slogans such as Gal 3:28) may have led to an appeal to these rule-like statements. On women see esp. David L. Balch, *Let Wives Be Submissive: The Domestic Code in 1 Peter* (Chico, Calif.: Scholars Press, 1981), 65–80. On slaves see esp. James E. Crouch, *The Origin and Intention of the Colossian Haustafel* (Göttingen: Vandenhoeck & Ruprecht, 1972), 126.

4   While this is generally true, some NT writings (e.g., the Pastoral Epistles, 2 Peter) may have been composed after or at about the same time as the writings of the Apostolic Fathers (e.g., *1 Clement*, the *Didache*).

5   Investigators have pointed out that esp. for the first two centuries CE, the use of the very terms "Judaism" and "Christianity" can be misleading and problematic. The categories do not do justice to the overlap between traditions and the actual historical circumstances of the evolution of communities. Among the extensive literature on this topic, see esp. D. Boyarin, *Border Lines: The Partition of Judaeo-Christianity* (Philadelphia: University of Pennsylvania Press, 2006); S. Mason, "Jews, Judeans, Judaizing, Judaism: Problems of Categorization in

Ancient History," *Journal for the Study of Judaism in the Persian, Hellenistic and Roman Periods* 38 (2007): 457–512.

6   The groundbreaking work of David L. Balch on 1 Peter (1981) is especially important for this explanation of the emergence of household code teaching. Balch noted how certain groups such as the Dionysus cult, the Egyptian Isis cult, and the Jews came to be accused in a stereotypical fashion of producing immorality among the population and of disrupting the order of the household. With respect to Judaism and on the basis of the writings of Philo of Alexandria and Josephus in particular, Balch pointed to the presence of household management discourse that served an apologetic function, calling for comparison with the NT household codes. See esp. Balch, *Let Wives Be Submissive*, 74. Scholars have applied the apologetic hypothesis to other household codes. For apologetic theories with respect to Colossians, e.g., see Angela Standhartinger, "The Origin and Intention of the Household Code in the Letter to the Colossians," *JSNT* 79 (2000): 117–30; James D. G. Dunn, *The Epistles to Colossians and to Philemon* (NIGTC; Grand Rapids: Eerdmans, 1996), 250.

7   E.g., John H. Elliott, in an influential study also appearing in 1981 (see reference to Balch above), argued the code of 1 Peter was part of a strategy to encourage cohesion in the face of external pressures to conform. In other words, rather than having an outward explanatory orientation, the code of 1 Peter should be read in light of the overall aim of the document to offer integration—to offer a home for the homeless, a home for the strangers and aliens who were now part of the community (cf. 1 Pet 1:1, 17; 2:11). See J. H. Elliott, *A Home for the Homeless: A Sociological Exegesis of 1 Peter* (Philadelphia: Fortress, 1981). Debate between John H. Elliott and David L. Balch led to helpful conversation about inward/outward outlook and where particular documents might fit on this continuum, with 1 Peter offering the most explicit evidence of apologetic intention and other documents displaying it to varying degrees. For this debate see David L. Balch, "Hellenization/Acculturation in 1 Peter," in *Perspectives on 1 Peter* (ed. Charles H. Talbert; Macon, Ga.: Mercer University Press), 79–101; and, in the same volume, John H. Elliott, "1 Peter, Its Situation and Strategy," 61–78; John H. Elliott, *1 Peter: A New Translation with Introduction and Commentary* (AB 37B; New York: Doubleday, 2000), 509–10.

8   On the contrast between Paul's perspective on marriage and 1 Corinthians 7 and the household codes, see Gillian Beattie, *Women and Marriage in Paul and His Early Interpreters* (JSNTSup 296; London: T&T Clark, 2005), 74–77.

9   On asceticism and the household codes, see esp. Margaret Y. MacDonald, "Citizens of Heaven and Earth: Asceticism and Social Integration in Colossians and Ephesians," in *Asceticism and the New Testament* (ed. Leif E. Vaage and Vincent L. Wimbush; New York: Routledge, 1999), 269–98.

10   From the mid-1970s to the mid-1980s, the research on this topic by a number of scholars converged, leading to a general consensus on this matter. See esp. D. Lührmann, "Wo man nicht mehr Sklave oder Freier is. Überlegungen zur

Struktur frühchristlicher Gemeinden," *WD* 13 (1975): 53–83; D. Lührmann, "Neutestamentliche Haustafeln und Antike Ökonomie," *NTS* 27 (1980–1981): 83–97; K. Thraede, "Zum historischen Hintergrund der 'Haustafeln' des NT," in *Pietas: Festschrift für B. Kötting* (ed. E. Dassmann and K. S. Frank; Münster: Aschendorff, 1980), 359–68; K. Müller, "Die Haustafel des Kolosserbriefes und das antike Frauenthema. Eine Kritische rückschau auf alte Ergebnisse," in *Die Frau im Urchristentum* (ed. Josef Blank, Gerhard Dautzenberg, Helmut Merklein, and Karlheinz Müller; QD 95; Freiburg: Herder, 1983), 263–319; Balch, *Let Wives Be Submissive*. In his 1996 commentary on Colossians, Dunn described the debate concerning the roots of the household codes as now settled (see *The Epistles to Colossians and to Philemon*, 243).

11   On these associations see Carolyn Osiek and Margaret Y. MacDonald, with Janet Tulloch, *A Woman's Place: House Churches in Earliest Christianity* (Minneapolis: Augsburg Fortress, 2006), 118–43.

12   On the question of whether the codes simply reproduce conventional ethics, feminist scholarship has spoken with a clear voice since the 1980s. Patriarchy found its way into the early church via the domestic code. Many (though not all) feminist interpreters have subscribed to the notion of the codes as representing retreat from the original visions of Jesus and Paul (esp. Gal 3:28) and an important step in the patriarchalization of the church. Here the work of Elisabeth Schüssler Fiorenza has been of special importance, esp. *In Memory of Her: A Feminist Theological Reconstruction of Christian Origins* (London: SCM Press, 1983), 253. On the impact of Fiorenza's work for the study of the household codes, see Margaret Y. MacDonald, "Beyond Identification of the *Topos* of Household Management: Reading the Household Codes in Light of Recent Methodologies and Theoretical Perspectives in the Study of the New Testament," *NTS* 57 (2010): 74–79. For a valuable discussion of differences of opinion with respect to the household codes more generally, some of which continue today, see David L. Balch, "Household Codes," in *Greco-Roman Literature and the New Testament* (ed. David E. Aune; Atlanta: Scholars Press, 1988), 25–50. For a thorough summary of research on the household codes, see also Johannes Woyke, *Die Neutestamentlichen Haustafeln: Ein kritischer und konstrucktiver Forschungsüberblick* (SBS 184; Stuttgart: Katholisches Bibelwerk, 2000).

13   See esp. David C. Verner, *The Household of God: The Social World of the Pastoral Epistles* (SBLDS 71; Chico, Calif.: Scholars Press, 1989). For thorough structural and semantic analysis of the codes, see Marlis Gielen, *Tradition und Theologie neutestamentlicher Haustafelethik: Ein Beitrag zur Frage einer christlichen Auseinandersetzung mit gesellschaftlichen Normen* (BBB 75; Frankfurt am Main: Anton Hain, 1990).

14   E.g., see Balch, "Household Codes," 37.

15   Dunn, *The Epistles to the Colossians and to Philemon*, 244.

16   See Philo, *Spec.* 3.137 and 2.67–68; Balch, "Household Codes," 37. See further discussion below, esp. nn. 36, 37, and 60.

17   David L. Balch, "Neopythagorean Moralists and the New Testament House-
      hold Codes," *ANRW* 2, no. 26.1 (1992): 389–404.

18   See *Sylloge inscriptionum graecarum* (SIG) 3.985, examined by Standhartinger,
      "The Origin and Intention of the Household Code," 126–27.

19   See J. Albert Harrill, *Slaves in the New Testament: Literary, Social, and Moral
      Dimensions* (Minneapolis: Fortress, 2006), 85–87.

20   See, e.g., Franz Laub, *Die Begegnung des frühen Christentums mit der antiken
      Sklaverei* (Stuttgart: Katholisches Bibelwerk, 1982), 90. For full discussion of
      implications of the reciprocal ethical exhortations and the unusual nature of the
      direct address, see Gielen, *Tradition und Theologie neutestamentlicher Haustafele-
      thik*, 37–38, 69–71, 102, 118, 145.

21   It will be argued in this book that this uniqueness or unusual quality also relates
      to children and slave children. See further discussion below.

22   The head of the household could, however, be a woman. See Osiek and Mac-
      Donald, *A Woman's Place*, 144–63.

23   This insight has played a prominent role in feminist scholarship. See Elisabeth
      Schüssler Fiorenza, *Bread Not Stone: The Challenge of Feminist Biblical Interpre-
      tation* (Boston: Beacon, 1985), 74–77. At the same time, however, the association
      of the codes with patriarchy and even misogyny has been forcefully highlighted
      in feminist work, including the use of highly problematic imagery. See Carolyn
      Osiek, "The Bride of Christ (Eph 5.22-33): A Problematic Wedding," *BTB* 32
      (2003): 29–39.

24   Elizabeth Schüssler Fiorenza's highly influential research deserves careful con-
      sideration, see esp. *Rhetoric and Ethic: The Politics of Biblical Studies* (Minneapo-
      lis: Fortress, 1999), ix.

25   Standhartinger, "The Origin and Intention of the Household Code," 125. See
      also Virginia Ramey Mollenkott, "Emancipative Elements in Ephesians 5.21-
      33: Why Feminist Scholarship Has (Often) Left Them Unmentioned, and Why
      They Should Be Emphasized," in *A Feminist Companion to the Deutero-Pauline
      Epistles* (ed. Amy-Jill Levine with Miriamme Blickerstaff; London: T&T
      Clark, 2003), 88–97; J. Barclay, "Ordinary but Different: Colossians and Hid-
      den Moral Identity," *ABR* 49 (2001): 34–52. Not all scholars, however, are in
      agreement. See, e.g., the discussion by J. Albert Harrill, who argues that even
      the theological ideas that offer justification for household teaching are based on
      conventional concepts. Harrill, *Slaves in the New Testament*, 85–87.

26   See Dunn, *The Epistles to the Colossians and to Philemon*, 244. On elements of
      resistance implied by scriptural references in Eph 5:22-33, see Osiek and Mac-
      Donald, *A Woman's Place*, 123–26.

27   For further discussion of this point, see chap. 2.

28   See, e.g., Valerius Maximus, *Memorable Deeds and Sayings* 7.8.2.

29   See Aristotle, *Pol.* 1.1253b–1260b26. Although written many centuries before
      the Roman era, Aristotle's discussion laid the basis for later discussions in

the Hellenistic and Roman worlds. Many of the fundamental familial ideals remained unchanged.

30 Aristotle, *Pol.* 1260b15–26 (Rackham, LCL).

31 Aristotle prefers a republican rather than monarchical model of rule in relation to a wife; *Pol.* 1259b10–18 (Rackham, LCL).

32 Aristotle, *Eth. nic.* 8.1160b23–1161a10.

33 In this paragraph I am following closely my discussion in "A Place of Belonging: Perspectives on Children from Colossians and Ephesians," in *The Child in the Bible* (ed. Marcia J. Bunge; Grand Rapids: Eerdmans, 2008), 281.

34 Xenophon, *Oec.* 7.

35 On familial strategies of slave management in the Roman world, see Harrill, *Slaves in the New Testament*, 85–87.

36 Xenophon, *Oec.* 9.

37 Xenophon, *Oec.* 13.9–12 .

38 The groundbreaking work of David L. Balch has been especially important here. See Balch, *Let Wives Be Submissive*, 118.

39 Balch, *Let Wives Be Submissive*, 55. On wives and husbands see Dionysius, *Ant. rom.* 2.25.4, and on children and fathers, see *Ant. rom.* 2.26.1 and 4. Balch points out that Dionysius did not elaborate on the slave-master relationship. For a very close parallel to the threefold structure of the household code material in Colossians and Ephesians, see esp. Seneca *Ep.* 94.1.

40 See Dionysius, *Ant. rom.* 2.26.1–27.5.

41 See Dionysius, *Ant. rom.* 2.26.1 (Cary, LCL).

42 On honoring parents as a value shared by Jews and Gentiles alike, see esp. Balch, "Neopythagorean Moralists," 402–3. See also Joseph Plevnik, "Honor/Shame," in *Biblical Social Values and Their Meaning: A Handbook* (ed. John J. Pilch and Bruce J. Malina; Peabody, Mass.: Hendrickson, 1993), 97.

43 This will be examined in detail in chap. 2.

44 See Dionysius, *Ant. rom.* 2.26.4 (Cary, LCL).

45 See Dionysius, *Ant. rom.* 2.27.1–2 (Cary, LCL).

46 See detailed discussion in chap. 2.

47 Against the use of excessive force, see Ps.-Plutarch, *Mor.* 8F [*Lib. ed.*]; Ps.-Phoc. 207.

48 See Balch, *Let Wives Be Submissive*, 18. On the limitations of the powers of the *pater familias*, see Balla, *The Child-Parent Relationship*, 46. He cites Richard P. Saller, *Patriarchy, Property and Death in the Roman Family* (Cambridge: Cambridge University Press, 1994), 72. There are texts that suggest children sometimes should disobey parents, especially to study philosophy. See Balla, *The Child-Parent Relationship*, 74–75.

49 See, e.g., Perictyone, *On the Harmony of a Woman*, 145.8–18, 23–26; Iamblichus, *Life of Pythagoras*, 22.13, 18–19; 23.8–9, cited in Balch, "Neopythagorean Moralists," 402. See also *Let Wives Be Submissive*, 57.

50   Doubt has been expressed about whether this fascinating text was actually written by a woman. Among the striking advice given is that women should turn a blind eye to their husbands' infidelities. For a full text see Ian Michael Plant, *Women Authors of Ancient Greece and Rome: An Anthology* (Norman: University of Oklahoma Press, 2004), 77–78.

51   Balch has called *Against Apion* "an apologetic encomium on the Jewish nation," arguing that Josephus was influenced in rhetorical outline by an encomium given by Menander of Laodicea. See *Let Wives Be Submissive*, 118, and, for comparison of Josephus to Dionysius of Halicarnassus, 54. This work will be discussed in detail in chap. 3.

52   An exception is Adele Reinhartz and Kim Shier, "Josephus on Children and Childhood," *Studies in Religion* 41 (2012): 364–75. On marriage see Josephus, *C. Ap.* 2.199; on the slave master-relationship see *C. Ap.* 2.216; on the rearing of children see *C. Ap.* 1.60; 2.202–4, 206; 2.173–74, 178.

53   *C. Ap.* 1.60 (Thackeray, LCL). To be discussed further in chap. 3, there are likely apologetic connotations inherent in the concept of *eusebeia*, which is closely associated with the Roman virtue of *pietas*, involving loyalty to gods, state, parents, and family. As noted above, this virtue is frequently linked to the obedience of children. See Beryl Rawson, *Children and Childhood in Roman Italy* (Oxford: Oxford University Press, 2003), 233.

54   *C. Ap.* 2.202 (Thackeray, LCL). See Reinhartz and Shier, "Josephus on Children and Childhood": on abortion and exposure they also cite Ps.-Phocylides; P. W. van der Horst, *The Sentences of Pseudo-Phocylides* (Studia in Veteris Testament Pseudepigrapha; Leiden: Brill, 1978), 232 (lines 184–85). Also Philo, *Spec.* 3.108–19.

55   *C. Ap.* 2.216–17 (Thackeray, LCL). See Reinhartz and Shier, "Josephus on Children and Childhood," 370. Reinhartz and Shier view this statement as "certainly apologetic."

56   *C. Ap.* 2.206; cf. Philo, *Spec.* 2.232 (Colson, LCL). See the following discussion of severe consequences for the disobedience of children in Proverbs: William P. Brown, "To Discipline without Destruction: The Multifaceted Profile of the Child in Proverbs," in *The Child in the Bible* (ed. Marcia J. Bunge; Grand Rapids: Eerdmans, 2008), 63–81.

57   Philo, *Spec.* 2.225–27; cf. 2.213; 4.184.

58   See Stobaeus, *Anthology* 4.79.53. Stobaeus, Extracts from Hierocles, *On Appropriate Acts*. For the translation adopted here, textual history, dating, and identity of Hierocles, see Ilaria Ramelli, *Hierocles the Stoic: Elements of Ethics, Fragments, and Excerpts* (translated into English from Italian, by David Konstan; Writings from the Greco-Roman World; Atlanta: SBL, 2009), 82–83.

59   Judith Gundry-Volf, "The Least and the Greatest: Children in the New Testament," in *The Child in Christian Thought* (ed. Marcia J. Bunge; Grand Rapids: Eerdmans, 2003), 56.

60   See Stobaeus, *Anthology* 4.84.20. Ramelli, *Hierocles the Stoic*, 87, 123.

61   Gundry-Volf, "The Least and the Greatest," 59.

62   See Halvor Moxnes, ed., *Constructing Early Christian Families: Family as Social Reality and Metaphor* (London: Routledge, 1997), 20–21; Carolyn Osiek and David L. Balch, *Families in the New Testament World: Households and House Churches* (Family, Religion, and Culture; Louisville, Ky.: Westminster John Knox, 1997), 6.

63   See Richard P. Saller, "Household and Gender," in *The Cambridge Economic History of the Greco-Roman World* (ed. W. Sheidel, I. Morris, and R. Saller; Cambridge: Cambridge University Press, 2007), 87–88.

64   Osiek and MacDonald, *A Woman's Place*, 154–55; Richard Saller, "*Pater Familias, Mater Familias*, and the Gendered Semantics of the Roman Household," *CP* 94 (1999): 184, 187.

65   Most scholars have viewed the household code exhortation as intended for young children living at home, but a minority has viewed the teaching as intended for adult children as well. See M. Gärtner, *Die Familienerziehung in der alten Kirche* (Cologne: Bohlau, 1985), 36–37. On the flexible concept of the beginning of adulthood among Romans, see Rawson, *Children and Childhood in Roman Italy*, 135–45.

66   See detailed discussion in chap. 4.

67   See Michele George, "Domestic Architecture and Household Relations: Pompeii and Roman Ephesos," *JSNT* 21 (2004): 7–25.

68   See Rawson, *Children and Childhood in Roman Italy*, 215.

69   Rawson, *Children and Childhood in Roman Italy*, 154–56, 187–91, citing Nepos, *Att.* 13. In this paragraph I am following closely my argument in "Reading the New Testament Household Codes in Light of New Research on Children and Childhood in the Roman World," *SR* 41 (2012): 376–87.

70   It is possible that some of these children have limited possibilities for actual attendance at church gatherings, but their status is nevertheless an important issue for consideration. See Margaret Y. MacDonald and Leif Vaage, "Unclean but Holy Children: Paul's Everyday Quandary in 1 Cor 7:14c," *Catholic Biblical Quarterly* 73 (2011): 526–46.

71   On the use of familial language to refer to slave alliances see Dale B. Martin, "Slave Families and Slaves in Families," in *Early Christian Families in Context: An Interdisciplinary Dialogue* (ed. David L. Balch and Carolyn Osiek; Grand Rapids: Eerdmans, 2003), 207–30.

72   I have examined the implications of the husband's role in determining the religion of the household for understanding the lives of early Christian women, including those married to nonbelievers, in *Early Christian Women and Pagan Opinion: The Power of the Hysterical Woman* (Cambridge: Cambridge University Press, 1996).

73   See esp. Jean Noël Aletti, *Saint Paul: Épitre aux Colossiens* (Paris: J. Galbalda, 1993), 250; Turid Karlsen Seim, "A Superior Minority: The Problem of Men's Headship in Ephesians 5," in *Mighty Minorities? Minorities in Early*

Christianity—Positions and Strategies: Essays in Honor of Jacob Jervell on His 70th Birthday, 21 May 1995 (ed. David Hellholm, Halvor Moxnes, and Turid Karlsen Seim; Oslo: Scandinavian University Press, 1995), 167–81.

74 The strategy being adopted in this book is to investigate the implications of the household code teaching for the lives of children in NT communities within the broader framework of families, including the familial space of the house church. In dialogue with Roman family studies, there have been several studies on early Christian families that place the household context (including its social, economic, and architectural components) at the center of investigation. See esp. Moxnes, *Constructing Early Christian Families*; Osiek and Balch, *Families in the New Testament World*; David L. Balch and Carolyn Osiek, eds., *Early Christian Families in Context: An Interdisciplinary Dialogue* (Religion, Marriage, and Family; Grand Rapids: Eerdmans, 2003); Osiek and MacDonald, *A Woman's Place*. The great advantage of this approach is that it will allow one to draw upon a wide range of comparative evidence and the sophisticated analyses of ancient historians who have access to material evidence such as housing remains and inscriptions; while not being early Christian in origin, this evidence nevertheless sheds light on the world of childhood that early Christians inhabited. In the past decade, Roman family historians have turned their attention specifically to children and childhood, and their findings are just beginning to enter into the discussions of scholars of early Christianity. Particularly important comprehensive studies include Rawson, *Children and Childhood in Roman Italy*; Christian Laes, *Children in the Roman Empire: Outsiders Within* (Cambridge: Cambridge University Press, 2011); original Dutch edition: *Kinderen bij de Romeinen: Zes Eeuwen Dagelijks Leven* (Leuven: Uitgeverij Davidsfonds, 2006); Véronique Dasen and Thomas Späth, eds., *Children, Memory, and Family Identity in Roman Culture* (Oxford: Oxford University Press, 2010).

75 See Rawson, *Children and Childhood in Roman Italy*, 259–61. See detailed discussion in chap. 2.

76 See chap. 3.

77 Christian Laes states the following: "Archaeologists have found hardly any children's beds, nor is there evidence of designated play rooms. Children would usually play near the atrium or around the galleries of the peristyle." Laes, *Children in the Roman Empire*, 37.

78 One of the benefits that could be identified in sending a child out to school rather than organizing home tutoring was, remarkably, protection from the corruption that comes from observing rowdy dinner parties, dalliances with mistresses, and associations with boy lovers. See esp. Quintilian, *Inst.* 1.2.8, to be discussed further in chap. 4. Rawson, *Children and Childhood in Roman Italy*, 214.

79 William Loader writes the following: "It would have made sense to Mark's Jewish and Gentile readers, for whom it would have been one of the major scandals in the Gentile world and one which might easily find its way into the Christian community of Gentile converts" (William Loader, *Sexuality and the*

Jesus Tradition [Grand Rapids: Eerdmans, 2005], 24). See 23–25, where he cites R. F. Collins, *Sexual Ethics and the New Testament: Behavior and Belief* (New York: Crossroad, 2000), 67; Will Demming, "Mark 9:42-10:12, Matthew 5:27-32 and B. Nid. 13b: A First Century Discussion of Male Sexuality," *NTS* 36 (1990): 130–41. Loader understands "little ones" as referring to children and not to all disciples, as is often suggested. Citing Demming, he also draws attention to the use of the verb *skandalizō* in a sexual context in *Pss. Sol.* 16.7 and Sir 9.5. In addition, see Loader's reading of Matt 18:6-9 as an interpretation of Mark 9:42-48. Unlike most interpreters, he takes Matt 18:6 as continuing a reference to children. He makes the same point about Matt 18:14, positing an intriguing interpretation of the parable of 18:12-13 as having a child focus: "Matthew would accordingly be using the parable of the ninety-nine sheep to reinforce a commitment to caring about children, especially those who have been led astray by sexual predators" (27).

80 Citing R. F. Collins, Loader refers to *Sib. Or.* 3.595–600 (cf. 3.185–87; 5.166, 387; 2 En. 10.4 MS P). See *Sexuality and the Jesus Tradition*, 24. To these references should probably added *Did.* 2.2, which refers to the sexual corruption of youths, and *Did.* 5.2, which refers to murderers of children and corruptors of what God has created (this could also be a reference to abortion). Similarly, *Barn.* 19.4 states: "Do not engage in sexual immorality, do not commit adultery, do not engage in pederasty" [Ehrman, LCL]. *Barnabas* 10.6 associates the eating of hare (cf. Lev 11:6; Deut 14:7) with the corruption of children. The rear-approach intercourse and the frequent pregnancies of the hare led to its association with sexual acts. Clement of Alexandria (*Paed.* 2.10.83.5; 2.10.88.3) also associates the hare with pederasty. See full discussion in Bernadette J. Brooten, *Love between Women: Early Christian Responses to Female Homoeroticism* (Chicago: University of Chicago Press, 1998), 330. With respect to the significance of this material for understanding the sexual ethics of Colossians and Ephesians, see chap. 2.

81 On attitudes concerning the inherent deficiencies of children in the Greco-Roman world, see Peter Müller, *In der Mitte der Gemeinde: Kinder im Neuen Testament* (Neukirchen Vluyn: Neukirchener, 1992), 89–90, 161–64.

82 All biblical citations are from the NRSV unless otherwise noted.

83 The latter has been noted by James Francis, "Children and Childhood in the New Testament," in *The Family in Theological Perspective* (ed. Stephen Barton; Edinburgh: T&T Clark, 1996), 82.

84 Francis, "Children and Childhood in the New Testament," 72–73.

85 It should be noted, however, that traditions with respect to the child-parent relationship and the family are complex and somewhat ambivalent in the Gospels. See J. T. Carroll, "'What Then Will This Child Become?': Perspectives on Children in the Gospel of Luke," in *The Child in the Bible* (ed. Marcia J. Bunge; Grand Rapids: Eerdmans, 2008), 177–94.

86 Origen, *Cels.* 3.55.

87   E.g., Herm. *Mand.* 8.10; Herm. *Sim.* 9.29.1–2; Herm. *Vis.* 2.4.3; *Barn.* 20.2; Ign. *Smyrn.* 6.2; Lucian of Samosata, *Peregr.* 12–13. For more detailed discussion of the gospel passages in the previous two paragraphs, see Osiek and MacDonald, *A Woman's Place*, 83. For full discussion of Celsus and Lucian of Samosata's account, see MacDonald, *Early Christian Women and Pagan Opinion*, 49–126.

88   As observed by Beverly Roberts Gaventa, "Finding a Place for Children in the Letters of Paul," in *The Child in the Bible* (ed. Marcia J. Bunge; Grand Rapids: Eerdmans, 2008), 234. As Gaventa notes, there are a few references to adult offspring. In Rom 16:13 Paul greets both Rufus and his mother, and in 1 Cor 5:1–5, Paul condemns the actions of a man who is living with his father's wife (apparently the stepmother). See Gaventa, "Finding a Place for Children," 233–35.

89   For a detailed discussion of translation and other issues discussed here, see MacDonald and Vaage, "Unclean but Holy Children," 526–46.

90   As noted by C. B. Horn and J. W. Martens, Paul is no longer concerned about the fate of the children by 1 Cor 7:16, and there are ambiguities in Paul's position. Without manuscript evidence, I would not go so far as Horn and Martens, however, as to suggest "that 1 Corinthians 7:12-16 contains two different solutions to the problem of mixed marriages, in which one or both of the statements on children of such marriages may reflect the Post-Pauline Church." See *"Let the little children come to me": Childhood and Children in Early Christianity* (Washington, D.C.: Catholic University of America Press, 2009), 105.

91   In agreement with Gaventa, I would understand references to churches meeting in the houses of believers (e.g., Rom 16:5) or to the extended households/families (e.g., Rom 16:10; 16:11) as including children. See Gaventa, "Finding a Place for Children," 234.

92   See esp. Reidar Aasgaard, "Like a Child: Paul's Rhetorical Uses of Childhood," in *The Child in the Bible* (ed. Marcia J. Bunge; Grand Rapids: Eerdmans, 2008), 249–77; but also Gaventa, "Finding a Place for Children," 233–48, in the same volume.

93   Aasgaard, "Like a Child," 265. On obedience see also O. Larry Yarbrough, "Parents and Children in the Letters of Paul," in *The Social World of the First Christians: Essays in Honor of Wayne A. Meeks* (ed. L. Michael White and O. Larry Yarbrough; Minneapolis: Fortress, 1995), 130–31.

94   See detailed discussion in chap. 4.

95   See detailed discussion in chap. 3.

96   On the theme of formation in Paul's letters, see Aasgaard, "Like a Child," 266–70.

97   On adoption see David L. Bartlett, "Adoption in the Bible," in *The Child in the Bible* (ed. Marcia J. Bunge; Grand Rapids: Eerdmans, 2008), 375–98.

98   Horn and Martens have drawn attention to later apocryphal literature in which the apostles are depicted as feeding their little ones milk (e.g., *Acts John* 45). See *"Let the little children come to me,"* 58.

99   As argued by Aasgaard, "Like a Child," 257–58.

100 This has been explored especially by Beverly Roberts Gaventa in *Our Mother Saint Paul* (Louisville: Westminster John Knox, 2007).

101 Aasgaard, "Like a Child," 258.

102 Reidar Aasgaard has offered the following insightful comment: "Thus what can be seen as rhetorical cleverness might just as likely be interpreted as the opposite, namely, as Paul here employing metaphors that in fact are not meant to enhance his authority *but to make him vulnerable and left to the mercy of his addressees*" ("Like a Child," 276, emphasis in original). On Paul's paradoxical expressions with respect to family and childhood, see also MacDonald and Vaage, "Unclean but Holy Children."

103 Over the past fifteen years, important volumes on Paul, politics, and empire edited by Richard Horsley have appeared. See Richard A. Horsley, ed., *Paul and Empire: Religion and Power in Roman Imperial Society* (Harrisburg, Pa.: Trinity International, 1997); *Paul and Politics: Ekklesia, Israel, Imperium, Interpretation. Essays in Honor of Krister Stendahl* (Harrisburg, Pa.: Trinity International, 2000); *Paul and the Roman Imperial Order* (Harrisburg, Pa.: Trinity International, 2004). Bringing together the work of several scholars on the setting of Paul's letters within the Roman imperial world, including its ideologies, these volumes have concentrated on the undisputed letters of Paul and therefore have paid comparatively little attention to the household codes.

104 See esp. N. Elliott, "Paul and the Politics of Empire," in *Paul and Politics: Ekklesia, Israel, Imperium, Interpretation* (ed. R. A. Horsley; Harrisburg, Pa.: Trinity, 2000), 26. See also N. Elliott's "The Anti-imperial message of the Cross," in *Paul and Empire: Religion and Power in Roman Imperial Society* (ed. R. A. Horsley; Harrisburg, Pa.: Trinity, 1997), 178; and *Liberating Paul: The Justice of God and the Politics of the Apostle* (Maryknoll, N.Y.: Orbis Books, 1994).

105 See, e.g., Harry O. Maier, "A Sly Civility: Colossians and Empire," *JSNT* 27 (2005): 323–49; Jerry L. Sumney, *Colossians: A Commentary* (NTL; Louisville, Ky.: John Knox, 2008); Margaret Y. MacDonald, "The Politics of Identity in Ephesians," *JSNT* 26 (2004): 419–44; see also Osiek and MacDonald, *A Woman's Place*, 118–43; Brian J. Walsh and Sylvia Keesmaat, *Colossians Remixed: Subverting the Empire* (Downers Grove, Ill.: InterVarsity, 2004). Most recently, see Harry O. Maier, *Picturing Paul in Empire: Imperial Image, Text, and Persuasion in Colossians, Ephesians, and the Pastoral Epistles* (Edinburgh: Bloomsbury, 2013).

106 This is the thesis of Harry Maier in "A Sly Civility."

107 See detailed discussion in chap. 2.

108 "Hidden transcript" is a concept developed by political theorist James C. Scott. Among the groups analyzed by Scott are the slaves of the U.S. South and their appropriation of texts like Eph 6:5-9. He points to the disjuncture between the deportment of slaves during public religious ceremonies and what happened away from surveillance with the use of devices that prevented sound from

carrying: "[A]n entirely different atmosphere reigned—one of release from the constant guardedness of domination, permitting shouts, clapping, and participation." Ephesians 6:5-9 might have called for "a plea for a sincere official transcript from slaves," but "the offstage Christianity . . . stressed the themes of deliverance, and redemption, Moses and the Promised Land, the Egyptian captivity, and emancipation" (James C. Scott, *Domination and the Arts of Resistance* [New Haven, Conn.: Yale University Press, 1990], 116). According to Jerry Sumney, Scott's theories should cause us to rethink the implications of the household codes. In comments on the code of Colossians, Sumney states: "The tension between what the code seems to require and what Colossians proclaims about the cosmos and believers' place in Christ, as well as some statements within the code itself . . . indicate that something other than the usual reading is in order." Sumney, *Colossians*, 237. He builds upon the earlier use of Scott by Walsh and Keesmaat in *Colossians Remixed*. Other scholars who have employed Scott in their analyses include, among others, David G. Horrell, *1 Peter* (London: T&T Clark, 2008); Warren Carter, "Going All the Way? Honoring the Emperor and Sacrificing Wives and Slaves in 1 Pet 2.13-3.6," in *A Feminist Companion to the Catholic Epistles and Hebrews* (ed. Amy-Jill Levine and Marya Mayo Robbins; London: T&T Clark, 2004), 14–33.

109   The difficulty of ascribing this type of scenario to the context of early Christianity, however, is that unlike the American South, where records of the speech and activities of the oppressed groups exist, "offstage" early Christianity can only be cautiously deduced from very fragmentary evidence. See esp. J. Albert Harrill, "Paul and Empire: Studying Roman Identity after the Cultural Turn," *Early Christianity* 2 (2011): 281–311, esp. 294–95, 309. On the theoretical implications of using Scott's theories for the study of the NT, see Richard A. Horsley, ed., *Hidden Transcripts and the Arts of Resistance: Applying the Work of James C. Scott to Jesus and Paul* (SemeiaSt 48; Atlanta: SBL, 2004).

110   This will be argued in detail in chap. 2.

111   The appeal to Scott's theories has tended to lead to a picture of greater internal consistency within NT documents (contradictory tendencies can be explained within the framework of a "hidden transcript") than some scholars would accept. See MacDonald, "Beyond Identification of the *Topos* of Household Management," 82.

112   Scott's theories and postcolonial analysis have been brought together, e.g., by David G. Horrell who argues that the author of 1 Peter is not purely conformist, even if he adopts a less radical, anti-imperial stance than the author of the book of Revelation. See *1 Peter*, 94. See also David G. Horrell, "Between Conformity and Resistance: Beyond the Balch-Elliott Debate towards a Postcolonial Reading of 1 Peter," in *Reading 1 Peter with New Eyes: Methodological Reassessments of the Letter of First Peter* (ed. Robert L. Webb and Betsy Bauman-Martin; Library of New Testament Studies; London: T&T Clark, 2007), 111–43.

113   R. S. Sugirtharajah, *Postcolonial Criticism and Biblical Interpretation* (Oxford:

Oxford University Press, 2002), 11. It should be noted that in recent years, feminist scholarship has increasingly engaged in dialogue with postcolonial scholarship. See esp. Elisabeth Schüssler Fiorenza, *The Power of the Word: Scripture and the Rhetoric of Empire* (Minneapolis: Fortress, 2007).

114 The most influential work has been Homi Bhabha, *The Location of Culture* (London: Routledge, 1994). For a theoretical discussion of the influence of Bhabha on NT scholars, see Stephen D. Moore, *Empire and Apocalypse: Postcolonialism and the New Testament* (Sheffield: Sheffield Phoenix, 2006). For specific examples of application of the theories of Bhabha, see Horrell, *1 Peter*; and "Between Conformity and Resistance"; Maier, "A Sly Civility"; Jennifer G. Bird, *Faithful Obedience: Reconsidering 1 Peter's Command to Wives* (London: T&T Clark, 2011).

115 See Homi Bhabha, "DissemiNation: Time, Narrative, and the Margins of the Modern Nation," in *Nation and Narration* (ed. Homi Bhabha; London: Routledge, 1990), 291–322; and *Location of Culture*, 129–38.

116 Bhabha, *Location of Culture*, 86 (emphasis in original).

117 Particularly intriguing is the idea that mimicry may in actual fact be a type of mockery. Bhabha, *Location of Culture*, 86.

118 According to Bhabha, hybridity is a type of "in-between" space: "A contingent, borderline experience opens up in-between colonizer and colonized. This is a space of cultural and interpretative undecidability" (Bhabha, *Location of Culture*, 206).

119 To some extent I am building upon the work of other scholars. Maier, e.g., argues that Colossians offers a "hybrid vision" wherein the *Haustafel* plays an important role. See Maier, "A Sly Civility," 349. See also MacDonald, "Beyond Identification of the *Topos* of Household Management," 80–81.

120 The programmatic essay was Bernadette J. Brooten, "Early Christian Women and Their Cultural Context: Issues of Method in Historical Reconstruction," in *Feminist Perspectives on Biblical Scholarship* (ed. Adela Yarbro Collins; Chico, Calif.: Scholars Press, 1985), 65–91. Such sentiments were at the heart of the development of the interdisciplinary field of women's studies, which to some extent are finding a parallel today in the emerging field of childhood studies. See, e.g., Mary Jane Kehily, ed., *An Introduction to Childhood Studies* (Maidenhead, UK: Open University Press, McGraw-Hill International, 2004); Dominic Wyse, ed., *Childhood Studies: An Introduction* (Oxford: Blackwell, 2004). For a theoretical discussion of how the interest in children and childhood across disciplines is influencing scholarship on early Christianity, see esp. Reidar Aasgaard, "Children in Antiquity and Early Christianity: Research History and Central Issues," *Familia* [Salamanca, Spain] 33 (2006): 23–46.

121 In the past fifteen years, there has been a definite move, especially under the influence of literary methods and rhetorical analysis and studies of the ancient novel, in the direction of significant pessimism with respect to the recovery of women's social experience. A programmatic essay has been that of Elizabeth A. Clark, "The Lady Vanishes: Dilemmas of a Feminist Historian after

the 'Linguistic Turn,'" *CH* 67 (1998): 1–31. It is worth noting that the ground-breaking historian on women and religion in the ancient world Ross Shepard Kraemer has clearly been influenced by the linguistic turn and has changed her mind on a variety of historical issues, admitting that she may have been "too optimistic about our ability to describe ancient social realities" in her earlier book *Her Share of the Blessings*. See Ross Shepard Kraemer, *Unreliable Witnesses: Religion, Gender, and History in the Greco-Roman Mediterranean* (Oxford: Oxford University Press, 2011), 6. See also Ross S. Kraemer, *Her Share of the Blessings: Women's Religions among Pagans, Jews, and Christians in the Roman World* (Oxford: Oxford University Press, 1993). On the importance of paying attention to metaphor and other literary devices in the study of children in early Christianity, see Gaventa, "Finding a Place for Children"; Aasgaard, "Like a Child."

122   See full discussions in chaps. 3 and 4.

Chapter 2

1   On the basis of Jewish (including rabbinic), Roman, and Greek sources, Horn and Martens write the following: "For males in Rome, most commentators point to the accession of a youth to the *toga virilis* at about the age of seventeen. In Greek areas youth seems to have come to an end and adulthood begun with a boy's ability to enter into the body politic as well as his entrance into the army. This would put the end of childhood at seventeen or eighteen. In a Jewish setting, a boy's transition to adulthood seems to have been completed between the ages of eighteen and twenty. . . . In all of the cultures we have examined, the basic point of transition to adulthood for girls was puberty, which was generally defined as occurring between twelve and fourteen, although sometimes girls were married at an earlier age" (Horn and Martens, *"Let the little children come to me,"* 18).

2   Rawson, *Children and Childhood in Roman Italy*, 135.

3   See Margaret Y. MacDonald, *Colossians and Ephesians* (SP 17; Collegeville, Minn.: Liturgical, 2000), 111.

4   See detailed discussion in chap. 4.

5   See, e.g., the seven stages of life of Hippocrates (fifth to fourth centuries BCE): infant, child, lad or teenager, young man, man, older man, and old man. These are discussed by the first-century Hellenistic Jewish author Philo of Alexandria in *Opif.* 103–4, who gives his own version of stages of childhood as part of the whole life course. As Horn and Martens point out, male physiology is at the heart of this discussion in both Hippocrates and Philo, with female development being apparently of no interest. According to Philo, the boy progresses from childhood to youth at about fourteen, which culminates finally in the growing of a beard and increasing strength, the ability to produce offspring and found a family. See Horn and Martens, *"Let the little children come to me,"* 6–7, commenting on *Opif.*

103–4. Other examples include Horace, *Ars* 156–78, and Seneca, *Ep.* 121, as discussed in Rawson, *Children and Childhood in Roman Italy*, 137.

6   Horn and Martens examine evidence from the Mishnah; see *"Let the little children come to me,"* 14. With respect to the education of girls, however, there is interesting evidence contained in the Damascus Document to be examined in chap. 3. See also Quintilian (*Inst.* 1.1.18) as discussed by Rawson in *Children and Childhood in Roman Italy*, 141.

7   Rawson, *Children and Childhood in Roman Italy*, 137 (citing Horace, *Ars* 156–78).

8   Rawson, *Children and Childhood in Roman Italy*, 142.

9   Rawson, *Children and Childhood in Roman Italy*, 145.

10   This is a key factor in the interpretation of the Pastoral Epistles. See chap. 4.

11   See chap. 1.

12   Rawson, *Children and Childhood in Roman Italy*, 141, citing H. G. Knothe, "Zur 7-Jahresgrenze der 'Infantia' im antiken römischen Recht," *Studia et Documenta Historiae et Iuris* 48 (1982): 239–56.

13   Laes, *Children in the Roman Empire*, 153–54.

14   Laes, *Children in the Roman Empire*, 156.

15   See *CIL* 6.6182, cited in Laes, *Children in the Roman Empire*, 190. In this paragraph I am following closely my discussion in my 2011 Presidential Address for the Canadian Society of Biblical Studies, "Making Room for the Little Ones: How New Research on Children and Slaves in Roman World Is Changing What We Think about the History of Early Christian Women" (published in *Bulletin 2011/12: The Canadian Society of Biblical Studies* 71 [2012]: 1–25).

16   See A. Wallace-Hadrill, "Houses and Households: Sampling Pompeii and Herculaneum," in *Marriage, Divorce, and Children in Ancient Rome* (ed. Beryl Rawson; Oxford: Clarendon, 1991), 191–227; *Houses and Society in Pompeii and Herculaneum* (Princeton, N.J.: Princeton University Press, 1994).

17   Beryl Rawson identifies such circumstances as underlying Celsus' description of the early Christian meetings (*Cels.* 3.55). See *Children and Childhood in Roman Italy*, 216.

18   Rawson, *Children and Childhood in Roman Italy*, 216. See also M. B. Flory, "Family in *familia*: Kinship and Community in Slavery," *American Journal of Ancient History* 3 (1978): 78–95.

19   Rawson, *Children and Childhood in Roman Italy*, 216.

20   W. Scheidel, "The Demographic Background," in *Growing Up Fatherless in Antiquity* (ed. S. R. Huebner and D. M. Razan; Cambridge: Cambridge University Press, 2009), 38–40. Cited in Henrik Mouritsen, "The Families of the Roman Slaves and Freedmen," in *A Companion to Families in the Greek and Roman Worlds* (ed. Beryl Rawson; Oxford: Blackwell, 2011), 129–44 (134). As Mouritsen notes, however, such assessments of the paternity of slave children remain a matter of debate.

21   There are several female slaves mentioned in early Christian literature, including the female slave with the spirit of divination at Philippi (Acts 16:16-19), the

doorkeeper in the house of Mary in Jerusalem (Acts 12:12-13), and the two *ancillae* called *ministrae* who are tortured by Pliny the Younger for information (*Ep.* 10.96). *The Acts of the Martyrs of Lyons and Vienne* (Eusebius, *Hist. eccl.* 5.1.2–63) refers to Blandina, the heroic figure of Lyons. For more examples and fuller discussion of the circumstances of Felicitas in *The Martyrdom of Perpetua and Felicitas*, see Osiek and MacDonald, *A Woman's Place*, 108.

22 See esp. Martin, "Slave Families and Slaves in Families."

23 Mouritsen, "The Families of the Roman Slaves and Freedmen," 138.

24 Mouritsen, "The Families of the Roman Slaves and Freedmen," 142–43.

25 Janet Hutchinson, "Picturing the Roman Family," in *A Companion to Families in the Greek and Roman Worlds* (ed. Beryl Rawson; Oxford: Blackwell, 2011), 521–41 (533). She comments specifically on the tomb relief from via Po, Rome, Augustan period.

26 Here it is helpful to consider the postcolonial concept of mimicry. See Bhabha, *Location of Culture*, 86. See detailed discussion in chap. 1.

27 Even the presence of the husbands of unbelieving wives cannot be ruled out entirely, though such a circumstance is rarely seen in early Christian literature.

28 The obedience of children is a virtue shared universally by pagans, Jews, and Christians. See discussion in chap. 1.

29 This has been recognized by Aletti in *Saint Paul*, 250.

30 Laes, *Children in the Roman Empire*, 164.

31 Véronique Dasen, "Childbirth and Infancy in Greek and Roman Antiquity," in *A Companion to Families in the Greek and Roman Worlds* (ed. Beryl Rawson; Oxford: Blackwell, 2011), 291–314, 309. See also Rawson, *Children and Childhood in Roman Italy*, 123.

32 See, e.g., Soranus, *Gynecology* 2.18–20.

33 Ps.-Plutarch, *Mor.* 3E [*Lib. ed.*].

34 For more detailed discussion see Osiek and MacDonald, *A Woman's Place*, 64–65.

35 Quintilian, *Inst.* 1.1.4–5, 8.

36 Seneca, *Ep.* 94.8–9.

37 See Rawson, *Children and Childhood in Roman Italy*, 214, citing Seneca, *Ep.* 94.8.

38 Rawson, *Children and Childhood in Roman Italy*, 154–56. On the education of slave children, see also 187–91. See Nepos, *Att.* 14.

39 There is no explicit reference to a communal meal in Colossians, but attitudes to food and consumption are certainly linked to communal identity. This is a matter of dispute within the community, and asceticism appears to be an aspect of the false teaching (Col 2:16, 21).

40 Quintilian, *Inst.* 1.2.8.

41 Minucius Felix, *Oct.* 8–9. The early Christian author Minucius Felix responded to this critique in his apologetic work, probably from the late second century, known as *Octavius*.

42   Origen, *Cels.* 3.5.

43   Origen cited Celsus in order to denounce his arguments. Despite the polemical context, a leading historian of the Roman family describes the setting depicted by Celsus as in keeping with ancient household and work arrangements and offering evidence of children frequenting slaves' quarters and neighborhood workshops. See Rawson, *Children and Childhood in Roman Italy*, 215–16.

44   See esp. John M. G. Barclay, "Paul, Philemon, and the Dilemma of Christian Slave Ownership," *NTS* 37 (1991): 161–86.

45   See, e.g., Chris Frilingos, "'For My Child Onesimus': Paul and Domestic Power in Philemon," *JBL* 119 (2000): 91–104; Scott S. Elliott, "'Thanks, but No Thanks': Tact, Persuasion, and the Negotiation of Power in Paul's Letter to Philemon," *NTS* 57 (2011): 51–64; Joseph H. Marshall, "The Usefulness of an Onesimus: The Sexual Use of Slaves and Paul's Letter to Philemon," *JBL* 130 (2011): 749–70.

46   There is a complicated relationship between Paul's letter to Philemon and Colossians that has figured prominently in the debate about the authenticity of Colossians. Particularly significant is the fact that the closing remarks of Col 4:7-18 closely resemble Phlm 23–24. Defenders of the authenticity of Colossians argue on the basis of this fact that both Onesimus and his master Philemon were from Colossae and that the two documents were written at roughly the same time. But it is also the case that the close relationship could also result from Colossians being composed very soon after Paul's death, or it could be based on an attempt to gain a hearing for the letter as a message from Paul. See MacDonald, *Colossians and Ephesians*, 7–10, 177–89.

47   For textual and grammatical considerations leading to this conclusion, see MacDonald, *Colossians and Ephesians*, 179.

48   In fact, it has recently been argued that the references to the usefulness of Onesimus in Phlm 11 should be read in light of a culture in which the sexual utility of slaves was taken for granted. In his highly original study, Marshall focuses on the presence of *chrēstos* terminology (usefulness) in ancient literature generally to refer to the sexual use of slaves. This terminology appears in Phlm 11 but has not previously been understood in this way. One potential problem with the theory, however, is the flexible use of this terminology, including its use in reference to the situation of slaves in 1 Cor 7:21, in which it clearly has different meaning altogether. I would like to thank Carolyn Osiek for pointing this out to me. Also potentially problematic for Marshall's interpretation is the clear association of the sexual use of slaves with the slave's lack of honor, which seems counter to other indications in early Christian texts as discussed below in nn. 100 and 101. See Marshall, "The Usefulness of an Onesimus," 760.

49   See, e.g., Carolyn Osiek, "Female Slaves, *Porneia*, and the Limits of Obedience," in *Early Christian Families in Context: An Interdisciplinary Dialogue* (ed. David L. Balch and Carolyn Osiek; Grand Rapids: Eerdmans, 2003), 269–70. In a detailed study, Jennifer Glancy goes further and suggests that in a society

in which slaves were viewed as morally neutral sexual outlets, Paul's command to "obtain a vessel" in 1 Thess 4:3-8 would be taken as a reference to a slave vessel. In other words, Paul's lack of explicit treatment according to Glancy should be understood as general acceptance of a cultural norm. See Jennifer A. Glancy, *Slavery in Early Christianity* (Oxford: Oxford University Press, 2002), 62.

50 Seneca, *Ep.* 47.8 (Gummere, LCL). In the most extreme cases, castration was employed to preserve boyish beauty and the emergence of the first beard. See Statius' description of the Emperor Domitian's favorite slave, Earinus, in *Silvae* 3.4. See Christian Laes, "*Delicia*-Children Revisited: The Evidence of Statius' *Silvae*," in *Children, Memory, and Family Identity in Roman Culture* (ed. V. Dasen and T. Späth; Oxford: Oxford University Press, 2010), 262–63. See further discussion of *delicia* children below in n. 55.

51 See the frequently cited comments of Seneca the Elder in which he defines the status of the slave in relation to the freeborn in terms of the necessity of sexual service of the master (Seneca the Elder, *Disputes* 4, pref. 10).

52 See, e.g., *Ben.* 3.17; *Ira.* 32. For further examples see Thomas Wiedemann, *Greek and Roman Slavery* (Baltimore, Md.: Johns Hopkins University, 1981), 224–51.

53 See discussion below in nn. 91–92.

54 Christian Laes, "Desperately Different? *Delicia* Children in the Roman Household," in *Early Christian Families in Context: An Interdisciplinary Dialogue* (ed. David L. Balch and Carolyn Osiek; Grand Rapids: Eerdmans, 2003), 318.

55 For use of the specific terminology, see, e.g., Martial, *Epigrams* 7.14. For other evidence see discussion in Laes, "Desperately Different," 318–19.

56 Laes, "Desperately Different," 20.

57 For the flexible and somewhat ambiguous use of the terminology, see Laes, "Desperately Different," 311–14. For a thorough analysis of the complex emotional components inherent in some relations with *delicia*, which were essentially pseudo-adoptions with no sexual relations (even if literary descriptions carry erotic overtones), see Christian Laes' examination of the evidence on *delicia* children offered by the Roman poet Publius Papanius Statius (45–96 CE) in "*Delicia*-Children Revisited," 244–71.

58 Laes, "Desperately Different," 321.

59 For survey of the evidence in Laes, "Desperately Different," see 322–23. Without coming to firm conclusions, Laes offers interesting theories about the absence of references to *delicia* in Christian sources.

60 Musonius Rufus, *Fragment* 12. A similar line of argument is made by Ambrose, who speaks of the destabilizing influence of masters forming relations with slave women, including the jealousy of the wives. See Ambrose, *Abr.* 1.4.

61 Trans. by Cora E. Lutz, "Musonius Rufus: The Roman Socrates," *Yale Classical Studies* 10 (1947): 32–47.

62 For the inscription see SIG 3.985, included with Greek text and interpretative notes in Franciszek Sokolwski, *Lois sacrées de l'Asie Mineure* (Paris: Boccard, 1955), 53–58. For the English translation cited in this essay and detailed

discussion of the meaning of the text, see S. C. Barton and G. H. R. Horsley, "A Hellenistic Cult Group and the New Testament Churches," *JAC* 24 (1981): 7–41. See also Stanley K. Stowers, "A Cult from Philadelphia: Oikos Religion or Cultic Association," in *The Early Church in Its Context: Essays in Honor of Everett Ferguson* (ed. Abraham J. Malherbe, Frederick W. Norris, and James W. Thompson; SNT 90; Leiden: Brill, 1998), 287–301. The following two paragraphs offer a condensed version of my argument in "Slavery, Sexuality and House Churches: A Reassessment of Colossians 3.18–4.1 in Light of New Research on the Roman Family," *NTS* 53 (2007): 98–100.

63 A detailed comparison between the inscription and Col 3:18–4:1 has been undertaken by Angela Standhartinger in "The Origin and Intention of the Household Code," 117–30.

64 Verses 25–27 of translation by Barton and Horsley in "A Hellenistic Cult Group."

65 See, e.g., Stowers, "A Cult from Philadelphia," 288–93.

66 Verses 20–21 of translation by Barton and Horsley in "A Hellenistic Cult Group."

67 William R. Shoedel, *Ignatius of Antioch: A Commentary on the Letters of Ignatius of Antioch* (Philadelphia: Fortress, 1985), 271.

68 In his 2003 (LCL) translation of this work, Bart. D. Ehrman, renders the expression as follows: "Do not engage in pederasty." In fact, *Did.* 2.2 closely resembles the language from the Philadelphian inscription cited above: "Do not engage in pederasty, do not engage in sexual immorality. Do not steal, do not practice magic, do not use enchanted potions, do not abort a fetus or kill a child that is born." The same Greek terminology to refer to the sexual corruption of children appears in Justin, *Dial.* 95 to refer to the sins of the nations.

69 The reference to corruption of what God has created has often been taken as prohibition against abortion, but other interpretations related to the ruin of children are possible especially given the use of similar terminology in *Did.* 2.2 and the general association of the language with moral depravity. See also relevant texts in the Epistle to Barnabas (*Barn.* 10.6–8; 19.4) as discussed in chap. 1. See also Laes, *Children in the Roman Empire*, 270–72, for discussion of later evidence.

70 With respect to the protection of children, see also discussion of gospel material in chap. 1.

71 See MacDonald, *Colossians and Ephesians*, 135.

72 On the setting of a moral standard in Colossians, see Barclay, "Ordinary but Different," 34–45.

73 Justin, *2 Apol.* 2.

74 *Ant. rom.* 2.26.1. See detailed discussion in chap. 1.

75 *Ant. rom.* 2.27.1–2.

76 See Laes, "*Delicia*-Children Revisited," 253.

77 Statius, *Silvae* 2.1. 172–73. See Laes, "*Delicia*-Children Revisited," 253.

78 See Glancy, *Slavery in Early Christianity*, 59.

79 *The Governance of God* 7.4, trans. Wiedemann, *Greek and Roman Slavery*, 179.

80 This could refer to slaves remaining faithful within their marriages or slaves responsible for other slaves, as in the case of slave managers (bailiffs).

81 For a discussion of ambiguities in this text, see MacDonald, *Colossians and Ephesians*, 158–59. See also MacDonald, "Slavery, Sexuality and House Churches," 104–5.

82 See Craig A. Williams, *Roman Homosexuality: Ideologies of Masculinity in Classical Antiquity* (Oxford: Oxford University Press, 1999), 141.

83 Cato the Elder, *Agr.* 143, trans. Jane F. Gardner and Thomas Wiedemann, *The Roman Household: A Sourcebook* (London: Routledge, 1991), 82.

84 Columella, *Rust.* 1.8.10., trans. Gardner and Weidemann, *The Roman Household*, 81.

85 The parallels between the household codes and the agricultural handbooks have been of special interest to J. Albert Harrill in *Slaves and the New Testament*. See esp. 107–8n83, 239–40.

86 Columella, *Rust.* 1.8.2–3.

87 Columella, *Rust.* 1.8.4.

88 Statius, *Silv.* 2.6.15–17. Cited by Laes in "*Delicia*-Children Revisited," 256.

89 See J. Albert Harrill, "The Domestic Enemy: A Moral Polarity of Household Slaves in Early Christian Apologies and Martyrdoms," in *Early Christian Families in Context: An Interdisciplinary Dialogue* (ed. David L. Balch and Carolyn Osiek; Grand Rapids: Eerdmans, 2003), 233. On the tenuous nature of masculinity, see Williams, *Roman Homosexuality*, 141.

90 Ps.-Plutarch, *Mor.* 4F [*Lib. ed.*] (Babbitt, LCL).

91 Seneca's terminology here is significant. Here *delicium* seems to refer mainly to the fact that the slave had been selected specially as a playmate for the young Seneca. See Laes, "Desperately Different," 303.

92 Seneca, *Ep.* 12.3 (Gummere, LCL).

93 Statius, *Silv.* 2.1.135–6. Cited in Laes, "*Delicia*-Children Revisited," 253.

94 *CIL* 6.18754. Cited in Laes, "*Delicia*-Children Revisited," 249.

95 *CIL* 6.22972, translated by and cited in Rawson, *Children and Childhood in Roman Italy*, 259.

96 For interpretation of these images see Rawson, *Children and Childhood in Roman Italy*, 260–61.

97 See Laes, "*Delicia*-Children Revisited," 249.

98 Many scholars have been influenced by the theories of James C. Scott on the "hidden transcript." See esp. Sumney, *Colossians*; Walsh and Keesmaat, *Colossians Remixed*. See also the discussion in chap. 1.

99 See Glancy, *Slavery in Early Christianity*, for analysis of Paul's complex use of slavery, kinship, and adoption imagery in Galatians 3–4.

100 See Sumney, *Colossians*, 108.

101 See Richard Saller, "Women Slaves and the Economy of the Roman

Household," in *Early Christian Families in Context: An Interdisciplinary Dialogue* (ed. David L. Balch and Carolyn Osiek; Grand Rapids: Eerdmans, 2003), 196.

102 This is a good example of what has been labeled as hybridity in postcolonial analysis: the colonized absorb and transform ideologies of colonial (in this case Roman imperial) power. See discussion in chap. 1.

103 See Rawson, *Children and Childhood in Roman Italy*, 53.

104 See R. R. R. Smith, "The Imperial Reliefs from the Sebasteion at Aphrodisias," *JRS* 77 (1987): 88–138, esp. 110. With slightly different interests, the Sebasteion has been compared with Colossians in an excellent article: Maier, "A Sly Civility." Offering a somewhat different interpretation of the visual imagery of the barbarian boy captive, see Rosemary Canavan, *Clothing the Body of Christ at Colossae* (WUNT 2/334; Tübingen: Mohr Siebeck, 2012), 123–25.

105 This has been noted by Douglas A. Campbell. See "Unravelling Colossians 3.11b," *NTS* 42 (1996): 120–32. He argues that "barbarian" and Scythians are actually opposing terms like "slave" and "free." In this case, "barbarian" would be a reference to free local populations such as Lydians, Phrygians, and Pisidians, who were slave owners. On the Scythians, see Strabo, *Geogr.* 7.3.12, and Horace, *Saec.* 53–56. On Ephesus as a port of entry for slaves, see Varro, *The Latin Language* 7.9.

106 This has been noted by Glancy in *Slavery in Early Christianity*, 77–78. Many have dated Colossians to approximately this period. See Josephus, *J.W.* 6.379–86.

107 Statius, *Silv.* 3.4.32–34. Cited in Laes, "*Delicia*-Children Revisited," 261.

108 Josephus, *B.J.* 7.384–87 (Thackeray, LCL). For a second reference to the violation of women and enslavement of children, see Josephus, *B.J.* 7.334–35.

109 On the concept of multiple identities as applied to slaves in early Christianity, see esp. Martin, "Slave Families and Slaves in Families."

110 This has been noted by David L. Balch, who drew attention to the sustained interest among the neopythagorean moralists (arguably the closest parallels to the NT household codes) in linking house loyalty and civic loyalty. See Balch, "Neopythagorean Moralists," 380–411, esp. 395.

111 See Mary Rose D'Angelo, "Colossians," in *Searching the Scriptures 2: A Feminist Commentary* (ed. Elisabeth Schüssler Fiorenza; New York: Crossroad, 1994), 313–24.

112 See, e.g., Ps.-Plutarch, *Mor.* 8F *[Lib. ed.]*; Ps.-Phoc. 207.

113 E.g., Herm. *Vis* 2.4.3; Ign. *Smyrn* 6.2.

114 Aristides, *Apology* 15.

115 *The Martyrdom of Perpetua and Felicitas*. See full discussion in Osiek and Mac-Donald, *A Woman's Place*, 47.

116 For an interpretation of Col 4:1 that identifies countercultural elements, see, e.g., Standhartinger, "The Origin and Intention of the Household Code," 127–28. She understands the term *isotēs* as the interpretative key to the whole letter. Scholars have paid particular attention to the meaning of *isotēs*, as it can actually mean equality (although it is most often translated as fairness, see

BAGD 381). This is how Philo of Alexandria uses the term when he refers to the absence of slaves among the Essenes (Philo, *Prob.* 79; cf. *Spec.* 2.66–68). But for the reasons outlined above, it seems more likely that the term refers to some type of equity in the treatment of slaves, rather than true equality.

117 Verses 30–40. See Barton and Horsley, "A Hellenistic Cult Group," 22. Barton and Horsley draw our attention to an interesting linguistic parallel with Colossians. There are particularly dire consequences for married free women failing to live up to moral ideals outlined in the inscription. Her lack of commitment is described as one of being "unworthy to reverence (*sebesthai*) this god." A related term (*phobeō*) is used in the description of the ultimate priority of slaves in Col 4.22. See Barton and Horsley, 14n28. For more detailed discussion, see MacDonald, "Slavery, Sexuality and House Churches," 103.

118 The idea of slaves as moral agents has, however, been questioned. See Harrill, *Slaves in the New Testament*, 85–87.

119 Other theories have been put forward. See Harrill, *Slaves in the New Testament*, 91.

120 Here the insights of postcolonial analysis may prove useful in helping us to understand the circumstances of the most vulnerable members of the community—the slave children—and the reason for the proclamation of traditional familial ethics in the household code genre that begins with Colossians. These ethical exhortations offer insights into what theorist Homi Bhabha calls the "borderline experience": "The margin of hybridity where cultural differences 'contingently' and conflictually touch, become moments of panic which reveals the borderline experience." See Bhabha, *Location of Culture*, 207. See also the discussion of postcolonial analysis in chap. 1.

121 The tendency to celebrate heavenly enthronement and citizenship becomes even more pronounced in Ephesians. The relationship between this tendency and household code discourse will be examined in more detail in chap. 3.

Chapter 3

1 See discussion in Balla, *The Child-Parent Relationship*, 74–75. It is interesting here to consider the testimony of Epictetus who, like the author of Colossians, recommends that children obey their parents "in everything," but at the same time cautions that the philosopher's commitment to the "good" should represent the top priority (*Diatr.* 2.10.7). See Balla, *The Child-Parent Relationship*, 175.

2 It should be noted that "in the Lord" (*en kyriō*) may not have been part of the original text as it is absent from several early manuscript witnesses. However, on balance, the longer reading is preferred. For evaluation of the evidence see MacDonald, *Colossians and Ephesians*, 332.

3 Here the presentation of the formation in the faith of Timothy in the Pastoral Epistles is particularly noteworthy. See 2 Tim 1:5; 3:15; see also chap. 4 in this volume.

4   See, e.g., Ps.-Plutarch, *Mor.* 8F [*Lib. ed.*]; Ps.-Phoc. 207.

5   Social constructionism has had a broad impact on many fields, including soci-
     ology and social psychology, and draws its origins especially from the seminal
     study of Peter L. Berger and Thomas A. Luckmann. See *The Social Construction
     of Reality* (Garden City N.Y.: Doubleday, 1966). For development of the inter-
     disciplinary theoretical perspectives, see, e.g., V. Burr, *Social Constructionism*
     (2nd ed.; London: Routledge, 2003). For more detail on how a social construc-
     tionist approach might shed light on Colossians and Ephesians, see Margaret
     Y. MacDonald, "Parenting, Surrogate Parenting and Teaching: Reading the
     Household Codes as Sources for Understanding Socialization and Education
     in Early Christian Communities," in *Theologische und soziologische Perspektiven
     auf früheristliche Lebenswelten* (ed. Dorothee Dettinger and Christof Land-
     messer; Leipzig: Evangelische Verlagsanstalt, 2014), 85–102.

6   Berger and Luckmann, *Social Construction of Reality*, 76–77. For a study of the
     applicability of these concepts to the life of the early church, see Margaret
     Y. MacDonald, *The Pauline Churches: A Socio-historical Study of the Institution-
     alization in the Pauline and Deutero-Pauline Writings* (Cambridge: Cambridge
     University Press, 1988).

7   This "taken for granted" quality, which has emerged so clearly in scholarly com-
     parisons to other ancient texts that reflect the household management theme,
     is one of the reasons why household code teaching is often characterized as
     thoroughly conventional with only a thin veneer of Christian ethos.

8   See full discussion of the significance of this text in the chap. 2.

9   The perspective of social constructionism draws attention to a balance between
     stability and fluidity in social construction as one moves from one community
     setting to another. On this dynamic see Kenneth J. Gergen, *An Invitation to
     Social Constructionism* (2nd ed.; London: Sage, 2009), 50.

10   Scholars adopting social constructionist approaches have been influenced by
     thinkers such as Michel Foucault. See Burr, *Social Constructionism*, 8

11   Burr, *Social Constructionism*, 9.

12   See more detailed discussion of this point in chap. 2.

13   On the multiple identities of slaves based especially on inscriptional evidence,
     see, e.g., Martin, "Slave Families and Slaves in Families." Here and in the next
     few paragraphs I am following closely the discussion in MacDonald, "Parent-
     ing, Surrogate Parenting and Teaching," 88–89, 92–93. See also chap. 2.

14   As indeed Ann-Cathrin Harders has done in "Roman Patchwork Families:
     Surrogate Parenting, Socialization, and the Shaping of Tradition," in *Chil-
     dren, Memory, and Family Identity in Roman Culture* (ed. Véronique Dasen and
     Thomas Späth; Oxford: Oxford University Press, 2010), 53.

15   Harders, "Roman Patchwork Families," 53.

16   The wet nurse offers one of the best examples of the influence of nonkin rela-
     tions and extended family to the experience of childhood in antiquity. Dasen,

"Childbirth and Infancy in Greek and Roman Antiquity," 309. See also Rawson, *Children and Childhood in Roman Italy*, 123.

17   Harders, "Roman Patchwork Families," 53, citing Berger and Luckmann, *Social Construction of Reality*, 129–37.

18   Soranus, *Gynecology* 2.18–20; Ps.-Plutarch, *Mor.* 3E [*Lib. ed.*].

19   On the selection of appropriate slave playmates to be brought up with a child, see Quintilian, *Inst.* 1.1.4–5, 8. For more detailed discussion see chap. 2 of this volume and Osiek and MacDonald, *A Woman's Place*, 64–65.

20   See Rawson, *Children and Childhood in Roman Italy*, 214, citing Seneca, *Ep.* 94.8. See also discussion in chap. 2 of this volume.

21   Rawson, *Children and Childhood in Roman Italy*, 154–56. On the education of slave children, see also 187–91. In intellectual homes, slave children sometimes received literary training, going on to establish their own literary careers as librarians, tutors, and skilled readers (Nepos, *Att.* 14).

22   It is interesting here to consider the role of Onesimus, who may well be the runaway slave about whom Paul writes to Philemon, who is described as a member of the Colossian community. Apparently, together with Tychicus (Col 4:7-9), Onesimus is delivering Paul's letter to the Colossians. While Onesimus' role appears to be somewhat secondary to that of Tychicus, both are presented as prepared to tell the Colossians "about everything" (Col 4:9), implying a further explanatory role in relation to the letter. See MacDonald, *Colossians and Ephesians*, 179. See also chap. 2 of this volume.

23   See Francesca Prescendi, "Children and the Transmission of Religious Knowledge," in *Children, Memory, and Family Identity in Roman Culture* (ed. Véronique Dasen and Thomas Späth; Oxford: Oxford University Press, 2010), 73–93; on children singing see esp. 82–83. There is also evidence that children sang at private gatherings, although the use of the word *pueri* makes it impossible to determine whether slaves or children are in view.

24   The strong reinforcement of the authority of the *pater familias* in law and in moral ideals is well known in the Roman world, and the household codes reflect this cultural priority. See discussion in chap. 2. Here and in the next few paragraphs I am following closely the discussion in MacDonald, "Parenting, Surrogate Parenting and Teaching," 93–95.

25   See esp. Seneca, *De providentia* 1.5–6, as discussed by Francesca Mencacci, "*Modestia* vs. *licencia*: Seneca on Childhood and Status in the Roman Family," in *Children, Memory, and Family Identity in Roman Culture* (ed. Véronique Dasen and Thomas Späth; Oxford: Oxford University Press, 2010), 223–25.

26   See John M. G. Barclay, "The Family as the Bearer of Religion," in *Constructing Early Christian Families* (ed. H. Moxnes; London: Routledge, 1997), 77.

27   Prescendi, "Children and Transmission of Religious Knowledge," 73–75, citing esp. Ovid, *Fast.* 5.431–2; Ps.-Plutarch, *Mor.* 9E [*Lib. ed.*].

28   See detailed discussion in chap. 4.

29   Prescendi, "Children and the Transmission of Religious Knowledge," 77, citing

Plutarch, *Cat. Maj.* 20. For the emphasis placed on the education of sons, see also Harders, "Roman Patchwork Families," 49–59.

30　Prescendi, "Children and the Transmission of Religious Knowledge," 78, citing Xenophon, *Anab.* 5.6.29.

31　On these dynamics see Harders, "Roman Patchwork Families," 52.

32　Epictetus, *Diatr.* 2.10.7 (Oldfather, LCL).

33　Josephus, *C. Ap.* 2.174. Here and in the next few paragraphs I am following closely the discussion in MacDonald, "Parenting, Surrogate Parenting and Teaching," 96–99.

34　Josephus, *C. Ap.* 2.181.

35　Josephus, *C. Ap.* 2.217. According to Shier and Reinhartz, Josephus' comments reflect familiarity with the Roman concept of *patria potestas*, which gave the *pater familias* absolute (life and death) authority over the members of his household, especially his children. See Reinhartz and Shier, "Josephus on Children and Childhood," 370.

36　Josephus, *C. Ap.* 1.60 (Thackeray, LCL).

37　Josephus, *C. Ap.* 2.202 (Thackeray, LCL). The language of Pseudo-Phocylides is particularly striking: "A woman should not destroy the unborn babe in her belly, nor after its birth throw it before dogs and the vultures of prey." The translation is from Horst, *The Sentences of Pseudo-Phocylides*, p. 232, II.184–85. See also Philo, *De Spec.* 3.119. Scholars have warned, however, that these statements may be more prescriptive than descriptive. See A. Reinhartz, "Philo on Infanticide," *Studia Philonica Annual* 4 (1992): 42–58.

38　Josephus, *C. Ap.* 2.204. For more extensive discussion of the role of children in Josephus' apologetic discourse, with parallel texts from Philo of Alexandria, see MacDonald, "A Place of Belonging," 267–88.

39　See Origen, *Cels.* 3.55; see also 3.44.

40　See Origen, *Cels.* 3.50. On how Celsus' discourse presents Christianity as violating the ideals of masculinity, see Osiek and MacDonald, *A Woman's Place*, 134–35.

41　*1 Clem.* 21.8–9 (Ehrman, LCL). The commitment to instruct children surfaces in the deuteropauline works and finds further articulation in the teaching of the Apostolic Fathers (e.g., 2 Tim 3.15; *1 Clem.* 21.6, 8; *Did.* 4.9; Pol. *Phil.* 4.2; Herm. *Vis.* 2.4.3).

42　Philo, *Decal.* 107.

43　Sir 3:1-8.

44　Josephus, *C. Ap.*, 2.217, citing Deut 21:18-21.

45　See esp. Exod 21:15, 17; Prov 19:26; 20:20; 28:24; Mark 7:9-13; Matt 15:4-6. See MacDonald, "A Place of Belonging," 283. That these exhortations refer primarily to adult children has been argued by M. Gärtner, *Die Familienerziehung in der alten Kirche* (Cologne: Bohlau, 1985), 36–37.

46　Josephus, *Ant.* 4.260–63. See L. H. Feldman, trans. and ed., *Jewish Antiquities* (Boston, Mass.: Brill, 2004).

47 See *Laudatio Turiae* LS 8393, col. i, 11.30–33. Cited in Geoffrey S. Nathan, *The Family in Late Antiquity: The Rise of Christianity and the Endurance of Tradition* (London: Routledge, 2000), 196. As can be witnessed, e.g., in the famous inscription celebrating the feminine virtue and long *univera* marriage (married only once) of the matron Turia, the *Laudatia Turiae*, the obedience of young children is closely linked to ideals about their prospective treatment of their parents. In the *Laudatio Turiae*, the wife receives the highest praise not only for being a model daughter, but also for treating her husband's mother with the same devotion she demonstrated to her own parents.

48 Seneca, *Ben.* 3.38.2.

49 On this topic, see esp. Rawson, *Children and Childhood in Roman Italy*, 142–45.

50 *1 Clem* 22.1 (Ehrman, LCL).

51 *1 Clem* 23.1.

52 Josephus, *C. Ap.* 2.173–74 (Thackeray, LCL). On the two schemes, see also *Ag. Ap.* 2.171–2.

53 The life-course approach to the teaching of the law in the Dead Sea Scrolls has recently also been highlighted by Cecilia Wassen in "On the Education of Children in the Dead Sea Scrolls," *SR* 41 (2012): 350–63.

54 This term was widely employed by Greek-speaking Jews to refer to the Scriptures. See L. T. Johnson, *The First and Second Letters to Timothy* (AB 35A; New York: Doubleday, 2001), 419.

55 Such links between the conceptual and the practical also can be found in the Greco-Roman world. In 2 Timothy, divinely inspired Scriptures impart wisdom in the context of teaching and training for righteousness (2 Tim 3:16). The saving role of education, as we see reflected in the Pastorals, draws its origins from "Hellenistic moral philosophy" (Dio Chrysostom, *Alex.* 15–16). This type of philosophical education is highly practical, centered on the pursuit of a life that is morally sound, and reflects the kind of teaching we see in the NT household codes (cf. Seneca, *Ep.* 94.1; Ps.-Plutarch, *Mor.* 7D–F [*Lib. ed.*]; cf. Titus 2:1-10). See B. Fiore, *The Pastoral Epistles* (SP 12; Collegeville, Minn.: Liturgical, 2007), 22.

56 I have previously argued this in depth. See MacDonald, *Colossians and Ephesians*, 21–22. On the topic of ethics and the treatment of the outside world in Ephesians, see esp. Daniel K. Darko, *No Longer Living as the Gentiles: Differentiation and Shared Ethical Values in Ephesians 4.17–6.9* (London: T&T Clark, 2008).

57 MacDonald, *Colossians and Ephesians*, 236–38. Although I remain convinced of the heuristic value of analyzing NT communities in seeking analogies with sects from other eras, some scholars have questioned the applicability of the concept within an ancient context. See Eyal Regev, "Were the Early Christians Sectarians?" *JBL* 130 (2011): 771–93.

58 See esp. Pheme Perkins, *Ephesians* (ANTC; Nashville: Abingdon, 1997). On sectarianism and the Qumran literature, see discussion by Phillip F. Esler, *The*

First Christians in Their Social World: Social Scientific Approaches to New Testament Interpretation (London: Routledge, 1994), 20–91.

59 These documents have been examined thoroughly in relation to this theme by Cecilia Wassen who also considers various translation and textual issues. See Wassen, "On the Education of Children in the Dead Sea Scrolls."

60 Wassen, "On the Education of Children in the Dead Sea Scrolls," 351–52. Wassen bases the text and translation from 1QSa on the following edition: J. Charlesworth and L. Stuckenbruck, *Rule of the Community and Related Documents* (vol. 1 of *The Dead Sea Scrolls: Hebrew, Aramaic, and Greek Texts with English Translations*; ed. J. Charlesworth et al.; Tübingen: JCB Mohr; Louisville, Ky.: Westminster John Knox, 1984), 109–117.

61 Wassen, "On the Education of Children in the Dead Sea Scrolls," 352–53. Wassen draws attention to comparative evidence from rabbinic literature, which speaks of levels of education in the teaching of Torah, beginning at age five (*m. Avot* 5.21).

62 Wassen, "On the Education of Children in the Dead Sea Scrolls," 353. According to Wassen, the meaning of the reference to the book of Hagu remains unclear (cf. CD 10:6; 13:2; 14:7–8). It may refer to the Torah, to a halakhic collection, or perhaps to a sapiential composition.

63 Wassen, "On the Education of Children in the Dead Sea Scrolls," 353. Wassen notes the popularity of Deuteronomy at Qumran based on the thirty copies preserved.

64 Josephus, *C. Ap.* 2.178 (Thackeray, LCL). On teaching children Scripture and the laws from the early stages of childhood see Philo, *Hypoth.* 7.14; Mishnah (*m. Pesahim* 10:4; *m. Avot* 5:21); Josephus, *Ag. Ap.* 2.204; *Ant.* 211. The Essenes, which many assume were linked to the Qumran movement, are described as "versed from the early years in holy books, various forms of purification, and sayings of the prophets" (Josephus, *B.J.* 2.159). See Wassen, "On the Education of Children in the Dead Sea Scrolls," 355.

65 Josephus, *C. Ap.* 2.175. The approach recommended in 1QS 6:7-8 is even more rigorous, with ongoing study of Torah day and night, with one man relieving the other in common recitation of the benedictions. See Wassen, "On the Education of Children in the Dead Sea Scrolls," 355. She discusses several features of lifelong learning.

66 See MacDonald, *Colossians and Ephesians*, 320.

67 See Plutarch, *Mor.* 488C; CD 7:2, 3.

68 E.g., Prov 4:10-14; 1QS 4:23-24.

69 See *Did.* 1–5; *Barn.* 18–20; 1QS 3–4, esp. 4:2-26. Commentators are divided as to whether this very long passage should be divided into sections. For arguments in favor of thematic unity, see MacDonald, *Colossians and Ephesians*, 319–20.

70 The issues of grammar and translation for Eph 5:21 are somewhat complex and subject to a few different interpretations. See MacDonald, *Colossians and Ephesians*, 303–4.

71 MacDonald, *Colossians and Ephesians*, 303–4.

72 Concepts of gender figure prominently in what is presented as shameful or honorable in the ancient world. See MacDonald, *Colossians and Ephesians*, 314–16. On the emphasis on sexuality in the ethical teaching of Eph 4:17–5.20, see also 311.

73 See MacDonald, "Slavery, Sexuality and House Churches," 94–113.

74 Here I am following closely the discussion by Wassen in "On the Education of Children in the Dead Sea Scrolls," 355. On the home as the primary location of the education of Jewish children in the Second Temple period, see C. Hertzer, *Jewish Literacy in Roman Palestine* (Texts and Studies in Ancient Judaism 81; Tübingen: Mohr Siebeck, 2001), 49. She argues that elementary schools for Jewish children become quite common from the third century CE. On the Dead Sea Scrolls providing the earliest evidence for the communal education of Jewish children, see also S. Fraade, "Interpretative Authority in the Studying Community at Qumran," *JJS* 44 (1993): 46–69. See esp. 55–56.

75 For Hebrew text and discussion of various textual and translation issues, see Wassen, "On the Education of Children in the Dead Sea Scrolls," 356. She cites the translation by J. Baumgarten, *Qumran Cave 4. XIII. The Damascus Document (4Q266-273)* (DJD 18; Oxford: Clarendon, 1996), 70–71. She compares the reference to the instruction of young children to Isaiah 28:9.

76 See Ps.-Plutarch, *Mor.* 8F [*Lib. ed.*]; Ps.-Phoc. 207.

77 Wassen offers the following conclusion: "The loving character of the Examiner in his role of teacher modifies the general impression of the sect as a harsh environment somewhat, and serves as a corrective to a too one-sided portrayal of the community. We can conclude that since the Examiner had some responsibility for the instruction of the children their education was considered highly important. This confirms that the correct instruction of children was held to be the key to maintaining perfection in the covenantal relationship in the community." Wassen, "On the Education of Children in the Dead Sea Scrolls," 357.

78 For Hebrew text and discussion of various textual and translation issues, see Wassen, "On the Education of Children in the Dead Sea Scrolls," 357.

79 Wassen astutely observes: "One may also infer that children of members would likely automatically be initiated into the muster of adults, since they otherwise would be in a liminal position in the community" (Wassen, "On the Education of Children in the Dead Sea Scrolls," 358). The seemingly automatic acceptance of children as holy in the Corinthian community (1 Cor 7:14) has often greatly perplexed commentators, and the evidence from the *Damascus Document* may well illuminate this text. While it is outside of the purview of our interests here, Wassen closely examines the teaching with respect to new members from the outside, as opposed to the members who are the children of full members of the community. Slightly different expectations seem to characterize the integration of both groups.

80　It possible, though unlikely, that "prophets" in Eph 2:20 refers to OT prophets. See MacDonald, *Colossians and Ephesians*, 249–50, 291–92. The use of the term prophet for teachers did, however, continue in certain circles into the second century (*Did.* 11–13; 15.1–2; *Herm. Mand.* 11).

81　MacDonald, *Colossians and Ephesians*, 291–92, 299; MacDonald, *The Pauline Churches*, 132–33; David G. Horrell, "Leadership Patterns and the Development of Ideology in Early Christianity," in *Social Scientific Approaches to New Testament Interpretation* (ed. David G. Horrell; Edinburgh: T&T Clark, 1999), 309–37.

82　This has been suggested by Rudolf Schnackenburg. See *Ephesians: A Commentary* (trans. Helen Heron; Edinburgh: T&T Clark, 1991), 186. The suggestion is somewhat speculative but is in keeping with the themes of Eph 4:11-16 and is not incompatible with the structure of the Greek text.

83　The terminology of Eph 4:13-14 has sometimes led commentators to suggest that the author of Ephesians is responding to gnostic false teaching, but the terminology can be accounted for in other ways, including the dependence of Ephesians upon Colossians. The evidence does not allow for the establishment of a gnostic background for Ephesians; the epistle makes only two references to false teaching (Eph 4:13; 5:6). See further discussion in MacDonald, *Colossians and Ephesians*, 294.

84　MacDonald, *Colossians and Ephesians*, 293–94. See also Jerome H. Neyrey, "Deception," in *Biblical Social Values and Their Meaning: A Handbook* (ed. John J. Pilch and Bruce J. Malina; Peabody, Mass.: Hendrickson, 1993), 42.

85　On the love in Ephesians, see esp. John Paul Heil, *Ephesians: Empowerment to Walk in Love for the Unity of All in Christ* (Studies in Biblical Literature 13; Atlanta: SBL, 2007).

86　See Epictetus, *Diatr.* 1.19.10; 3.24.6.

87　It is possible that "saints" in Eph 3:16 refers to the "heavenly hosts," but this would not change the meaning significantly. See MacDonald, *Colossians and Ephesians*, 277, 283–84. For arguments in favor of the saints referring to the whole community, see Andrew T. Lincoln, *Ephesians* (Word Biblical Commentary 42; Dallas: Word Books, 1990), 313.

88　See Ville Vuolanto, "Children and the Memory of Parents in the Late Roman World," *Children, Memory, and Family Identity in Roman Culture* (ed. Véronique Dasen and Thomas Späth; Oxford: Oxford University Press, 2010), 174.

89　Vuolanto, "Children and the Memory of Parents," 176.

90　Vuolanto, "Children and the Memory of Parents," 174. Vuolanto concentrates especially on asceticism in early Christianity in the fourth and fifth centuries, noting that "the desire for children and lineage is one of the most frequently mentioned excuses for not opting for asceticism" (181).

91　Later early Christian literature concerned with asceticism explicitly articulated the conflict between the values of the spiritual family and the cultural concern for lineage. In the second century, in the *Acts of Paul and Thecla*, the opponents of Paul, Demas and Hermogenes, comfort Thecla's fiancé, Tamyris, with the proclamation that Paul will be brought to the governor, who will destroy Paul, and Tamyris will then have Thecla as his wife. In turn, they promise to teach Tamyris about the resurrection that Paul says is to come (and only for those who remain celibate), which in reality has already taken place in the children—an apparent reference to the immortality that is secured through one's children. See *Acts of Paul and Thecla* 14. Cf. 12–15. See "Acts of Thecla" in J. K. Elliott, ed., *The Apocryphal New Testament: A Collection of Apocryphal Christian Literature in an English Translation* (Oxford: Oxford University Press, 1993). The notion of children leading to immortality is even more developed in the fifth-century *Life of Thecla*. See Vita Theclae 5, in which "the opponents of Paul and Thecla pointed out the function of children in providing true resurrection, and in preserving and renewing the image of the parents." See Vuolanto, "Children and the Memory of Parents," 181.

92 In later centuries church authors could be highly critical of cultural mores. The mocking tone of Gregory of Nyssa in the fourth century CE is illustrative of the point, but also highlights the ongoing dominance of traditional values. According to Gregory a man "must not be thought inferior to his forefathers; he must be deemed a great man by the generation to come by leaving his children records of himself." See Gregory of Nyssa, *Virg.* 4.3, cited in Vuolanto, "Children and the Memory of Parents," 175.

93 Vuolanto, "Children and the Memory of Parents," 183.

94 See esp. Elliott, *A Home for the Homeless*. On the apologetic function of the household codes, see Balch, *Let Wives Be Submissive*. Balch and Elliott have engaged in important debate on the extent to which the code of 1 Peter should be viewed as truly apologetic, i.e., designed explicitly to appease tension with outsiders, with an external focus. Elliott has understood the code to be primarily designed to encourage internal cohesion. On the debate see Balch, "Hellenization/Acculturation in 1 Peter," 79–101; Elliott, "1 Peter, Its Situation and Strategy," 61–78; Elliott, *1 Peter*, 509–10; Horrell, "Between Conformity and Resistance," 111–43. See also discussion in chap. 1 of this volume.

95 This is the name I gave to these women in my 1996 work, *Early Christian Women and Pagan Opinion*, 195–206.

96 For the ancient evidence condemning the allegiance of women to superstitious religious groups in defiance of the authority of husbands see MacDonald, *Early Christian Women and Pagan Opinion*.

97 Descriptions of the conversions of entire households/families are in fact quite rare in the NT and are found mainly in Acts (e.g., Acts 11:14; 16:14-15, 31-34; 18:8).

98 Such family violence became a popular theme in the Apocryphal Acts of the Apostles as apostles and their female devotees were presented in conflict with mothers, fathers, and fiancés. See Ross S. Kraemer, "The Conversion of Women to Ascetic Forms of Christianity," *Signs* 6 (1980): 298–307.

99 Postcolonial analysis has been useful in bringing out this combination of elements. See Horrell, *1 Peter*, 94. See also the discussion in chap. 1 of this volume.

100 While believing or apostate masters cannot be ruled out entirely, it seems more likely that the text refers to unbelieving masters, given the use of similar language in Acts 2:40 and Phil 2:14 to refer to the unbelieving world as a perverse generation.

101 Flogging of slaves was generally accepted, although some authors called for moderation. See, e.g., Seneca, *Ira* 3.32, cited in Harrill, *Slaves in the New Testament*, 106.

102 On this specific topic see Pedar Foss, "Watchful Lares: Roman Household Organization and the Rituals of Cooking and Eating," in *Domestic Space in the Roman World: Pompeii and Beyond* (ed. Ray Laurence and Andrew Wallace-Hadrill; Journal of Roman Archaeology Supplementary Series 22; Portsmouth, R.I.: Journal of Roman Archaeology, 1997), 197–218; Michele George, "Repopulating the Roman House," in *The Roman Family in Italy: Status, Sentiment, Space* (ed. Beryl Rawson and Paul Weaver; Oxford: Clarendon, 1997), 316–17; R. A. Tybout, "Domestic Shrines and 'Popular Painting': Style and Social Context," *Journal of Roman Archaeology* 9 (1996): 367–70. On domestic religion generally see David G. Orr, "Roman Domestic Religion: The Evidence of the Household Shrines," *ANRW* 2.16.2 (1978): 1569–75.

103 An exception here is the work on this topic by Caroline Johnson Hodge. See "Married to an Unbeliever: Households, Hierarchies, and Holiness in 1 Corinthians 7:12-16," *HTR* 103, no. 1 (2010): 1–25; "'Holy Wives' in Roman Households: 1 Peter 3:1-6," *Journal of Interdisciplinary Feminist Thought* 4, no. 1 (2010): 1–24.

104 See Cato, *Agr.* 143. See more detailed discussion of this text in chap. 2.

105 See Plutarch, *Conj. Praec.* (*Mor.* 140D). Note that I have discussed this text and related ones at length in *Early Christian Women and Pagan Opinion*, 49–126.

106 Cited in Johnson Hodge, "Married to an Unbeliever," 6. Translation amended from *Catullus, Tibullus, Pervigilium Veneris* (3.12.1–4, 14–15, with Tibullus translation by John Percival Postgate, rev. by George Patrick Goold) (2nd ed.; LCL 6; Cambridge, Mass.: Harvard University Press, 1988), 331.

107 Marcus Cornelius Fronto (100–166 CE) is believed to be the author of a critique of Christianity later used in a work entitled "Octavius" by the Christian apologist Minucius Felix. See *Oct.* 8–9, in G. Clarke, trans., *The Octavius of Marcus Minucius Felix* (New York: Newman, 1974). The involvement of children in some types of early Christian rites is also suggested by Lucian of Samosata in his account of the imprisonment of the Christian philosopher Peregrinus. Lucian refers to orphans together with widows visiting the imprisoned philosopher; this will be discussed in chap. 4.

108 For full discussion see MacDonald, *Early Christian Women and Pagan Opinion*, 10–162.

109 The idealistic nature of the household code in Ephesians, which masks the presence of wives in complex circumstances, has been highlighted by Seim in "A Superior Minority."

110   For more detailed discussion of this point, see Osiek and MacDonald, *A Woman's Place*, 131–32.

111   See esp. Suzanne Dixon, *The Roman Mother* (London: Croom Helm, 1988), 62–63. Dixon offers several examples from Roman literature illustrating that some women were very active in arranging matches, citing the letters of Cicero and Pliny in particular. On marriage more generally see Susan Treggiari, "Marriage and Family in Roman Society," in *Marriage and Family in the Biblical World* (ed. Ken M. Campbell; Downers Grove, Ill.: InterVarsity, 2003), 132–82.

112   Ambrose, *Virg.* 1.7.32. Cited in Vuolanto, "Children and the Memory of Parents," 187.

113   There are significant sexual nuances within Eph 5:22-33. See esp. Osiek, "The Bride of Christ."

114   See *Acts of Paul and Thecla* and the *Martyrdom of Perpetua and Felicitas*.

115   See Laes, *Children in the Roman Empire*, 46, 252–55.

116   Laes, *Children in the Roman Empire*, 243. Laes cites Plutarch, *Quaest. rom.* 288 a–b among other ancient texts. He notes the association of children with virginity in the Roman world.

117   See detailed discussion in chap. 4.

118   On the role of mothers among the slave families and freed-slave families of Rome, see Dixon, *The Roman Mother*, 233.

119   On imperial ideology and Ephesians see esp. Eberhard Faust, *Pax Christi et Pax Caesaris: Religionsgeschichtliche, traditionsgeschichtliche und sozialgeschichtlich Studien zum Epheserbrief* (NTOA 24; Göttingen: Vandenhoek & Ruprecht, 1993); Carmen Bernabé Ubieta, "'Neither *Xenoi* nor *parakoi, sympolitai* and *oikeioi tou theou*' (Eph 2.19) Pauline Christian Communities: Defining a New Territoriality," *Social-Scientific Models for Interpreting the Bible* (ed. John J. Pilch; Leiden: Brill, 2001), 260–80; MacDonald, "The Politics of Identity in Ephesians," 419–44. For the current discussion see also the study by Harry O. Maier, which concerns the points of conjuncture of the disputed Pauline literature with imperial iconography, *Picturing Paul in Empire*. On the importance of empire studies for investigations of the household codes generally, see also discussion in chap. 1 of this book.

120   See esp. Suzanne Dixon, "The Sentimental Ideal of the Roman Family," in *Marriage, Divorce, and Children in Ancient Rome* (ed. Beryl Rawson; Oxford: Clarendon, 1991), 99–113. On the influence of imperial marriage ideals in the east see Bruce W. Winter, *Roman Wives, Roman Widows: The Appearance of the New Women and Pauline Communities* (Grand Rapids: Eerdmans, 2003), 35.

121   See Rawson, *Children and Childhood in Roman Italy*, 27.

122   Rawson, *Children and Childhood in Roman Italy*, 27–28.

123   Rawson, *Children and Childhood in Roman Italy*, 34.

124   Rawson, *Children and Childhood in Roman Italy*, 34–35. From the period of Ephesians, Rawson offers the following example: "Domitian continued to use

children in his imperial symbolism. The Secular Games of 88 had a prominent role for children, and coins of 88 commemorating these games . . . had representations of children. For instance, a child and adult citizen are depicted as recipients of Domitian's distribution of largess; and three children take part in a procession before Domitian" (41; see fig. 1.7).

125 Rawson discusses especially the relief of the Seruilli family: freeborn son and freed couple (Rome, 30–20 BCE). Rawson, *Children and Childhood in Roman Italy*, 30–31. For other examples, see Rawson, "The Iconography of Roman Childhood," in *The Roman Family in Italy: Status, Sentiment, Space* (ed. B. Rawson and P. Weaver; Oxford: Clarendon, 1997), 205–32.

126 Rawson, *Children and Childhood in Roman Italy*, 53. Although they come from the second century CE, the columns of Trajan and Marcus Aurelius offer particularly graphic examples. Closer to the era under discussion, Rawson (53–54) describes a monument of the 70s CE: the memorial to the senatorial commander Ti. Plautius Siluanus Aelianus: "His civil and military achievements were inscribed on a large slab in front of the Plautii family tomb beside the Anio river near Tibur (Tivoli). His achievements included protection of his province of Moesia on the Danube, 'in which he brought across the river more than 100,000 from the population of Transdanubians to pay tribute, along with their wives and children and leaders and kings.' The impact of this mass forced movement of people, its procession into Moesia, and associated ceremonies, on the now settled, but vulnerable province is not difficult to imagine. The submissive leaders, and the women and children who represented the future of their people, personified the end of a separate, independent people." Closer in geography is the temple complex of Sebasteion at Aphrodisias dedicated to the Julio-Claudian emperors and located about 100 km from Colossae. See discussion in chap. 2 of the present volume.

127 The relationship between these texts is examined in detail in Osiek and MacDonald, *A Woman's Place*, 127–131. Notions of citizenship are tied to concepts of Jewish identity in a complex manner. See MacDonald, "The Politics of Identity in Ephesians."

128 See chap. 1.

129 The use of postcolonial analysis in NT interpretation has been highly influential here. See MacDonald, "Beyond Identification of the *Topos* of Household Management."

130 Josephus, *C. Ap.* 2.174.

131 Josephus, *C. Ap.* 2.181.

132 For the influence of this myth on Roman culture see Rawson, *Children and Childhood in Roman Italy*, 32–34.

133 On the relationship between the household codes of Ephesians and emerging rules of endogamy, see Osiek and MacDonald, *A Woman's Place*, 124–26.

Chapter 4

1   On the significance of the address to Paul's delegates, see esp. L. T. Johnson, *Letters to Paul's Delegates: 1 Timothy, 2 Timothy, Titus* (New Testament in Context; Valley Forge, Pa.: Trinity International, 1996), 34–40. Although authorship remains an issue of debate among commentators, I am persuaded by the body of scholarship that views 1 Timothy, 2 Timothy (many have viewed the letter as based on authentic Pauline notes or an earlier letter), and Titus as pseudonymous. For detailed discussion see I. H. Marshall, *A Critical and Exegetical Commentary on the Pastoral Epistles* (ICC; Edinburgh: T&T Clark, 1999), 57–92.

2   For parallels, see Johnson, *Letters to Paul's Delegates*, 30.

3   Similar sentiments are expressed with respect to Timothy. In 1 Thess 3:2, e.g., Paul informs the Thessalonians that he has sent them Timothy to establish them in the faith and to exhort them. In this text Timothy is presented as Paul's peer, his brother, sharing in his divine commission.

4   On the use of parenting and childhood metaphors in the letters of Paul, see esp. Aasgaard, "Like a Child," 249–77.

5   John Barclay has argued that 1 Tim 4:12 is the exception that proves the rule; the endorsement of Timothy's youthful leadership is with "words . . . carefully chosen to validate this unusual phenomenon." See J. M. G. Barclay, "There Is neither Old nor Young? Early Christianity and Ancient Ideologies of Age," *NTS* 53 (2007): 238.

6   On Titus see Johnson, *Letters to Paul's Delegates*, 30–31.

7   See Raymond F. Collins, "Titus: Introduction," in *Anselm Academic Study Bible* (ed. Carolyn Osiek; Winona, Minn.: Anselm Academic, 2012), 1991.

8   See R. A. Kaster, *Guardians of Language: The Grammarian and Society in Late Antiquity* (Berkeley: University of California Press, 1997), 68. On the symbolic association of teaching and parenting, see also Teresa Morgan, "Ethos: The Socialization of Children in Education and Beyond," in *A Companion to Families in the Greek and Roman Worlds* (ed. Beryl Rawson; Oxford: Blackwell, 2011), 504–20.

9   Juvenal, *Sat.* 7. 236–41 (Braund, LCL). See also discussion in Morgan, "The Socialization of Children in Education," 504.

10   See Osiek and MacDonald, *A Woman's Place*, 68–94.

11   See, e.g., Quintilian, *Inst.* 2.6.7. For similar examples, see Morgan, "The Socialization of Children in Education," 515. As Morgan notes, however, it is difficult to know whether such notions really represent how children were actually viewed in the family or whether "this viewpoint is a conceit of educational theory."

12   The role of Timothy as Paul's delegate has recently been examined from a social-scientific perspective by Bruce Malina. He argues that Timothy is essentially an ideal local supervisor/overseer. See B. J. Malina, *Timothy: Paul's Closest Associate* (Collegeville, Minn.: Liturgical, 2008).

13   The terms *presbyteros* and *episcopos* are variously translated as presbyter or elder

and overseer or bishop, respectively. They are not identical to the church offices of later times but seem to represent an intermediary stage in the development of offices. There has been much speculation about the origins of these offices. In Titus 1:5-9, the terms seem to be interchangeable.

14 Increasingly scholars are seeking to understand the individual perspectives of each of the Pastoral Epistles. The highly personal nature of 2 Timothy, among other factors, has led to the suggestion that it was written by Paul himself or it incorporates genuine Pauline fragments. While 2 Timothy may come from a different author, there are enough similarities to suggest that all three epistles belong to the same corpus of literature. For a good summary of the issues, see Raymond F. Collins, "The Second Letter to Timothy: An Introduction," in *Anselm Academic Study Bible* (ed. Carolyn Osiek; Winona, Minn.: Anselm Academic, 2012), 1982–84. On the similarities between Titus and the other Pastoral Epistles, see Collins, "Titus," 1990.

15 According to Luke Timothy Johnson, 2 Tim 4.1-8 represents the climax of Paul's exhortation in 2 Timothy. See Johnson, *The First and Second Letters to Timothy*, 425.

16 Pol. *Phil.* 4.2.

17 See discussion in chap. 3.

18 See Valerius Maximus, *Memorable Deeds and Sayings* 8.3. Note that Valerius Maximus also reports the laughable and unsuccessful efforts of two women, Carfania and Maesia Sentia, who sought to appear in court. The example of women philosophers should also be considered, but often such women achieved philosophical heights by abandoning women's conventional lifestyles, including marriage. The fourth-century CE Hypatia of Alexandria offers a very good example. See Morgan, "The Socialization of Children in Education," 518–19.

19 Juvenal, *Sat.* 6.435-55 (Braund, LCL).

20 See Morgan, "The Socialization of Children in Education," 518–19.

21 On this topic, see esp. Winter, *Roman Wives, Roman Widows*.

22 See Musonius Rufus, *On the Education of Women* 4, and Pliny the Younger, *Ep.* 4.19.4, respectively. See also Morgan, "The Socialization of Children in Education," 518.

23 Ps.-Plutarch 14B–C [*Lib. ed.*].

24 Plutarch, *Ti. C. Gracch.* 1.6-7. For translation see M. Joyal, I. McDougall, and J. C. Yardley, *Greek and Roman Education: A Sourcebook* (London: Routledge, 2009), 157–58.

25 Cicero, *Brut.* 104.

26 Cicero, *Brut.* 211; cf. Cicero, *De. or.* 3.45; Pliny, *Ep.* 1.16.6. For translation see Joyal, McDougall, and Yardley, *Greek and Roman Education*, 158.

27 Quintilian, *Inst.* 1.1.6-7.

28 The term widely employed by Greek-speaking Jews to refer to the Scriptures. For a list of relevant texts referring to Scriptures, see Johnson, *The First and Second Letters to Timothy*, 419.

29   Scripture and tradition in the Pastoral Epistles appear to be given a function which is much like that of the Jewish law. The law is that which makes a person wise (LXX Ps 18:8 "making wise the babes") as in the expression "making you wise (*sophizō*) concerning salvation" in 2 Tim 3:15. This is the translation offered by Johnson, *The First and Second Letters to Timothy*, 419–20.

30   On the practical function of Scriptures see Johnson, *The First and Second Letters to Timothy*, 424. For an examination of the use of educational terminology in the Pastoral Epistles, see esp. Claire S. Smith, *Pauline Communities as "Scholastic Communities": A Study of the Vocabulary of "Teaching" in 1 Corinthians, 1 and 2 Timothy and Titus* (Tübingen: Mohr Siebeck, 2012).

31   See Smith, *Pauline Communities as "Scholastic Communities,"* 313–14. The verb and its derivatives are found frequently in the Pastoral Epistles (1 Tim 1:20; 2 Tim 2:23, 25; 3:16; Titus 2:12).

32   On the association of lifelong learning with *paideia*, see also Josephus, *Ag. Ap.* 2.171–72. For discussion of this text and others from Josephus concerning education, see chap. 3 in this volume.

33   Barclay, *There Is neither Old nor Young?*, 237.

34   The expression typically refers to special representatives of God, especially Moses. For a list of relevant citations, see esp. Johnson, *The First and Second Letters to Timothy*, 421.

35   The background to this expression is the philosophical debates of the era concerning the practices of rhetoricians. Philosophers of the day criticized especially the Cynic philosophers for ignoring the emotions and moral conditions of their audiences—those they purportedly sought to benefit. See esp. A. J. Malherbe, "'In Season and Out of Season': 2 Timothy 4:2," *JBL* 103 (1984): 235–43. It is important to note, however, that there are in fact several texts in the Pastoral Epistles that support conventional viewpoints about speech, advising being gentle, patient, and discriminating in speech and in relations with all people (1 Tim 4:12; 6:11; 2 Tim 2:24-26; Titus 3:2).

36   See esp. Jennifer A. Glancy, "Protocols of Masculinity in the Pastoral Epistles," in *New Testament Masculinities* (ed. S. D. Moore and J. C. Anderson; Semeia 45; Atlanta: SBL, 2003), 235–64.

37   See Marshall, *Critical and Exegetical Commentary on the Pastoral Epistles*, 41.

38   Because gossip is feminized in ancient discourse, there may be an indirect connection to the false teaching as attractive to women (2 Tim 3:6) and the characterization of those drawn to the false teaching as having "itchy ears" (2 Tim 4.3). Clement of Alexandria associates the expression with a lack of manliness (*Strom* 1, 3.22.5). M. B. Kartzow, *Gossip and Gender: Othering of Speech in the Pastoral Epistles* (Berlin: Walter de Gruyter, 2009), 198. She cites the text and translation of Clement of Alexandria in Martin Dibelius and Hans Conzelmann, *The Pastoral Epistles* (Philadelphia: Fortress, 1972), 120.

39   An exception to this is Mona T. Lafosse, *Age Matters: Age, Aging and Intergenerational Relationships in Early Christian Communities with a Focus on 1 Timothy 5* (Ph.D. diss., University of Toronto, 2011).

40 *CIL* 6.5534; *Carmina Latina Epigraphica* 1035 Rome. Cited and discussed in Laes, *Children in the Roman Empire*, 54.

41 Rawson, *Children and Childhood in Roman Italy*, 145. On the end of childhood as a flexible concept, see 134–45. On marriage, motherhood, and the transition from childhood to adulthood for young women see also discussion in chap. 3 of this volume.

42 The story is recounted in the writings of Aulus Gellius, the Latin author and grammarian who wrote a twenty-book compendium called *Attic Nights*. See esp. Gellius, *Noct. att.* 12.1.1–24. The critique of the practice of engaging wet nurses by the philosopher-teacher of the baby's father is recounted in great detail. Mothers nursing their own children were considered praiseworthy by various philosophers and social commentators who also lamented the decline of this practice. See, e.g., Tacitus, *Dial.* 28.4–5. See a more detailed discussion in Osiek and MacDonald, *A Woman's Place*, 64–65. See also Juvenal's satirical critique of well-to-do women who are unwilling to undergo the dangers of childbirth and the work of nursing children (*Sat.* 6.590–600).

43 See Osiek and MacDonald, *A Woman's Place*, 90–91.

44 Juvenal, *Sat.* 6.230–40 (Braund, LCL).

45 Laes, *Children in the Roman Empire*, 28. Laes builds upon the work of Saller in *Patriarchy, Property and Death in the Roman Family*.

46 Juvenal, *Sat.* 6.398–409 (Braund, LCL).

47 This is the simulation of Roman historian T. Parkin, "The Roman Life Course and the Family," in *A Companion to Families in the Greek and Roman Worlds* (ed. Beryl Rawson; Oxford: Blackwell, 2011), 276–90, 280. See also *Old Age in the Roman World: A Cultural and Social History* (Baltimore, Md.: Johns Hopkins University Press, 2003).

48 The distinction between the various categories of widows, including "real" and "enrolled" widows in 1 Tim 5.3-16 is not quite clear in the text and subject to various interpretations by commentators. See discussion in MacDonald, *Early Christian Women and Pagan Opinion*, 154–65.

49 Herm. *Vis.* 2.4.3.

50 Ign. *Smyrn.* 13.1.

51 This controversial text is discussed in the next section.

52 On this text, see esp. Barclay, "*There Is neither Old nor Young?*"

53 The issue of whether age or church office is in view also has some bearing on the question of whether there were female presbyters. First Timothy 5:1-2 refers to both *presbyteroi* (males) and *presbyterai* (females). See Kevin Madigan and Carolyn Osiek, *Ordained Women in the Early Church: A Documentary History* (Baltimore, Md.: Johns Hopkins University Press, 2005), 162.

54 Although the same terms are used, the Pastorals appear to not reflect the same type of threefold ministry we see in the writings of Ignatius of Antioch, with the bishop having authority over the presbyters and deacons. It is beyond the scope of this study to solve various problems of interpretation related to the

terminology used for office. But see full discussion in MacDonald, *The Pauline Churches*, 207–20.

55 David C. Verner, *The Household of God*, 132.

56 See, e.g., Plutarch, *Conj. praec.* 144C (Babbitt, LCL). On this topic and its relationship to the defense of masculinity in the Roman world, see Osiek and MacDonald, *A Woman's Place*, 133–34. On control and dominion as prime directives of masculinity, see esp. Williams, *Roman Homosexuality*, 141.

57 For a discussion of institutionalization, see esp. MacDonald, *The Pauline Churches*.

58 On the role of the steward and its implications for understanding household code discourse, see esp. Harrill, *Slaves in the New Testament*, 103–5. He writes, "Ideally the master's own character is 'stamped' upon the steward. The master sets the elite slave in charge of other slaves while yet remaining their ultimate Lord" (87).

59 On the concept of pseudo-parenting see chap. 3.

60 The interpretation of 1 Tim 3:11 as referring to female deacons is supported by much patristic interpretation. See Madigan and Osiek, *Ordained Women in the Early Church*, 18–21.

61 See, e.g., Harry O. Maier, *The Social Setting of Ministry as Reflected in the Writings of Hermas, Clement, and Ignatius* (Studies in Christianity and Judaism/Études sur le christianisme et le judaïsme 12; Waterloo, Ontario: Wilfrid Laurier University Press, 2002).

62 On this role see also chap. 3.

63 This has been emphasized by Malherbe, "'In Season and Out of Season,'" 240–41. In this paragraph, I am following closely the argument I developed in *The Pauline Churches*, 174–76.

64 Quintilian, *Inst.* 1.1.1ff. (Russell, LCL). See Teresa Morgan, *Literate Education in the Hellenistic and Roman Worlds* (Cambridge: Cambridge University Press, 1998), 244.

65 Quintilian, *Inst.* 2.2.5, 9.1; Philo, *Congr.* 6. See Morgan, *Literate Education*, 269.

66 See Morgan, *Literate Education*, 246, 269. See also discussion of how the teacher molds the pupil, 259–60.

67 Ps.-Plutarch, 12B–C [*Lib. ed.*] (Babbitt, LCL); see Morgan, *Literate Education*, 256.

68 Ps.-Plutarch, 13e–f. Morgan, *Literate Education*, 256. See 256–57.

69 See discussion in chap. 1.

70 Morgan, *Literate Education*, 258–59.

71 Morgan, *Literate Education*, 243.

72 It is not clear whether the statement in the first half of 1 Tim 3:1 "The saying is sure" refers to this endorsement or to the previous exhortation concerning women. See discussion by Frances Young, who is in favor of the latter, in *The Theology of the Pastoral Epistles* (Cambridge: Cambridge University Press, 1994), 56–57.

73 On the relationship between these teachings and concepts of good citizenship and benefaction see Young, *The Theology of the Pastoral Epistles*, 101. See also MacDonald, *The Pauline Churches*, 210. Throughout the Pastorals, the doing of good works is associated with service to the less privileged (cf. 1 Tim 2:10; 5:10; 6:18; Titus 3:14) and is a major responsibility of the well-to-do (1 Tim 6:18).

74 On this text and various problems of interpretation, see the excellent discussion by Elsa Tamez, *Struggles for Power in Early Christianity: A Study of the First Letter to Timothy* (Maryknoll, N.Y.: Orbis Books, 2007), 40–47. This text raises many questions with respect to women and sexuality. See especially William Loader, *The New Testament on Sexuality* (Grand Rapids: Eerdmans, 2012).

75 See discussion of this text in chap. 1.

76 This is the opinion of Teresa Morgan in "The Socialization of Children in Education," 518.

77 On the obligation to raise and educate children, see Tamez, *Struggles for Power*, 46.

78 Tamez, *Struggles for Power*, 45.

79 That some kind of communal gathering for worship involving men and women is involved is indicated especially by 1 Tim 2:1, 8. See Smith, *Pauline Communities as "Scholastic Communities*," 60–61.

80 Here I am following closely the argument of Elsa Tamez, who writes, "The men of the community do not have to listen to them. Their condition does not permit it because they, being women, are easily tricked and seduced by strange teaching (as was Eve, the mother of all the living), and they might teach that which is unadvisable. If they teach in front of the community, the men who listen could fall into transgression, as Adam fell upon listening to Eve. To avoid 'this catastrophe' according to the author, the communities should respect order: the women must become subordinate and stop dominating the men of the community. The author tells them that women have their place ordained by God and must not usurp the place of men" (43). See *Struggles for Power*, 42–43.

81 See Morgan, "The Socialization of Children in Education," 518–19.

82 The sources do not provide identical lists of subjects, but generally agree on what constitutes common or ordinary education (*enkyklios paideia*). Morgan, *Literate Education*, 33–39.

83 Morgan, *Literate Education*, 33–39. In actual fact a wide variety of materials have survived, all generally under the label of papyri, but including "fragments of papyrus, ostraka, waxed or whitened wood tablets and, occasionally, pieces of parchment" (39).

84 *Les Papyrus Bouriant* (*Pbour*) 1. Cited in Morgan, "The Socialization of Children in Education," 514.

85 For various *nomai* on women, see Morgan, *Literate Education*, 136.

86 Morgan, *Literate Education*, 137.

87 Morgan, *Literate Education*, 137–38.

88 See esp. Gerard L. Ellespermann, *The Attitude of the Early Christian Latin*

Writers toward Pagan Literature and Learning (Washington, D.C.: Catholic University of America Press, 1949).

89   The seminal work on early Christianity as a "scholastic community" or school has been conducted by Edwin A. Judge, "The Early Christians as a Scholastic Community," *JRH* III (1960): 4–15. Now see the detailed response to Judge, including his numerous publications by Smith in *Pauline Communities as "Scholastic Communities,"* 1–14, 377–93. Smith examines an extensive range of "teaching" vocabulary to test the appropriateness of the category. Because of problems and potential misunderstanding associated with the category "scholastic community," she helpfully suggests an alternative of "learning community" (388–91). For an important comparative analysis of the relationship between early church groups and various associations and institutions in the Roman world, see Meeks, *Urban Christians*, who includes a response to Judge. For a more recent survey, see Richard S. Ascough, *What Are They Saying about the Formation of the Pauline Churches?* (Mahwah, N.J.: Paulist, 1998). See also Edward Adams, "First-Century Models for Paul's Churches: Selected Scholarly Development since Meeks," in *After the First Urban Christians: The Social-Scientific Study of Pauline Christianity Twenty-Five Years Later* (ed. Todd D. Still and David G. Horrell; London: T&T Clark, 2009), 60–78.

90   Frances Young has written, insightfully, "Timothy or Titus are the 'philosopher-chaplains' who represent Paul, passing on his teaching and moral advice. The teaching is codified according to accepted traditions, and largely consists of delineations of virtuous character and appropriate behavior, expressed in proper relations between different grades in the hierarchy of the household." See *The Theology of the Pastoral Epistles*, 90. See also 79–96.

91   E. A. Judge refers to "adult education," which he defines as "a kind of higher education 'in Christ' that presupposes existing Jewish and Hellenic systems of education, but discounts and supersedes both." See "The Conflict of Educational Aims in the New Testament," *Journal of Christian Education* 9 (1966): 32–45.

92   For other differences between early Christian communities and philosophical schools, see Smith, *Pauline Communities as "Scholastic Communities,"* 9–10.

93   This has been carefully documented by Smith in *Pauline Communities as "Scholastic Communities."* She offers the following helpful general definition of teaching: "to impart a message from an addresser to an addressee, where the purpose and/or result of the act is to cause the addressees to gain knowledge, understanding, a skill, attitude or belief or to transform thought, belief or conduct" (378).

94   On etymology and meaning of the Greek term see Smith, *Pauline Communities as "Scholastic Communities,"* 54–55.

95   The formulaic statement may also refer to the statement about bishops that begins at 3:1b, and many translators have preferred this option. The question cannot be settled on the basis of the Greek text alone.

96   Aristotle presented the household as the microcosm of the state, and his basic notion penetrated classical civilization. See discussion in chap. 1. Reflecting

this type of framework, 1 Timothy 2 begins with an appeal for prayer for heads of state.

97 On the emergence of a male teaching role see Smith, *Pauline Communities as "Scholastic Communities,"* 69–70.

98 Smith, *Pauline Communities as "Scholastic Communities,"* 77.

99 Smith, *Pauline Communities as "Scholastic Communities,"* 72. Notions of active learning and training throughout the life course are also tied to the use of *paideia* in 2 Tim 3:16: "training in righteousness" (cf. 1 Tim 1:20; 2 Tim 2:25; Titus 2:12). See discussion above and chap. 3.

100 The Greek text is lit. "husband of one wife" or "man of one woman," and commentators have puzzled over its meaning. The expression also occurs in 1 Tim 3:12 and Titus 1:6 (cf. 1 Tim 5:9). Other interpretations include a prohibition against bigamy or, in keeping with some patristic interpretation, a prohibition against second marriage. Raymond F. Collins has recently examined the question at length, and I agree that the most likely meaning in this context is exemplary marital fidelity. See Raymond F. Collins, *Accompanied by a Believing Wife: Ministry and Celibacy in the Earliest Christian Communities* (Collegeville, Minn.: Liturgical, 2013), 180–210. On the double standard on fidelity in marriage in law and society in the Roman world, see Osiek and MacDonald, *A Woman's Place,* 22–23.

101 On this text see chap. 3.

102 This is true even with respect to false or different teaching (Titus 1:11; 1 Tim 1:3; 6:3).

103 Smith, *Pauline Communities as "Scholastic Communities,"* 77.

104 See Morgan, *Literate Education,* 26. With respect to Vespasian, she cites evidence from Emperor Suetonius.

105 Morgan, *Literate Education,* 27–28, citing Pliny the Younger, *Ep.* 4.13.3ff.

106 Even the terminology applied to teachers, which in some theoretical discussions suggests levels of education ranging from elementary literacy to rhetoric, has been shown in practice to have been used much more flexibly. There is also some limited evidence for female teachers in the papyri (*grammatike* and *deskale*; that these terms refer to the wives of teachers, however, cannot be ruled out). Morgan, *Literate Education,* 28.

107 Morgan, *Literate Education,* 29–32. Morgan observes the following: "The infrequency, the vagueness and the inconsistency of our references to places of education, numbers and ages of pupils, methods of teaching and the structures of the 'school day', if any, are in sharp contrast with the wealth of relatively precise and consistent information we have about the content of education" (32). With respect to schools and teachers, however, the (albeit fictional) narrative account of Jesus' schooling in the *Infancy Gospel of Thomas* is worthy of note. See Osiek and MacDonald, *A Woman's Place,* 87–89. See Reidar Aasgaard, *The Childhood of Jesus* (Eugene, Ore.: Cascade, 2009).

108 See Osiek and MacDonald, *A Woman's Place*; Rawson, *Children and Childhood in Roman Italy*, 154–56. Note that the home has been stressed as important for the instruction of Jewish girls in contrast to the "public" education of boys in schools. See Shoshana Pantel Zolty, *"And All Your Children Shall Be Learned": Women and the Study of Torah in Jewish Law and History* (Northvale, N.J.: Aronson, 1993), 114–17.

109 Quintilian, *Inst.* 1.2. For a discussion of the importance of Quintilian's writing for understanding educational practices in house churches, see Osiek and MacDonald, *A Woman's Place*, 84–85.

110 Quintilian, *Inst.* 1.2.8.

111 See Rawson, *Children and Childhood in Roman Italy*, 54–56; on the education of slave children see also 187–91.

112 See Minucius Felix, *Oct.* 8–9. For a citation and full detailed discussion of the text, see MacDonald, *Early Christian Women and Pagan Opinion*, 59–67.

113 See Lucian of Samosata, *Peregr.* 12–13, For a citation and full detailed discussion of the text, see MacDonald, *Early Christian Women and Pagan Opinion*, 73–82.

114 Origen, *Cels.* 3.55. See also 3.44; 3.50. For a translation see Origen, *Contra Celsum* (trans. Henry Chadwick; Cambridge: Cambridge University Press, 1953). For full discussion of this text see MacDonald, *Early Christian Women and Pagan Opinion*, 109–120.

115 There is considerable interest, e.g., in associations providing meeting spaces such as banquet houses. For a good summary of the current debate see Annette Weissenrieder, "Contested Spaces in 1 Cor 11:17-33 and 14:30: Sitting or Reclining in Ancient Houses, in Associations and in the Space of the *ekklesia*," in *Contested Spaces* (ed. David L. Balch and Annette Weissenrieder; WUNT 285; Tübingen: Mohr Siebeck, 2012), 59–107.

116 Weissenrieder offers the following thought-provoking remark: "I will consider specific concrete spaces (house, meeting place, gathering place for the *ekklēsia*), keeping in mind that the choice of the word *ekklēsia* does not evoke a specific concrete space, but rather the concept is generated by a certain way of behaving within the space." Weissenrieder, "Contested Spaces in 1 Cor 11:17-33 and 14:30," 66.

WORKS CITED

Aasgaard, Reidar. *The Childhood of Jesus*. Eugene, Ore.: Cascade, 2009.

———. "Children in Antiquity and Early Christianity: Research History and Central Issues." *Familia* [Salamanca, Spain] 33 (2006): 23–46.

———. "Like a Child: Paul's Rhetorical Uses of Childhood." Pages 249–77 in Bunge, *The Child in the Bible*.

Adams, Edward. "First-Century Models for Paul's Churches: Selected Scholarly Development since Meeks." Pages 60–78 in *After the First Urban Christians: The Social-Scientific Study of Pauline Christianity Twenty-Five Years Later*. Edited by Todd D. Still and David G. Horrell. London: T&T Clark, 2009.

Aletti, Jean Noël. *Saint Paul: Épitre aux Colossiens*. Paris: J. Galbalda, 1993.

Apostolic Fathers, The. Translated by Bart D. Ehrman. 2 vols. Loeb Classical Library. Cambridge, Mass.: Harvard University Press, 2003.

Aristotle. *Politics*. Translated by H. Rackham. Loeb Classical Library 264. Cambridge, Mass.: Harvard University Press, 1932.

Ascough, Richard S. *What Are They Saying about the Formation of the Pauline Churches?* New York: Paulist, 1998.

Balch, David L. "Hellenization/Acculturation in 1 Peter." Pages 79–101 in Talbert, *Perspectives on 1 Peter*.

———. "Household Codes." Pages 25–50 in *Greco-Roman Literature and the New Testament*. Edited by David E. Aune. Atlanta: Scholars Press, 1988.

———. *Let Wives Be Submissive: The Domestic Code in 1 Peter*. Chico, Calif.: Scholars Press, 1981.

———. "Neopythagorean Moralists and the New Testament Household Codes." *Aufstieg und Niedergang der römischen Welt* 2, no. 26.1 (1992): 389–404.

Balch, David L., and Carolyn Osiek, eds. *Early Christian Families in Context: An Interdisciplinary Dialogue.* Grand Rapids: Eerdmans, 2003.

Balla, P. *The Child-Parent Relationship in the New Testament and Its Environment.* Tübingen: Mohr Siebeck, 2003.

Barclay, John M. G. "The Family as the Bearer of Religion in Judaism and Early Christianity." Pages 66–80 in Moxnes, *Constructing Early Christian Families.*

———. "Ordinary but Different: Colossians and Hidden Moral Identity." *Australian Biblical Review* 49 (2001): 34–52.

———. "Paul, Philemon, and the Dilemma of Christian Slave Ownership." *New Testament Studies* 37 (1991): 161–86.

———. "There Is neither Old nor Young? Early Christianity and Ancient Ideologies of Age." *New Testament Studies* 53 (2007): 225–41.

Bartlett, David L. "Adoption in the Bible." Pages 375–98 in Bunge, *The Child in the Bible.*

Barton, S. C., and G. H. R. Horsley. "A Hellenistic Cult Group and the New Testament Churches." *Jahrbuch für Antike und Christentum* 24 (1981): 7–41.

Baumgarten, J. *Qumran Cave 4. XIII. The Damascus Document (4Q266-273).* Discoveries in the Judaean Desert 18. Oxford: Clarendon, 1996.

Beattie, Gillian. *Women and Marriage in Paul and His Early Interpreters.* Journal for the Study of the New Testament Supplement Series 296. London: T&T Clark, 2005.

Becker, Jürgen, and Ulrich Luz, *Die Briefer und die Galater, Epheser und Kolosser.* Das Neue Testament Deutsch 8/1. Göttingen: Vandenhoeck & Ruprecht, 1998.

Berger, Peter L., and Thomas A. Luckmann. *The Social Construction of Reality.* Garden City, N.Y.: Doubleday, 1966.

Bhabha, Homi. "DissemiNation: Time, Narrative, and the Margins of the Modern Nation." Pages 291–322 in *Nation and Narration.* Edited by H. Bhabha. London: Routledge, 1990.

———. *The Location of Culture.* London: Routledge, 1994.

Bird, Jennifer G. *Faithful Obedience: Reconsidering 1 Peter's Command to Wives.* London: T&T Clark, 2011.

Boyarin, D. *Border Lines: The Partition of Judaeo-Christianity.* Philadelphia: University of Pennsylvania Press, 2006.

Brooten, Bernadette J. "Early Christian Women and Their Cultural Context: Issues of Method in Historical Reconstruction." Pages 65–91 in *Feminist Perspectives on Biblical Scholarship.* Edited by Adela Yarbro Collins. Chico, Calif.: Scholars Press, 1985.

———. *Love between Women: Early Christian Responses to Female Homoeroticism.* Chicago: University of Chicago Press, 1998.

Brown, William P. "To Discipline without Destruction: The Multifaceted

Profile of the Child in Proverbs." Pages 63–81 in Bunge, *The Child in the Bible.*

Bunge, Marcia J., ed. *The Child in the Bible.* Grand Rapids: Eerdmans, 2008.

Burr, V. *Social Constructionism.* 2nd ed. London: Routledge, 2003.

Campbell, Douglas A. "Unravelling Colossians 3.11b." *New Testament Studies* 42 (1996): 120–32.

Canavan, Rosemary. *Clothing the Body of Christ at Colossae.* Wissenschaftliche Untersuchungen zum Neuen Testament 2/334. Tübingen: Mohr Siebeck, 2012.

Carroll, J. T. "'What Then Will This Child Become?': Perspectives on Children in the Gospel of Luke." Pages 177–94 in Bunge, *The Child in the Bible.*

Carter, Warren. "Going All the Way? Honoring the Emperor and Sacrificing Wives and Slaves in 1 Pet 2.13–3.6." Pages 14–33 in *A Feminist Companion to the Catholic Epistles.* Edited by Amy-Jill Levine and Marya Mayo Robbins. London: T&T Clark, 2004.

Catullus, Tibullus, Pervigilium Veneris. Translated by F. W. Cornish, J. P. Postgate, and J. W. Mackail. 2nd ed. Loeb Classical Library 6. Cambridge, Mass.: Harvard University Press, 1988.

Charlesworth, J., and L. Stuckenbruck. *Rule of the Community and Related Documents.* Vol. 1 of *The Dead Sea Scrolls: Hebrew, Aramaic, and Greek Texts with English Translations.* Edited by J. Charlesworth et al. Tübingen: J. C. B. Mohr; Louisville, Ky.: Westminster John Knox, 1984.

Clark, Elizabeth A. "The Lady Vanishes: Dilemmas of a Feminist Historian after the 'Linguistic Turn.'" *Church History* 67 (1998): 1–31.

Clarke, G. *The Octavius of Marcus Minucius Felix.* New York: Newman, 1974.

Cohick, L. H. *Women in the World of the Earliest Christians: Illuminating Ancient Ways of Life.* Grand Rapids: Baker Academic, 2009.

Collins, Raymond F. *Accompanied by a Believing Wife: Ministry and Celibacy in the Earliest Christian Communities.* Collegeville, Minn.: Liturgical, 2013.

———. "The Second Letter to Timothy: An Introduction." Pages 1982–84 in Osiek, *Anselm Academic Study Bible.*

———. *Sexual Ethics and the New Testament: Behavior and Belief.* New York: Crossroad, 2000.

———. "Titus: Introduction." Pages 1990–92 in Osiek, *Anselm Academic Study Bible.*

Crouch, J. E. *The Origin and Intention of the Colossian Haustafel.* Göttingen: Vandenhoeck & Ruprecht, 1972.

D'Angelo, Mary Rose. "Colossians." Pages 325–48 in *Searching the Scriptures: A Feminist Commentary.* Edited by Elisabeth Schüssler Fiorenza. New York: Crossroad, 1997.

Darko, Daniel K. *No Longer Living as the Gentiles: Differentiation and Shared Ethical Values in Ephesians 4.17–6.9.* London: T&T Clark, 2008.

Dasen, V. "Childbirth and Infancy in Greek and Roman Antiquity." Pages 291–314 in Rawson, *A Companion to Families in the Greek and Roman Worlds.*

Dasen, Véronique, and Thomas Späth, eds. *Children, Memory, and Family Identity in Roman Culture.* Oxford: Oxford University Press, 2010.

Demming, Will. "Mark 9:42–10:12, Matthew 5:27-32 and *B. Nid.* 13b: A First Century Discussion of Male Sexuality." *New Testament Studies* 36 (1990): 130–41.

Dibelius, Martin, and Hans Conzelmann. *The Pastoral Epistles.* Philadelphia: Fortress, 1972.

Dionysius of Halicarnassus. *Roman Antiquities. Books 1–2.* Translated by Earnest Cary. Loeb Classical Library 319. Cambridge, Mass.: Harvard University Press, 1937.

Dixon, Suzanne. *The Roman Mother.* London: Croom Helm, 1988.

———. "The Sentimental Ideal of the Roman Family." Pages 99–113 in Rawson, *Marriage, Divorce, and Children in Ancient Rome.*

Dunn, James D. G. *The Epistles to Colossians and to Philemon.* New International Greek Testament Commentary. Grand Rapids: Eerdmans, 1996.

Ellespermann, Gerard L. *The Attitude of the Early Christian Latin Writers toward Pagan Literature and Learning.* Washington, D.C.: Catholic University of America Press, 1949.

Elliott, J. K., ed. *The Apocryphal New Testament: A Collection of Apocryphal Christian Literature in an English Translation.* Oxford: Oxford University Press, 1993.

Elliott, John H. *1 Peter: A New Translation with Introduction and Commentary.* Anchor Bibl. 37B. New York: Doubleday, 2000.

———. "1 Peter, Its Situation and Strategy: A Discussion with David Balch." Pages 61–78 in Talbert, *Perspectives on 1 Peter.*

———. *A Home for the Homeless: A Sociological Exegesis of 1 Peter.* Philadelphia: Fortress, 1981.

Elliott, N. "The Anti-imperial Message of the Cross." Pages 167–83 in Horsley, *Paul and Empire.*

———. *Liberating Paul: The Justice of God and the Politics of the Apostle.* Maryknoll, N.Y.: Orbis Books, 1994.

———."Paul and the Politics of Empire." Pages 17–39 in Horsley, *Paul and Politics.*

Elliott, Scott S. "'Thanks, but No Thanks': Tact, Persuasion, and the Negotiation of Power in Paul's Letter to Philemon." *New Testament Studies* 57 (2011): 51–64.

Epictetus. *Discourses. Books 1–2.* Translated by W. A. Oldfather. Loeb Classical Library 131. 1925; Cambridge, Mass.: Harvard University Press, 2000.

Esler, Phillip F. *The First Christians in Their Social World: Social Scientific Approaches to New Testament Interpretation.* London: Routledge, 1994.

Faust, Eberhard. *Pax Christi et Pax Caesaris: Religionsgeschichtliche, traditionsgeschichtliche und sozialgeschichtlich Studien zum Epheserbrief.* Novum Testamentum et Orbis Antiquus 24. Göttingen: Vandenhoek & Ruprecht, 1993.

Feldman, L. H., trans. and ed. *Jewish Antiquities.* Leiden: Brill, 2004.

Fiore, B. *The Pastoral Epistles.* Sacra pagina 12. Collegeville, Minn.: Liturgical, 2007.

Fiorenza, Elisabeth Schüssler. *Bread Not Stone: The Challenge of Feminist Biblical Interpretation.* Boston: Beacon, 1985.

———. *In Memory of Her: A Feminist Theological Reconstruction of Christian Origins.* London: SCM Press, 1983.

———. *The Power of the Word: Scripture and the Rhetoric of Empire.* Minneapolis: Fortress, 2007.

———. *Rhetoric and Ethic: The Politics of Biblical Studies.* Minneapolis: Fortress, 1999.

Flory, M. B. "Family in *familia*: Kinship and Community in Slavery." *American Journal of Ancient History* 3 (1978): 78–95.

Foss, Pedar. "Watchful Lares: Roman Household Organization and the Rituals of Cooking and Eating." Pages 196–218 in *Domestic Space in the Roman World: Pompeii and Beyond.* Edited by Ray Laurence and Andrew Wallace-Hadrill. Journal of Roman Archaeology Supplementary Series 22. Portsmouth, R.I.: Journal of Roman Archaeology, 1997.

Fraade, S. "Interpretative Authority in the Studying Community at Qumran." *Journal of Jewish Studies* 44 (1993): 46–69.

Francis, James. "Children and Childhood in the New Testament." Pages 65–85 in *The Family in Theological Perspective.* Edited by Stephen Barton. Edinburgh: T&T Clark, 1996.

Frilingos, Chris. "'For My Child Onesimus': Paul and Domestic Power in Philemon." *Journal of Biblical Literature* 119 (2000): 91–104.

Gardner, Jane F., and Thomas Wiedemann, *The Roman Household: A Sourcebook.* London: Routledge, 1991.

Gärtner, M. *Die Familienerziehung in der alten Kirche.* Cologne: Bohlau, 1985.

Gaventa, Beverly Roberts. "Finding a Place for Children in the Letters of Paul." Pages 233–48 in Bunge, *The Child in the Bible.*

———. *Our Mother Saint Paul.* Louisville: Westminster John Knox, 2007.

George, Michele. "Domestic Architecture and Household Relations: Pompeii and Roman Ephesos." *Journal for the Study of the New Testament* 21 (2004): 7–25.

———. "Repopulating the Roman House." Pages 299–320 in Rawson and Weaver, *The Roman Family in Italy: Status, Sentiment, Space*.

Gergen, Kenneth J. *An Invitation to Social Constructionism.* 2nd ed. London: Sage, 2009.

Gielen, Marlis. *Tradition und Theologie neutestamentlicher Haustafelethik: Ein Beitrag zur Frage einer christlichen Auseinandersetzung mit gesellschaftlichen Normen.* Bonner biblische Beiträge 75. Frankfurt am Main: Anton Hain, 1990.

Glancy, Jennifer A. "Protocols of Masculinity in the Pastoral Epistles." Pages 235–64 in *New Testament Masculinities.* Edited by S. D. Moore and J. C. Anderson. *Semeia* 45. Atlanta: Society of Biblical Literature, 2003.

———. *Slavery in Early Christianity.* Oxford: Oxford University Press, 2002.

Gundry-Volf, Judith. "The Least and the Greatest: Children in the New Testament." Pages 29–60 in *The Child in Christian Thought.* Edited by Marcia J. Bunge. Grand Rapids: Eerdmans, 2003.

Harders, Ann-Catherin. "Roman Patchwork Families: Surrogate Parenting, Socialization, and the Shaping of Tradition." Pages 49–72 in Dasen and Späth, *Children, Memory, and Family Identity in Roman Culture.*

Harrill, J. Albert. "The Domestic Enemy: A Moral Polarity of Household Slaves in Early Christian Apologies and Martyrdoms." Pages 234–54 in Balch and Osiek, *Early Christian Families in Context.*

———. "Paul and Empire: Studying Roman Identity after the Cultural Turn." *Early Christianity* 2 (2011): 281–311.

———. *Slaves in the New Testament: Literary, Social, and Moral Dimensions.* Minneapolis: Fortress, 2006.

Heil, John Paul. *Ephesians: Empowerment to Walk in Love for the Unity of All in Christ.* Studies in Biblical Literature 13. Atlanta: Society of Biblical Literature, 2007.

Hertzer, C. *Jewish Literacy in Roman Palestine.* Texts and Studies in Ancient Judaism 81. Tübingen: Mohr Siebeck, 2001.

Horn, C. B., and J. W. Martens. *"Let the little children come to me": Childhood and Children in Early Christianity.* Washington, D.C.: Catholic University of America Press, 2009.

Horrell, David G. *1 Peter.* London: T&T Clark, 2008.

———. "Between Conformity and Resistance: Beyond the Balch-Elliott Debate towards a Postcolonial Reading on 1 Peter." Pages 111–43 in *Reading 1 Peter with New Eyes: Methodological Reassessments of the Letter of First Peter.* Edited by Robert L. Webb and Betsy Bauman-Martin. Library of New Testament Studies. London: T&T Clark, 2007.

————. "Leadership Patterns and the Development of Ideology in Early Christianity." Pages 309–38 in *Social Scientific Approaches to New Testament Interpretation.* Edinburgh: T&T Clark, 1999.

Horsley, R. A., ed. *Hidden Transcripts and the Arts of Resistance: Applying the Work of James C. Scott to Jesus and Paul.* Semeia Studies 48. Atlanta: Society of Biblical Literature, 2004.

————, ed. *Paul and Empire: Religion and Power in Roman Imperial Society.* Harrisburg, Pa.: Trinity International, 1997.

————, ed. *Paul and Politics: Ekklesia, Israel, Imperium, Interpretation. Essays in Honor of Krister Stendahl.* Harrisburg, Pa.: Trinity International, 2000.

————, ed. *Paul and the Roman Imperial Order.* Harrisburg, Pa.: Trinity International, 2004.

Horst, P. W. van der. *The Sentences of Pseudo-Phocylides.* Studia in Veteris Testamenti Pseudepigrapha. Leiden: Brill, 1978.

Hutchinson, Janet. "Picturing the Roman Family." Pages 521–41 in Rawson, *A Companion to Families in the Greek and Roman Worlds.*

Johnson, L. T. *The First and Second Letters to Timothy.* Anchor Bible 35A. New York: Doubleday, 2001.

————. *Letters to Paul's Delegates: 1 Timothy, 2 Timothy, Titus.* New Testament in Context. Valley Forge, Pa.: Trinity International, 1996.

Johnson Hodge, Caroline. "'Holy Wives' in Roman Households: 1 Peter 3:1-6." *Journal of Interdisciplinary Feminist Thought* 4, no. 1 (2010): 1–24.

————. "Married to an Unbeliever: Households, Hierarchies, and Holiness in 1 Corinthians 7:12–16." *Harvard Theological Review* 103, no. 1 (2010): 1–25.

Josephus. Translated by H. St. J. Thackeray et al. 10 vols. Loeb Classical Library. Cambridge, Mass.: Harvard University Press, 1926–1965.

Joyal, M., I. McDougall, and J. C. Yardley. *Greek and Roman Education: A Sourcebook.* London: Routledge, 2009.

Judge, Edwin A. "The Conflict of Educational Aims in the New Testament." *Journal of Christian Education* 9 (1966): 32–45.

————. "The Early Christians as a Scholastic Community." *Journal of Religious History* III (1960): 4–15, 125–137.

Juvenal and Persius. Translated by Susanna Morton Braund. Loeb Classical Library 91. Cambridge, Mass.: Harvard University Press, 2004.

Kartzow, M. B. *Gossip and Gender: Othering of Speech in the Pastoral Epistles.* Berlin: de Gruyter, 2009.

Kaster, R. A. *Guardians of Language: The Grammarian and Society in Late Antiquity.* Berkeley: University of California Press, 1997.

Kehily, Mary Jane, ed. *An Introduction to Childhood Studies*. Maidenhead, U.K.: Open University Press, McGraw-Hill International, 2004.

Knothe, H. G. "Zur 7-Jahresgrenze der 'Infantia' im antiken römischen Recht." *Studia et Documenta Historiae et Iuris* 48 (1982): 239–562.

Kraemer, Ross Shepard. "The Conversion of Women to Ascetic Forms of Christianity." *Signs* 6 (1980): 298–307.

———. *Her Share of the Blessings: Women's Religions among Pagans, Jews, and Christians in the Roman World*. Oxford: Oxford University Press, 1993.

———. *Unreliable Witnesses: Religion, Gender, and History in the Greco-Roman Mediterranean*. Oxford: Oxford University Press, 2011.

Laes, Christian. *Children in the Roman Empire: Outsiders Within*. Cambridge: Cambridge University Press, 2011. Original Dutch edition: *Kinderen bij de Romeinen: Zes Eeuwen Dagelijks Leven*. Leuven: Uitgeverij Davidsfonds, 2006.

———. "*Delicia*-Children Revisited: The Evidence of Statius' Silvae." Pages 245–72 in Dasen and Späth, *Children, Memory, and Family Identity in Roman Culture*.

———. "Desperately Different? *Delicia* Children in the Roman Household." Pages 298–324 in Balch and Osiek, *Early Christian Families in Context*.

Lafosse, Mona T. *Age Matters: Age, Aging and Intergenerational Relationships in Early Christian Communities with a Focus on 1 Timothy 5*. Ph.D. diss., University of Toronto, 2011.

Laub, Franz. *Die Begegnung des frühen Christentums mit der antiken Sklaverei*. Stuttgart: Katholisches Bibelwerk, 1982.

Lincoln, Andrew T. *Ephesians*. Word Biblical Commentary 42. Dallas: Word Books, 1990.

Loader, William. *The New Testament on Sexuality*. Grand Rapids: Eerdmans, 2012.

———. *Sexuality and the Jesus Tradition*. Grand Rapids: Eerdmans, 2005.

Lührmann, D. "Neutestamentliche Haustafeln und Antike Ökonomie." *New Testament Studies* 27 (1980): 83–97.

———. "Wo man nicht mehr Sklave oder Freier ist. Überlegungen zur Struktur frühchristlicher Gemeinden." *Wort und Dienst* 13 (1975): 53–83.

Lutz, Cora E. "Musonius Rufus: The Roman Socrates." *Yale Classical Studies* 10 (1947): 32–47.

MacDonald, Margaret Y. "Beyond Identification of the *Topos* of Household Management: Reading the Household Codes in Light of Recent Methodologies and Theoretical Perspectives in the Study of the New Testament." *New Testament Studies* 57 (2010): 74–79.

———. "Citizens of Heaven and Earth: Asceticism and Social Integration in Colossians and Ephesians." Pages 269–98 in *Asceticism and the New*

Testament. Edited by Leif E. Vaage and Vincent L. Wimbush. New York: Routledge, 1999.

———. *Colossians and Ephesians*. Sacra pagina 17. Collegeville, Minn.: Liturgical, 2000.

———. *Early Christian Women and Pagan Opinion: The Power of the Hysterical Woman*. Cambridge: Cambridge University Press, 1996.

———. "Making Room for the Little Ones: How New Research on Children and Slaves in Roman World Is Changing What We Think about the History of Early Christian Women." *Bulletin 2011/12: The Canadian Society of Biblical Studies* 71 (2012): 1–25.

———. "Parenting, Surrogate Parenting and Teaching: Reading the Household Codes as Sources for Understanding Socialization and Education in Early Christian Communities." Pages 85–102 in *Theologische und soziologische Perspektiven auf früheristliche Lebenswelten*. Edited by Dorothee Dettinger and Christof Landmesser. Leipzig: Evangelische Verlagsanstalt, 2014.

———. *The Pauline Churches: A Socio-historical Study of the Institutionalization in the Pauline and Deutero-Pauline Writings*. Cambridge: Cambridge University Press, 1988.

———. "A Place of Belonging: Perspectives on Children from Colossians and Ephesians." Pages 278–304 in Bunge, *The Child in the Bible*.

———. "The Politics of Identity in Ephesians." *Journal for the Study of the New Testament* 26 (2004): 419–44.

———. "Reading the New Testament Household Codes in Light of New Research on Children and Childhood in the Roman World." *Studies in Religion* 41 (2012): 376–87.

———. "Slavery, Sexuality and House Churches: A Reassessment of Colossians 3.18–4.1 in Light of New Research on the Roman Family." *New Testament Studies* 53, no. 1 (2007): 94–113.

MacDonald, Margaret Y., and Leif Vaage. "Unclean but Holy Children: Paul's Everyday Quandary in 1 Cor 7:14C." *Catholic Biblical Quarterly* 73 (2011): 526–46.

Madigan, Kevin, and Carolyn Osiek. *Ordained Women in the Early Church: A Documentary History*. Baltimore, Md.: Johns Hopkins University Press, 2005.

Maier, Harry O. *Picturing Paul in Empire: Imperial Image, Text, and Persuasion in Colossians, Ephesians, and the Pastoral Epistles*. Edinburgh: Bloomsbury, 2013.

———. "A Sly Civility: Colossians and Empire." *Journal for the Study of the New Testament* 27 (2005): 323–49.

———. *The Social Setting of Ministry as Reflected in the Writings of Hermas, Clement, and Ignatius*. Studies in Christianity and Judaism/Études sur le christianisme et le judaïsme 12. Waterloo, Ontario: Wilfrid Laurier University Press, 2002.

Malherbe, A. J. "'In Season and Out of Season': 2 Timothy 4:2." *Journal of Biblical Literature* 103 (1984): 235–43.

Malina, B. J. *Timothy: Paul's Closest Associate*. Collegeville, Minn.: Liturgical, 2008.

Martin, Dale B. "Slave Families and Slaves in Families." Pages 207–30 in Balch and Osiek, *Early Christian Families in Context*.

Marshall, I. H. *A Critical and Exegetical Commentary on the Pastoral Epistles*. International Critical Commentary. Edinburgh: T&T Clark, 1999.

Marshall, Joseph H. "The Usefulness of an Onesimus: The Sexual Use of Slaves and Paul's Letter to Philemon." *Journal of Biblical Literature* 130 (2011): 749–70.

Mason, S. "Jews, Judeans, Judaizing, Judaism: Problems of Categorization in Ancient History." *Journal for the Study of Judaism in the Persian, Hellenistic and Roman Periods* 38 (2007): 457–512.

Mencacci, Francesca. "*Modestia* vs. *licentia*: Seneca on Childhood and Status in the Roman Family." Pages 223–44 in Dasen and Späth, *Children, Memory, and Family Identity in Roman Culture*.

Mollenkott, Virginia Ramey. "Emancipative Elements in Ephesians 5.21-33: Why Feminist Scholarship Has (Often) Left Them Unmentioned, and Why They Should Be Emphasized." Pages 88–97 in *A Feminist Companion to the Deutero-Pauline Epistles*. Edited by Amy-Jill Levine with Miriamme Blickerstaff. London: T&T Clark, 2003.

Moore, Stephen D. *Empire and Apocalypse: Postcolonialism and the New Testament*. Sheffield: Sheffield Phoenix, 2006.

Morgan, Teresa. "Ethos: The Socialization of Children in Education and Beyond." Pages 504–20 in Rawson, *A Companion to Families in the Greek and Roman Worlds*.

_____ . *Literate Education in the Hellenistic and Roman Worlds*. Cambridge: Cambridge University Press, 1998.

Mouritsen, Henrik. "The Families of the Roman Slaves and Freedmen." Pages 129–44 in Rawson, *A Companion to Families in the Greek and Roman Worlds*.

Moxnes, Halvor, ed. *Constructing Early Christian Families: Family as Social Reality and Metaphor*. London: Routledge, 1997.

Müller, K. "Die Haustafel des Kolosserbriefes und das antike Frauenthema. Eine Kritische rückschau auf alte Ergebnisse." Pages 263–319 in *Die Frau im Urchristentum*. Edited by Josef Blank, Gerhard Dautzenberg, Helmut Merklein, and Karlheinz Müller. Quaestiones disputatae 95. Freiburg: Herder, 1983.

Müller, Peter. *In der Mitte der Gemeinde: Kinder im Neuen Testament*. Neukirchen Vluyn, Germany: Neukirchener, 1992.

Nathan, Geoffrey S. *The Family in Late Antiquity: The Rise of Christianity and the Endurance of Tradition*. London: Routledge, 2000.

Neyrey, Jerome H. "Deception." Pages 38–42 in Pilch and Malina, *Biblical Social Values and Their Meaning*.

Origen, *Contra Celsum*. Translated by Henry Chadwick. Cambridge: Cambridge University Press, 1953.

Orr, David G. "Roman Domestic Religion: The Evidence of the Household Shrines." *Aufstieg und Niedergang der römischen Welt: Geschichte und Kultur Roms im Spiegel der neueren Forschung* 2.16.2 (1978): 1557–91.

Osiek, Carolyn, ed. *Anselm Academic Study Bible*. Winona, Minn.: Anselm Academic, 2012.

———. "The Bride of Christ (Eph 5.22-33): A Problematic Wedding." *Biblical Theology Bulletin* 32 (2003): 29–39.

———. "Female Slaves, *Porneia*, and the Limits of Obedience." Pages 255–273 in Balch and Osiek, *Early Christian Families in Context*.

Osiek, Carolyn, and David L. Balch. *Families in the New Testament World: Households and House Churches*. Family, Religion, and Culture. Louisville, Ky.: Westminster John Knox, 1997.

Osiek, Carolyn, and Margaret Y. MacDonald, with Janet Tulloch. *A Woman's Place: House Churches in Earliest Christianity*. Minneapolis: Augsburg Fortress, 2006.

Parkin, T. *Old Age in the Roman World: A Cultural and Social History*. Baltimore, Md.: Johns Hopkins University Press, 2003.

———. "The Roman Life Course and the Family." Pages 276–90 in Rawson, *A Companion to Families in the Greek and Roman Worlds*.

Perkins, Pheme. *Ephesians*. Abingdon New Testament Commentaries. Nashville: Abingdon, 1997.

Philo. *On the Special Laws, On the Virtues. On Rewards and Punishments*. Translated by F. H. Colson. Loeb Classical Library 341. Cambridge, Mass.: Harvard University Press, 1939.

Pilch, John J., and Bruce J. Malina, eds. *Biblical Social Values and Their Meaning: A Handbook*. Peabody, Mass.: Hendrickson, 1993.

Plant, Ian Michael. *Women Authors of Ancient Greece and Rome: An Anthology*. Norman: University of Oklahoma Press, 2004.

Plevnik, Joseph. "Honor/Shame." Pages 95–104 in Pilch and Malina, *Biblical Social Values and Their Meaning*.

Plutarch. *Moralia*. Translated by Frank Cole Babbitt. Cambridge, Mass.: Harvard University Press; London: William Heinemann, 1927.

Prescendi, Francesca. "Children and the Transmission of Religious Knowledge." Pages 73–93 in Dasen and Späth, *Children, Memory, and Family Identity in Roman Culture*.

Quintilian. *Institutio Oratoria (The Orator's Education). Books 1–5*. Translated by Donald A. Russell. Loeb Classical Library 124 and 125. Cambridge, Mass.: Harvard University Press, 2001.

Ramelli, Ilaria. *Hierocles the Stoic: Elements of Ethics, Fragments, and Excerpts.* Translated by David Konstan. Writings from the Greco-Roman World. Atlanta: Society of Biblical Literature, 2009.

Rawson, Beryl. *Children and Childhood in Roman Italy.* Oxford: Oxford University Press, 2003.

———, ed. *A Companion to Families in the Greek and Roman Worlds.* Oxford: Blackwell, 2011.

———. "The Iconography of Roman Childhood." Pages 205–32 in Rawson and Weaver, *The Roman Family in Italy: Status, Sentiment, Space.*

———, ed. *Marriage, Divorce, and Children in Ancient Rome.* Oxford: Clarendon, 1991.

Rawson, Beryl, and Paul Weaver, eds. *The Roman Family in Italy: Status, Sentiment, Space.* Oxford: Clarendon, 1997.

Regev, Eyal. "Were the Early Christians Sectarians?" *Journal of Biblical Literature* 130 (2011): 771–93.

Reinhartz, Adele. "Philo on Infanticide." *Studia Philonica Annual* 4 (1992): 42–58.

Reinhartz, Adele, and Kim Shier. "Josephus on Children and Childhood." *Studies in Religion* 41 (2012): 364–75.

Saller, Richard P. "Household and Gender." Pages 87–112 in *The Cambridge Economic History of the Greco-Roman World.* Edited by W. Scheidel, I. Morris, and R. Saller. Cambridge: Cambridge University Press, 2007.

———. "*Pater Familias, Mater Familias,* and the Gendered Semantics of the Roman Household." *Classical Philology* 94 (1999): 182–97.

———. *Patriarchy, Property and Death in the Roman Family.* Cambridge: Cambridge University Press, 1994.

———. "Women Slaves and the Economy of the Roman Household." Pages 185–206 in Balch and Osiek, *Early Christian Families in Context.*

Scheidel, W. "The Demographic Background." Pages 31–40 in *Growing Up Fatherless in Antiquity.* Edited by S. R. Huebner and D. M. Razan. Cambridge: Cambridge University Press, 2009.

Schnackenburg, Rudolf. *Ephesians: A Commentary.* Translated by Helen Heron. Edinburgh: T&T Clark, 1991.

Scott, James C. *Domination and the Arts of Resistance.* New Haven, Conn.: Yale University Press, 1990.

Seim, Turid Karlsen. "A Superior Minority: The Problem of Men's Headship in Ephesians 5." Pages 167–81 in *Mighty Minorities? Minorities in Early Christianity—Positions and Strategies: Essays in Honor of Jacob Jervell on His 70th Birthday, 21 May 1995.* Edited by David Hellholm,

Halvor Moxnes, and Turid Karlsen Seim. Oslo: Scandinavian University Press, 1995.

Seneca. *Epistles 1–65.* Translated by Richard M. Gummere. Loeb Classical Library 75. Cambridge, Mass.: Harvard University Press, 1917.

Shoedel, William R. *Ignatius of Antioch: A Commentary on the Letters of Ignatius of Antioch.* Philadelphia: Fortress, 1985.

Smith, Claire S. *Pauline Communities as "Scholastic Communities": A Study of the Vocabulary of "Teaching" in 1 Corinthians, 1 and 2 Timothy and Titus.* Tübingen: Mohr Siebeck, 2012.

Smith, R. R. R. "The Imperial Reliefs from the Sebasteion at Aphrodisias." *Journal of Roman Studies* 77 (1987): 88–138.

Sokolwski, Franziskek. *Lois sacrées de l'Asie Mineure.* Paris: Boccard, 1955.

Standhartinger, Angela. "The Origin and Intention of the Household Code in the Letter to the Colossians." *Journal for the Study of the New Testament* 79 (2000): 117–30.

Stowers, Stanley K. "A Cult from Philadelphia: Oikos Religion or Cultic Association?" Pages 287–301 in *The Early Church in Its Context: Essays in Honor of Everett Ferguson.* Edited by Abraham J. Malherbe, Frederick W. Norris, and James W. Thompson. Studien zum Neuen Testament 90. Leiden: Brill, 1998.

Sugirtharjah, R. S. *Postcolonial Criticism and Biblical Interpretation.* Oxford: Oxford University Press, 2002.

Sumney, Jerry L. *Colossians: A Commentary.* Louisville, Ky.: Westminster John Knox, 2008.

Talbert, Charles H., ed. *Perspectives on 1 Peter.* Macon, Ga.: Mercer University Press, 1986.

Tamez, Elsa. *Struggles for Power in Early Christianity: A Study of the First Letter to Timothy.* Maryknoll, N.Y.: Orbis Books, 2007.

Thraede, K. "Zum historischen Hintergrund der Haustafeln des NT." Pages 359–68 in *Pietas: Festschrift für B. Kötting.* Edited by E. Dassmann and K. S. Frank. Münster: Aschendorff, 1980.

Treggiari, Susan. "Marriage and Family in Roman Society," Pages 132–82 in *Marriage and Family in the Biblical World.* Edited by Ken M. Campbell. Downers Grove, Ill.: InterVarsity, 2003.

Tybout, R. A. "Domestic Shrines and 'Popular Painting': Style and Social Context." *Journal of Roman Archaeology* 9 (1996): 367–70.

Ubieta, Carmen Bernabé. "'Neither *Xenoi* nor *parakoi, sympolitai* and *oikeioi tou theou*' (Eph 2.19) Pauline Christian Communities: Defining a New Territoriality." Pages 260–80 in *Social-Scientific Models for Interpreting the Bible.* Edited by John J. Pilch. Leiden: Brill, 2001.

Verner, David C. *The Household of God: The Social World of the Pastoral*

Epistles. Society of Biblical Literature Dissertation Series 71. Chico, Calif.: Scholars Press, 1983.

Vuolanto, Ville. "Children and the Memory of Parents in the Late Roman World." Pages 173–92 in Dasen and Späth, *Children, Memory, and Family Identity in Roman Culture.*

Wallace-Hadrill, A. "Houses and Households: Sampling Pompeii and Herculaneum." Pages 191–227 in Rawson, *Marriage, Divorce, and Children in Ancient Rome.*

———. *Houses and Society in Pompeii and Herculaneum.* Princeton, N.J.: Princeton University Press, 1994.

Walsh, Brian J., and Sylvia Keesmaat. *Colossians Remixed: Subverting the Empire.* Downers Grove, Ill.: InterVarsity, 2004.

Wassen, Cecilia. "On the Education of Children in the Dead Sea Scrolls." *Studies in Religion* 41 (2012): 350–63.

Weissenrieder, Annette. "Contested Spaces in 1 Cor 11:17-33 and 14:30: Sitting or Reclining in Ancient Houses, in Associations and in the Space of the *ekklesia.*" Pages 59–107 in *Contested Spaces.* Edited by David L. Balch and Annette Weissenrieder. Wissenschaftliche Untersuchungen zum Neuen Testament 285. Tübingen: Mohr Siebeck, 2012.

Wiedemann, Thomas. *Greek and Roman Slavery.* Baltimore, Md.: Johns Hopkins University Press, 1981.

Williams, Craig A. *Roman Homosexuality: Ideologies of Masculinity in Classical Antiquity.* Oxford: Oxford University Press, 1999.

Winter, Bruce W. *Roman Wives, Roman Widows: The Appearance of the New Women and Pauline Communities.* Grand Rapids: Eerdmans, 2003.

Woyke, Johannes. *Die Neutestamentlichen Haustafeln: Ein kritischer und konstrucktiver Forschungsüberblick.* Stuttgarter Bibelstudien 184. Stuttgart: Katholisches Bibelwerk, 2000.

Wyse, D., ed. *Childhood Studies: An Introduction.* Oxford: Blackwell, 2004.

Yarbrough, O. Larry. "Parents and Children in the Letters of Paul." Pages 126–44 in *The Social World of the First Christians: Essays in Honor of Wayne A. Meeks.* Edited by L. Michael White and O. Larry Yarbrough. Minneapolis: Fortress, 1995.

Young, Frances. *The Theology of the Pastoral Epistles.* Cambridge: Cambridge University Press, 1994.

Zolty, Shoshana Pantel. *"And All Your Children Shall Be Learned": Women and the Study of Torah in Jewish Law and History.* Northvale, N.J.: Aronson, 1993.

Index of Ancient Sources

Index of Modern Authors

Subject Index